CHRISTIAN RECONSTRUCTION

What It Is, What It Isn't

CHRISTIAN RECONSTRUCTION

What It Is, What It Isn't

Gary North

and

Gary DeMar

Institute for Christian Economics
Tyler, Texas

Library of Congress Cataloging-in-Publication Data

North, Gary.
  Christian Reconstruction : what it is, what it isn't / Gary North and
Gary DeMar.
         p.   cm.
  Includes bibliographical references and indexes.
  ISBN 0-930464-52-4 : $25.00 (alk. paper) -- ISBN 0-930464-53-2
(pbk.) : $8.95 (alk. paper)
      1. Dominion theology. 2. Law (theology) 3. Christianity and
politics -- Protestant churches. 4. Millennialism. 5. Jewish law.
I. DeMar, Gary. II. Title
BT82.25.N67   1991
231.7'6--dc20   90-22956
                                                                      CIP

Institute for Christian Economics
P. O. Box 8000
Tyler, TX 75711

This book is dedicated to the memory of

Cornelius Van Til

whose expertise in epistemological
demolitions created a new movement
as a wholly unintended consequence.

TABLE OF CONTENTS

Preface, by *Gary North* ix
Introduction, by *Gary DeMar* 1

Part I: **God's Covenantal Kingdom**, by *Gary North*
1. The Nature of God's Kingdom 27
2. The Pietist-Humanist Kingdom 33
3. Humanism and Politics 38
4. God and Government 44
5. The Myth of Neutrality 51
6. The Four Covenants of God 56
7. Postmillennialism's "Faith in Man" 62
8. Premillennialism's Faith in Bureaucracy 66
9. The Pietist-Humanist Alliance 70
Conclusion, Part I 76

Part II: **Questions Frequently Asked About
Christian Reconstruction**, by *Gary DeMar*
1. What Is Christian Reconstruction? 81
2. Will Christians Bring in the Kingdom of God
in History? 96
3. Are Christians Still Under the Law? 100
4. Are We Sanctified by the Law? 103
5. Are We Now Under the "Law of Christ" Rather
Than the "Law of Moses"? 106
6. Isn't Natural Law the Standard of Righteousness
for the Nations? 108
7. What About "Democracy"? 120
8. What About "Salvation by Politics"? 123
9. Isn't Postmillennialism Really Liberalism? 127
10. What Role Does Israel Play in Postmillennialism? 132
11. Is Revolution the Way to Advance God's Kingdom? 140

Part III: **Why Are Christian Reconstructionists Confrontational?**
12. Are Our Critics Honest? *Gary DeMar* 147
13. What Is the Proper Response? *Gary North* 160

Conclusion, by *Gary DeMar* 183
Books for Further Reading and Study 191
Scripture Index 203
General Index 208

PREFACE

Gary North

In the summer of 1962, I first met Rousas John Rushdoony. I had read *Intellectual Schizophrenia* (1961) in the second semester of my junior year in college (1962), and I had corresponded with him. I was initially interested in his views regarding the possible connection between the Bible and the insights of economist Ludwig von Mises, since he had referred to Mises in his book.[1] It was a connection that I had begun pursuing on my own as a freshman in 1960. (I am still pursuing it.)

Rushdoony was teaching at a two-week summer seminar for college students sponsored by what was then called the Intercollegiate Society of Individualists, today called the Intercollegiate Studies Institute. It was, and remains, the most intellectual of the student conservative organizations.[2] Rushdoony had been brought to the St. Mary's College campus to lecture each morning on the Christian roots of early America. These lectures became *This Independent Republic* (1964).

He had only recently left the pastorate in the Orthodox Presbyterian Church to become a staff member of the William Volker Fund, which was then one of the best endowed conservative-free market foundations. (It was shut down in 1965, on the late founder's written instructions. The millions of dollars in funds were eventually given to the Hoover Institution.) The Volker Fund financed the research and writing of several of his

---

1. Rousas J. Rushdoony, *Intellectual Schizophrenia: Culture, Crisis and Education* (Philadelphia: Presbyterian & Reformed, 1961), p. 14n.
2. Its headquarters are in Bryn Mawr, Pennsylvania.

early books. It put him on a retainer to write *The One and the Many* (1971) after the Fund began to be shut down in 1964. That retainer income financed his move to Southern California in 1965.[3] He later dedicated the book to the administrator of the Fund, Harold Luhnow, the nephew of the late William Volker ("Mr. Anonymous"). It was Luhnow who had agreed to hire him in 1962, when Luhnow fired a group of libertarian scholars under the leadership of F. A. Harper.[4]

Rushdoony sent me Cornelius Van Til's apologetics syllabus in the fall of 1962, which I read and came to accept before I graduated from college that June. He hired me to come to the Volker Fund as a summer intern in 1963, and I lived with his family in Palo Alto.[5] Essentially, I was paid $500 a month (a princely sum in those days) to read books. It was during that summer that I read the major works of Ludwig von Mises, F. A. Hayek, Murray N. Rothbard, and Wilhelm Roepke. It was the most important "summer vacation" of my life.

At Rushdoony's insistence, I also read Van Til's *Defense of the Faith*. He had brought me to work at the Fund to provide the money for me to attend Westminster Theological Seminary in Philadelphia, specifically to study under Van Til. I had originally planned to attend Dallas Seminary. I was a hyper-dispensationalist at the time (Cornelius Stam, J. C. O'Hair), though a predestinarian. The problem was, as I learned that fall, Van Til never assigned any of his own books to his classes, and his classroom lecture style was as close to Werner Heisenberg's indeterminacy principle as anything I have ever seen. I left Westminster after one academic year, but not before Professor

---

3. He did not return to the pastorate. He sought and received formal permission to labor outside the bounds of the Northern California Presbytery of the OPC, a status he maintained until he left the denomination in the early 1970's.

4. Harper had answered by mail some of my questions about economics as early as summer, 1961, and he brought me to the Volker Fund, located in Burlingame, California, that fall, a semester before I heard of Rushdoony. He gave me several books at that time, and a year later sent me Murray Rothbard's incomparable *Man, Economy, and State*, after he set up his own organization, the Institute for Humane Studies, in 1962.

5. Another staff member was Rev. C. John Miller, who later went to Westminster Seminary as a faculty member. Miller wrote a three-volume manuscript against public education while on the staff. It was never published.

John Murray's lectures on Romans 11 converted me to postmillennialism. (I became a Presbyterian after reading Meredith Kline's 1964-65 *Westminster Theological Journal* essays on baptism that later became *By Oath Consigned*.)

In 1962, there was no Christian Reconstruction movement. There was not even an outline of it. Over the next decade, Rushdoony developed the fundamental theological and sociological principles of what was later to become a movement. I did sporadic work on biblical economics after 1964. He persuaded Hays Craig of Craig Press to publish my *Marx's Religion of Revolution* (1968). He put me on a part-time salary in 1970 ($300 a month) to help me complete my Ph.D. By then, I was writing almost every other month for *The Freeman*, and I was hired by Leonard E. Read in the fall of 1971 to join the senior staff of the Foundation for Economic Education. I completed my doctoral dissertation while on the FEE staff.

Rushdoony had been deeply influenced by Van Til, whose dual classification of *covenant-keeper* and *covenant-breaker* had persuaded him of the irreconcilable nature of Christianity and its rivals. Rushdoony wrote *By What Standard*, published in 1959, as an introduction to Van Til's uncompromising rejection of humanism. Like Van Til, Rushdoony believed that Christians need to abandon all traces of natural law theory. But this radical belief inevitably creates a monumental sociological problem for Christianity — a problem that Van Til never addressed publicly in his career:

"If Not Natural Law, Then What?"

Van Til was analogous to a demolitions expert. He placed explosive charges at the base of every modern edifice he could locate, and book by book, syllabus by syllabus, he detonated them. One by one, the buildings came down. But he left no blueprints for the reconstruction of society. He saw his job as narrowly negative: blowing up dangerous buildings with their weak (schizophrenic) foundations. This narrowly defined task was not good enough for Rushdoony. He recognized early that there has to be an alternative to the collapsed buildings. There have to be blueprints. But where are they to be found? Step by step in the 1960's, he concluded that the source of the missing blueprints is Old Testament law.

This was not a new idea. The New England Puritans in the first generation (1630-60) had also believed that Old Testament law is still binding on men and institutions. But after 1660, this faith in God's law steadily faded. By 1700, it was dead. The ancient discipline of *casuistry* — the study of how moral principles are applied to concrete historical circumstances — was abandoned by Protestant scholars. In its place came a new religion: Newtonian rationalism. This Unitarian import is still with us, though its luster has faded with the steady replacement of Newtonian physics by modern quantum physics.

Neither was Van Til's Calvinism a new idea. But Van Til added one new element: an uncompromising rejection of both the rationalism and irrationalism of covenant-breaking man. He rejected neutrality in every area of life. Van Til launched a revolution. It is this, and *only* this, that is clearly a new element in the Christian Reconstruction movement. In this sense, the movement is intellectually revolutionary. But this rejection of neutrality is not confined to Van Tilianism today. Protestant Christians in other traditions have now begun to insist that the Bible, not the mind of man, is authoritative: the foundation of all thought and the final court of appeal. They at least say they believe this; and when they really do believe it, they become the chief targets of Christian Reconstruction's recruiting program. To believe that the philosophy of autonomous man is all wrong is to accept the necessity of a positive alternative. But Christian Reconstruction is the only Bible-affirming movement on earth that offers an uncompromisingly biblical alternative.

Over the next ten years, Rushdoony wrote a series of path-breaking books critical of modern education, theology, science, and politics. In 1965, he launched the Chalcedon Foundation, under the auspices of a local Southern California foundation, Americanism Education, Inc., which had been founded by Walter Knott of Knott's Berry Farm fame. The mimeographed monthly report that became the *Chalcedon Report* began in that year. Slowly but steadily, Rushdoony's influence kept growing.

From Negative Criticism to Positive Reconstruction

It was not until the publication of Rushdoony's *Institutes of Biblical Law* in 1973 that the movement could be said to have completed the first stage of its development. Prior to his lectures on biblical law, which began in 1968, Rushdoony's work, like Van Til's, had been primarily negative: exposing the myth of neutrality in philosophy, education, politics, historiography, and science. Also in 1968, Francis Schaeffer's *The God Who Is There* appeared. Schaeffer extended the critique of neutrality. He had studied under Van Til at Westminster Theological Seminary, 1935-37, and while he never revealed whose system he was at least partially incorporating, he nonetheless did yeoman service in extending its devastating effects. So, as Schaeffer began to bring the implications of Van Til's negative critique to the attention of the general Christian public, Rushdoony began his presentation of a positive alternative. Out of the rubble of humanism will come a new society, the Bible teaches:

> And they shall build the old wastes, they shall raise up the former desolations, and they shall repair the waste cities, the desolations of many generations. And strangers shall stand and feed your flocks, and the sons of the alien shall be your plowmen and your vinedressers. But ye shall be named the Priests of the LORD: men shall call you the Ministers of our God: ye shall eat the riches of the Gentiles, and in their glory shall ye boast yourselves (Isaiah 61:4-6).

In 1973, Greg Bahnsen and I joined the staff of Chalcedon. Bahnsen had just completed his Master's thesis at Westminster, which was published as *Theonomy in Christian Ethics* in 1977. (A series of delays beyond Bahnsen's control kept it from appearing earlier.) I had completed my Ph.D. in history, specializing in the economic thought of Puritan New England, the year before. Turmoil began soon, when Bahnsen came under fire in the Southern California Presbytery of the Orthodox Presbyterian Church, where he was seeking ordination. It took him two years to gain it, and some of the same elders who fought him then are still trying to undermine him today. The ecclesiastical war against biblical law had begun in earnest by the mid-1970's. A malicious elder, a physician, was the primary instigator.

When the Presbytery finally dismissed his objections, his local church's session began to investigate him, so he wisely transferred to another OPC congregation on the morning that his session was scheduled to consider pressing charges, thereby escaping a fight. Ecclesiastical procedure and Robert's Rules of Order were his cloak and dagger; what he really committed to was suppression of a rival viewpoint. There are many other Presbyterian elders who share both his opinion and his tactics, and as theonomy has spread to their denominations by means of younger candidates for the ministry, they have staged similar procedural battles at the presbytery level to keep out "the plague" of belief in God's law. (Meanwhile, a real plague has arrived: AIDS, God's eloquent response to the myth of moral neutrality. Robert's Rules of Order won't solve *this* problem.)

The Late 1970's: Building Institutional Foundations

My *Introduction to Christian Economics* appeared in 1973. Rushdoony's *Revolt Against Maturity* appeared in 1974. Bahnsen's *Theonomy* appeared in 1977; his *Homosexuality: A Biblical View* appeared in 1978. But no other major Reconstructionist works were forthcoming in the 1970's. The 1970's were years of building institutional foundations. I began editing Chalcedon's *Journal of Christian Reconstruction* in 1974, the same year I started *Remnant Review*. I started the Institute for Christian Economics in 1975, but it remained dormant for two years. I joined the Congressional staff of Dr. Ron Paul in the second half of 1976. Bahnsen meanwhile journeyed to Jackson, Mississippi, to join the faculty of Reformed Theological Seminary. Three years later, he left RTS just as he came: fired with enthusiasm! In his brief stay, he taught James Jordan, David Chilton, Ken Gentry, and Gary DeMar. His colleagues were rightly concerned that he would continue to pick off the brighter, activist students. They eliminated this possibility when they got the opportunity.

Rushdoony was working hard to expand the mailing list of his Chalcedon Foundation, and generally ceased writing and publishing his older style academic books after 1973. In 1978, *Infallibility: An Inescapable Concept* (69 pages) appeared, and the next year came *The Necessity for Systematic Theology* (74 pages) and *Tithing and Dominion*, co-authored by Edward Powell. In the 1980's, a few of the books that he had written for the most part around 1973 begin to appear in print: *The Philosophy of the Christian Curriculum* (1981), *Law and Society* (1982), and *Salvation and Godly Rule* (1983).[6] These books are more popular in tone, with very short chapters and fewer footnote references. Rushdoony's goal had visibly shifted: presenting the case for Christian Reconstruction to a new audience — wider, but less theologically rigorous. The new books now came from other places.

The 1980's: High Gear Book Production in Tyler and Atlanta

In 1981, with Remnant Review and the ICE on their feet, I began to write in earnest. This began with *Unconditional Surrender* (1981), and *The Dominion Covenant: Genesis* followed the next year. ICE newsletters also multiplied. I began to recruit younger men to write books that could not be published through the conventional Christian book industry.

At the same time, Gary DeMar went to work for American Vision. He was hired to write what became the three-volume set, *God and Government*. By the mid-1980's, the board of American Vision decided to replace its founder with DeMar. At about that time, George Grant appeared on the scene: *Bringing in the Sheaves*, published originally by American Vision.

The ten-volume Biblical Blueprints series followed in 1986-87, with the first four volumes co-published by Thomas Nelson Sons, but abandoned soon thereafter. Dominion Press took over exclusive rights in late 1987. This series was a self-conscious attempt to prove that the thesis of Christian Reconstruction is correct; biblical law does apply to real-world situations: economics, education, civil government, welfare, politics, foreign policy, and family relations. We initially intended to write these books for high school students, but as it turned out, they are more geared to college students. But they are relatively easy to read. Over half of them are structured by the Bible's five-point cove-

---

6. As is true of most authors who comment on contemporary events, you can determine the original date of authorship by checking the latest dates in the books and newspaper articles cited in the footnotes.

nantal model, discovered by Ray Sutton in late 1986, and developed in his book, *That You May Prosper* in 1987. It was applied immediately by David Chilton in structuring his commentary on the Book of Revelation, *The Days of Vengeance* (1987). The five-point covenant model was the most recent major breakthrough of the Christian Reconstruction movement, and it will remain as the integrating structure for the ICE-Dominion Press books.

Confidence or Arrogance?

In my Forewords, Introductions, and Prefaces to ICE and Dominion Press books, I have expressed the opinion that our theological opponents are incapable of either answering us or developing a real-world, Bible-based alternative. This tactic is quite self-conscious: I am trying to break the seminaries' academic black-out by exasperating them. I try to get the critics to reply in print. This tactic generally works, but it takes time and a great deal of publication money. My targets eventually respond, thus enabling me to publish two or three volumes demonstrating why their responses proved my point: no answers.

This tactic has made me very unpopular. It has also raised questions of propriety and good taste among our followers. Should I make such public claims? Should I tell the whole Christian world that what we have is better than anything they have? I get letters warning me that such an attitude is unchristian and evidence of my arrogance. Perhaps so. But I have a model: David. He also made some seemingly outrageous claims, and they were tied to the very thing I proclaim: biblical law.

> I have more understanding than all my teachers: for thy testimonies are my meditation. I understand more than the ancients, because I keep thy precepts (Psalm 119:99-100).

No one can accurately accuse David of having been a shrinking violet. He blew his horn about as loudly as possible. He had the theological goods, and he let everyone know this fact in no uncertain terms. He had the law of God, and this placed him above his teachers and the ancients. It also placed him above any of his contemporaries who rejected God's law.

Outraged Critics

Can you imagine the outrage we would hear if he were alive today and made such a public statement? For that matter, we can be confident that the priests and civic officials of his day would have had a thing or two to say about such an attitude, had he not occupied the throne. I can almost hear them:

> Just who do you think you are? You claim far too much for yourself. By what authority do you claim such wisdom? Where did you, a mere shepherd by birth, get the idea that you excel your teachers, let alone the ancients? Have you studied under a master? Have you devoted years of work to a study of modern theology? No? Well, then, it is clear to us that you are ill-equipped to evaluate your own performance. You are an arrogant man, sir. You are puffed up with your own importance. You think you have great insights, but you are out of step with the latest findings of contemporary theologians. Your attitude is unbiblical. You lack deep spirituality. You are spiritually shallow. No thinking person is going to take seriously anything a strutting, self-inflated character like you has to say. Your style proves that you have nothing important to say. Therefore, we need not examine the content of your position.

David knew the authority in history that the revealed law of God offers to those who take it seriously and conform themselves to it. He announced his reliance on biblical law and the tremendous advantage it gave him: *wisdom*. The law of God is a tool of dominion, a means of spiritual advancement, and the foundation of progress: personal, spiritual, intellectual, and cultural. This is the message of the 119th psalm, the longest passage in the Bible, a psalm devoted to praising the law of God. By understanding the law of God and applying it in his life, a person advances the kingdom of God in history. So it was with David. He identified himself as one who had advanced beyond previous generations. David reminded his listeners:

> I have refrained my feet from every evil way, that I might keep thy word. I have not departed from thy judgments: for thou hast taught me. How sweet are thy words unto my taste! yea, sweeter than honey to my mouth! Through thy precepts I get understanding: therefore I hate every false way. Thy word is a lamp unto my

feet, and a light unto my path. I have sworn, and I will perform it,
that I will keep thy righteous judgments (vv. 101-6).

The law of God repels men. It is a lamp unto their feet, but
they walk in crooked paths. They resent the exposure that this
lamp brings. They love the darkness, for their deeds are evil.
They do not want to hear about God's law. They do not want to
believe that he who gains mastery over it and over himself in
terms of it becomes the master of his environment.

One group of critics of biblical law believes that power, not
biblical wisdom, is the basis of progress in history. They defend
the *power religion*. The other group of critics believes that in-
ward spirituality is alone the basis of progress, at least personal
progress — the only progress they acknowledge. They look deep
within themselves, adopt various spiritual disciplines, and seek
to remove themselves from the material concerns of this world.
This is the *escape religion*. They escape the exercise of authority
as self-consciously as the other critics pursue power. But both
groups are united on this: a rejection of God's revealed law and
the authority it brings to those who obey it. Both sides are
antinomian. Both sides reject Christian Reconstruction.

Anyone who publicly proclaims the unique, Holy Spirit-
empowered benefits of biblical law is dismissed by the critics as
arrogant. If such claims are true, the critics stand condemned.
They refuse to admit that such claims are true. They insist that
public humility regarding God's claims for His own law is God's
requirement, and they proclaim this loudly, with total confidence. They are experts in humility assertiveness. When it comes
to exercising proper humility, they will tell you in no uncertain
terms just where you are out of line. Their model is Shimei (II
Sam. 16:5-8). It is a dangerous model to adopt (I Kings 2).

The Offense of Christian Reconstruction

Modern Christianity implicitly sings this hymn: "O, how hate
I thy law; O, how hate I thy law; it is my consternation all the
day." It is the offense of Christian Reconstruction that its pro-
moters call upon all men to reconsider God's Bible-revealed
law. This law is the only God-given, authoritative means of

evaluation: self-evaluation first, and then the evaluation of everything else. God's law tells us what God thinks of the works of self-proclaimed autonomous man: "But we are all as an unclean thing, and all our righteousnesses are as filthy rags; and we all do fade as a leaf; and our iniquities, like the wind, have taken us away" (Isaiah 64:6). It is not a pretty self-portrait, so autonomous men refuse to look at it. Meanwhile, Christians today are afraid to mention its existence, out of concern for the sensibilities of autonomous men, with whom they have an unspoken alliance.[7]

Nevertheless, covenant-breakers cannot escape the testimony of God in everything they think, see, and do. They know the truth, and they actively hinder it, to their own damnation.

> For the wrath of God is revealed from heaven against all ungodliness and unrighteousness of men, who hold [back] the truth in unrighteousness;[8] Because that which may be known of God is manifest in them; for God hath shewed it unto them. For the invisible things of him from the creation of the world are clearly seen, being understood by the things that are made, even his eternal power and Godhead; so that they are without excuse: Because that, when they knew God, they glorified him not as God, neither were thankful; but became vain in their imaginations, and their foolish heart was darkened. Professing themselves to be wise, they became fools, And changed the glory of the uncorruptible God into an image made like to corruptible man, and to birds, and fourfooted beasts, and creeping things. Wherefore God also gave them up to uncleanness through the lusts of their own hearts, to dishonour their own bodies between themselves: Who changed the truth of God into a lie, and worshipped and served the creature more than the Creator, who is blessed for ever. Amen (Romans 1:18-25).

Common Ground: Disinheritance

Each person is made in God's image. This is the common ground among men — the *only* common ground. We are born the rebellious sons of the Creator God. We are all of one blood: "God that made the world and all things therein, seeing that he

---

7. See below, Chapter 9.
8. Murray, *Romans*, I, pp. 36-37.

is Lord of heaven and earth, dwelleth not in temples made with hands; Neither is worshipped with men's hands, as though he needed any thing, seeing he giveth to all life, and breath, and all things; And hath made of one blood all nations of men for to dwell on all the face of the earth, and hath determined the times before appointed, and the bounds of their habitation" (Acts 17:24-26). We are all born as God's disinherited children.

Christian Reconstructionists insist that there is no common ground among men other than this: the image of God. While all men know the *work* of the law (Romans 2:15), this know-ledge is not enough to save them.[9] It brings them under God's eternal wrath. They hinder in unrighteousness whatever truth they possess as men (Romans 1:18). The more consistent they are with their covenant-breaking presuppositions, the more they hate God's law and those who preach it. The more consistent they become with their rebellious view of God, man, law, and time, the more perverse they become. They prefer to worship creatures rather than the Creator:

> For this cause God gave them up unto vile affections: for even their women did change the natural use into that which is against nature: And likewise also the men, leaving the natural use of the woman, burned in their lust one toward another; men with men working that which is unseemly, and receiving in themselves that recompence of their error which was meet. And even as they did not like to retain God in their knowledge, God gave them over to a reprobate mind, to do those things which are not convenient; Being filled with all unrighteousness, fornication, wickedness, covetousness, maliciousness; full of envy, murder, debate, deceit, malignity; whis-perers, Backbiters, haters of God, despiteful, proud, boasters, inven-tors of evil things, disobedient to parents, Without understanding, covenantbreakers, without natural affection, implacable, unmerciful: Who knowing the judgment of God, that they which commit such things are worthy of death, not only do the same, but have pleasure in them that do them (Romans 1:26-32).

This means that natural law theory is a myth, the creation of Hellenistic Greek philosophers to offer hope in a world in

---

9. *Ibid.*, I, pp. 74-76.

which the Greek city-state (the *polis*) had fallen to Alexander the Great and then to Rome. But if natural law theory is a myth, what can take its place? To what *other* standard can men safely cling if they reject the abiding authority of God's law in history? Christian Reconstructionists have an answer: *none*. This answer is hated, rejected, and ridiculed by Christians in our day. This answer is the offense of Christian Reconstruction.

The 1990's: Crisis in Society

The collapse of the European Communist economies in late 1989 launched a new era, though not a true New World Order (Jesus launched that). A new European state was already on the drawing board. Immediately, 1990 was heralded as the dawn of man's New World Order. In August, 1990, the invasion of Kuwait by Saddam Hussein's Iraq signaled the first test of this New World Order. AIDS will prove to be a more broadly based, long-term problem. Meanwhile, the U.S. government's budget is $350+ billion a year in the red, the public schools continue to decline, and the optimism of the Reagan years is fading.

God is plowing up the modern world. This is softening the Establishment's resistance to many new ideas and movements, among which Christian Reconstruction is barely visible at present. This is good for us now; we need the noise of contemporary events to hide us from humanist enemies who, if they fully understood the long-term threat to their civilization that our ideas pose, would be wise to take steps to crush us.

And so we go about our work. We have time on our side; our opponents don't. We have a sovereign God on our side; our opponents don't. We cannot afford to be complacent; we can, however, afford to be confident, and for the same reasons that David was. Plus, we have word processors and mailing lists. That makes all the difference. A dozen men armed with word processors can inflict enormous damage on those whose paradigms are in a state of collapse.

You can't beat something with nothing. Theonomists alone proclaim this crucial something: biblical law. I say this with great confidence, not in myself but in God's law. And does this make our opponents angry! Read this book to find out why.

INTRODUCTION

Gary DeMar

In truth, "prolific" is hardly adequate to suggest the veritable flood of publications from these writers. It seems unlikely that anyone, and certainly not this writer, could honestly claim that he keeps up with every article, monograph, and tome laying out the latest advances and revisions of theonomist teaching.[1]

As the above quotation demonstrates, Mr. Neuhaus admits that he does not keep up with Reconstructionist publications. After reading his critique, one comes away with the impression that Mr. Neuhaus has read little of what has been published by Reconstructionist authors, and what he has read or heard seems to be secondhand. These secondhand sources are easy to spot. It seems that with contemporary Christian scholarship, one heresy hunter's misrepresentations are simply copied by other heresy hunters and passed off as facts. This is not scholarship. Christians who write highly critical review essays should take seriously the words of the Ninth Commandment: "Thou shalt not bear false witness against thy neighbour" (Ex. 20:16). This is especially true when the neighbor is in print on the particular topics involved. It leaves the critic vulnerable to the negative sanction against perjury: "Then shall ye do unto him, as he had thought to have done unto his brother: so shalt thou put the evil away from among you" (Deut. 19:19).

---

1. Richard John Neuhaus, "Why Wait for the Kingdom?: The Theonomist Temptation," *First Things*, No. 3 (May 1990), p. 14.

Mr. Neuhaus comments that he cannot keep up with "the latest advances and revisions of theonomist teaching." What he describes as "advances and revisions" are nothing more than the basic premises of Reconstructionism restated again and again because our critics fail to read the existing material. Here is how the process works: a critic goes into print with unsupported accusations; we respond in print within six months, sometimes in 30 days, sometimes in a full-length book; the original critic fails to respond or even acknowledge our refutation; and then a new critic picks up the original criticisms and repeats them. In Hal Lindsey's case, he allowed *The Road to Holocaust* to be reprinted in a paperback version without even correcting misspelled names, e.g., "John Rousas Rushdoony" for the actual Rousas John Rushdoony. Gary North offers the suggestion that the actions of the original published critics reveal that they are not involved in a quest for truth; they are involved in a quest for royalty checks, and sensationalism sells.

The flood of critiques of Christian Reconstruction by popular writers[2] began in earnest in 1985, twelve years after Rushdoony's *Institutes of Biblical Law* appeared. The initial attack came as a series of brief comments in Dave Hunt's book, *The Seduction of Christianity*, and was followed by *Beyond Seduction*[3] and *Whatever Happened to Heaven?*, all published by Harvest House.[4] The last-named book was a direct attack on Christian Reconstruction. Then came House and Ice's *Dominion Theology: Blessing or Curse?* This seemingly scholarly attempt at refutation

---

2. The debate over Christian Reconstruction has being going on for quite some time. See Greg L. Bahnsen, *Theonomy in Christian Ethics*, 2nd ed. (Phillipsburg, NJ: Presbyterian and Reformed, [1977] 1984), pp. xi-xxvii.

3. *The Seduction of Christianity* (1985) and *Beyond Seduction* (1987) were answered by Gary DeMar and Peter Leithart in *The Reduction of Christianity: A Biblical Response to Dave Hunt* (Ft. Worth, TX: Dominion Press, 1988).

4. Harvest House also published *Satan's Underground* by Lauren Stratford. This book and its author were exposed as frauds by an article appearing in *Cornerstone Magazine*, "Satan's Side Show" (Vol. 18, Issue 90, pp. 23-28). While Dave Hunt does not perpetrate the same kind of fraud as Stratford and her book, his work is still fraudulent in that he never accurately describes Christian Reconstructionist distinctives. Nor does he inform his readers that there are various eschatological positions that have had wide acceptance in the church long before dispensational premillennialism gained a foothold in the nineteenth century.

was itself refuted in great detail by two prominent Reconstructionist authors.[5] Hal Lindsey continued the attack with his poorly researched and badly reasoned *The Road to Holocaust*.

Most critics of Christian Reconstruction do not read carefully what we have written; even fewer acknowledge to their readership that comprehensive answers have been given to their attacks. For example, Hal Lindsey's *The Road to Holocaust* levels a charge of "anti-semitism" against Reconstructionists and all other groups that do not espouse a dispensational premillennial eschatology. In my book *The Debate over Christian Reconstruction*, two appendixes were included that answered this charge, one written by a Reconstructionist who happens to be Jewish! Lindsey nowhere in his book mentions this material. The charge of "anti-semitism" is a lie.[6] But it sells.

How to Play the Sensationalism Game

As Peter Leithart and I point out in *The Legacy of Hatred Continues*, and as I argue in **Question 10** in Part II of this book, by using a bit of "Lindsey-logic," dispensational premillennialism can be made to look "anti-semitic." This is how it's done. It takes very little imagination. The more trusting one's readers are, the less imagination it takes. There are two targeted groups of victims: one's opponents and one's overly trusting readers. We begin with a factual historical statement regarding the postmillennial view of the Jews. We begin with the truth.

Postmillennialists have always taught that the Jews have a prominent place in God's prophetic plan prior to the so-called "rapture": a great number of Jews will come to Christ before Jesus' return. Long before dispensationalism came on the scene in the early nineteenth century, the conversion of the Jews was a pillar of postmillennial thought and still is. The Westminster Assembly's *Directory for the Pub-*

---

5. Greg L. Bahnsen and Kenneth L. Gentry, Jr., *House Divided: The Break-Up of Dispensational Theology* (Tyler, TX: Institute for Christian Economics, 1989).

6. Steve Schlissel and David Brown, *On Hal Lindsey and the Restoration of the Jews* (Edmonton, Alberta: Still Waters Revival Books, 1990). Steve Schlissel pastors Messiah's Christian Reformed Church in Brooklyn, New York. Rev. Schlissel is a Jewish-born Christian Reconstructionist.

4   CHRISTIAN RECONSTRUCTION

lick Worship of God, published in 1645, nearly 200 years before anyone even heard of dispensational premillennialism, contains the following instruction on "Publick Prayer before the Sermon": "To pray for the propagation of the gospel and kingdom of Christ to all nations; *for the conversion of the Jews*, the fullness of the Gentiles, etc."

Next, we move to modern dispensationalism. We also report only the facts. No misrepresentations at this stage:

> In contrast, dispensationalism does not have a prophetic role for the Jews until *after* the "rapture." After the church is raptured, according to dispensationalism, "Two thirds of the children of Israel in the land will perish."[7] (There is nothing in postmillennialism that consigns Jews to this horrible fate.) The rapture immediately precedes the beginning of the Great Tribulation, in which Armageddon will occur, and Armageddon brings the slaughter of the Jews. Thus, anyone who preaches the imminent rapture also necessarily preaches the near-term massacre of Jews. To want the rapture to take place in one's own lifetime is to accept the inescapable slaughter of the Jews a few years later.

Third, we begin to sensationalize. We defame our opponents, not directly, but by innuendo. We make an unwarranted leap: from theology to supposedly inevitable implications — implications that foster anti-semitism. The sin begins here.

> Dispensationalists need the near-term slaughter of the Jews, if they want to escape life's problems in the rapture. They desperately want this escape, as the popularity of Dave Hunt's books testifies. It is obvious that the dispensationalist doctrine of the coming slaughter of the Jews leads inevitably to anti-semitism. Of course, not all dispensationalists are anti-semitic. But the fact remains, their system creates an attitude favorable to the destruction of Jews. Whenever we see such an attitude, even among those who publicly profess their support of national Israel, we are close to anti-semitism.
> We know why the dispensationalists support the nation of Israel: *self-interest*. Without the state of Israel, there can be no attack by the Antichrist against the Jews. Such an attack is prophetically inescapable, dispensationalists teach. It will take place shortly after the rap-

---

7. John F. Walvoord, *Israel in Prophecy* (Grand Rapids, MI: Zondervan/Academie, [1962] 1988), p. 108.

ture, they say. We know that dispensationalists long for the rapture. They therefore long for the slaughter of the Jews. These two imminent events – the church's rapture and Jews' slaughter – are separated by no more than seven years. If a dispensationalist prays "Come quickly, Lord Jesus," he is also implicitly praying, "Come slightly less quickly, Antichrist, to slaughter the Jews, after I'm out of here!" So, the whole mindset of dispensationalism inevitably leads to anti-semitism.

What is wrong with these two paragraphs? Surely not the theological specifics of dispensationalism. This really is what the system teaches about the Jews during Armageddon. What is wrong is this: an attempt to link a theological interpretation of prophecy with a particular set of conclusions about the inevitability of anti-semitism in our day. We imply (or even state openly) that a particular millennial viewpoint or approach to Bible interpretation necessarily leads to a particular mental attitude towards others, or at least a *subconscious* attitude. (How does someone consciously refute an accusation regarding his subconscious?) This makes our targeted victims the implicit accomplices of anti-semites. "After all," we have them say, "what good does it do to oppose the inevitable?"

The problem with dispensationalism's view of the Jews is theological, not emotional. Dispensationalists are seldom anti-semitic, but they do not interpret biblical prophecy accurately. Theirs is an intellectual error, not a racist evil. Dispensationalism has taken a first-century fulfillment of prophecy, when many Jews did perish at the hands of the Roman armies (the destruction of Jerusalem in A.D. 70),[8] and has projected this event nearly 2000 years into the future: to what is described as the coming "Great Tribulation." They teach that this event will follow the rapture of the church. A series of false interpretations then leads to sensational expectations about the immediate future. *The dispensational system creates an emotional demand for sensationalism.* Book sales prove it. The most successful Christian theological books today (as distinguished from self-help books on the family) are all linked to current events in relation to

---

8. David Chilton, *The Great Tribulation* (Ft. Worth, Texas: Dominion Press, 1987).

Bible prophecy: the New Age, demons, last-days cults, etc. It all began with *The Late, Great Planet Earth*. There is big money and personal fame in making millennial predictions, even when they do not come true (and they never do). When they do not come true, the author then can write another sensational book showing that they really will come true. Like an addiction, sensationalism feeds on itself, both for the pusher and the addict.

History has recorded for us the fulfillment of this prophecy concerning Jerusalem and Old Covenant Israel.[9] But because dispensationalism sees this as unfulfilled prophecy, an escalation of anti-semitism in these "last days" becomes a "sign" of the end. Anti-semitism becomes a prophetic inevitability under dispensationalism. So, they go around looking for anti-semites under every eschatological bed except their own.

What the sensationalists neglect to mention is that the existence in the Bible of an anti-Old Covenant Israel prophecy, fulfilled or unfulfilled, in and of itself tells us nothing about the intent or attitude of the person who believes it. Only the specific content of his exposition tells us what he thinks about the proper interpretation. That a Bible expositor faithfully refers to an anti-Old Covenant Israel prophecy says nothing about his attitude toward Jews, either as a group or as individuals. But to admit this is to reduce the moral legitimacy of sensationalism.

What is the result? *The Road to Holocaust*.

The Roots of Genocide

"Anti-semitism" has nothing to do with eschatology. There are as many reasons for "anti-semitism" as there are reasons for all types of national and racial hatred. Dozens of religious, racial, and ethnic groups have been persecuted over the centuries. The martyrdom of Christians began as soon as the gospel called upon people to repent, and it continues to this day (Acts

---

9. Flavius Josephus, *The Wars of the Jews or The History of the Destruction of Jerusalem* in *The Works of Josephus*, trans. William Whiston (Peabody, MA: Hendrickson Publishers, 1987), pp. 543-772. For an excerpted reading of the material pertinent to Jerusalem's A.D. 70 destruction, see David Chilton, *Paradise Restored: A Biblical Theology of Dominion* (Ft. Worth, TX: Dominion Press, 1985), pp. 237-90.

7:54-60). Few historians write about the Turkish massacre of the Armenian Christians, described as "the first genocide of the twentieth century."[10]

Maxim Gorky, the leading Soviet writer under Joseph Stalin, invented the following formula to justify genocide: "If the enemy does not surrender, he must be destroyed."[11] Stalin spoke openly about the "liquidation of the kulaks as a class."[12] "It was the green light for a policy of extermination, more than three years before Hitler came to power, twelve years before the ordering of the 'final solution'."[13] And who was a "kulak"? "Anyone who employed hired labor . . . , anyone who owned two horses or two cows or a nice house."[14] How many "kulaks" were executed? No one knows for sure. Winston Churchill wrote that Stalin told him that ten million peasants had been dealt with: One-third murdered, one-third in concentration camps, and one-third transported against their will to Siberia or central Asia.

A large percentage of the generation that knew Joseph Stalin died as a result of his directives. These were purely political killings, "exterminations," "liquidations" of "the enemy class" and "undesirable elements. "How many were involved? Solzhenitsyn's estimates reach as high as sixty million. Robert Conquest, author of *The Great Terror*, fixed the number at well into the millions. It is doubtful if we will ever know the true total – God alone knows.[15]

Religious persecution dominated both the Soviet Union and Nazi Germany. Not a few lost their lives in systematic purges. Stalin and Hitler "had done everything in their power to destroy the Polish Church. Hitler had closed its schools, universi-

10. Mikhail Heller and Alexsandr M. Nekrich, *Utopia in Power: The History of the Soviet Union from 1917 to the Present* (New York: Summit Books, 1986), p. 236.

11. *Idem.*

12. *Idem.*

13. Paul Johnson, *Modern Times: The World from the Twenties to the Eighties* (New York: Harper & Row, 1983), p. 271.

14. Heller and Nekrich, *Utopia in Power*, p. 234.

15. Lloyd Billingsley, *The Generation that Knew Not Josef: A Critique of Marxism and the Religious Left* (Portland, OR: Multnomah Press, 1985), p. 37.

ties and seminaries and murdered a third of the clergy."[16] A study of the history of Nazi Germany will show that Hitler had designs to eliminate Christians if they got in the way of his socialist-inspired millennium.

Adolf Hitler's disenfranchisement of the Jews in Germany in the 1930s and 1940s is a prominent theme in any study of World War II, Germany, and political tyranny. The Jews were methodically and efficiently barred from economic, educational, and political participation. Eventually they were driven from the nation, and millions died at the hands of power gone mad. What many people do not know is that the Christian church was put on notice either to follow the Nazi Party line or be closed down. Under the leadership of Alfred Rosenberg, an outspoken pagan, "the Nazi regime intended eventually to destroy Christianity in Germany, if it could, and substitute the old paganism of the early tribal Germanic gods and the new paganism of the Nazi extremists. As Bormann, one of the men closest to Hitler, said publicly in 1941, 'National Socialism and Christianity are irreconcilable.' "[17] William Shirer, an eyewitness to Hitler's rise to power, would later write: "We know now what Hitler envisioned for the German Christians: the utter suppression of their religion."[18]

Hitler's anti-semitism was probably associated with his adoption of pagan gnostic beliefs.[19] But Hitler was as anti-Christian as he was anti-semitic. The same can be said for Lenin and Stalin. So, not only does Lindsey egregiously misrepresent the views of fellow Christians, but he distorts history with sophomoric scholarship. He has not done his homework.

Witch Hunt

The front cover copy of *Witch Hunt*, a book critical of the methodology used by a number of self-proclaimed heresy hunt-

---

16. Johnson, *Modern Times*, p. 699.

17. William L. Shirer, *The Rise and Fall of the Third Reich* (New York: Simon and Schuster, 1960), p. 240.

18. William L. Shirer, *The Nightmare Years: 1930-1940* (Boston, MA: Little, Brown and Company, 1984), p. 156.

19. Dusty Sklar, *The Nazis and the Occult* (New York: Dorset Press, [1977] 1989).

ers intent on exposing every hint of error in the Christian community, describes the contemporary theological climate: "Christians are attacking Christians, charging one another with heresy. But are the accusations fair? Is the reasoning valid?"[20] The book you now are reading is about fairness. There is certainly no doubt that Christians disagree on numerous issues. At this point in history the Christian church has not attained theological consensus. When disagreements arise over variant theological positions, it is incumbent upon opposing sides to at least represent the opposing doctrinal opinions accurately. Has this been done? For the most part, it has not.

Honest Reporting as Heresy

Probably the most infamous attack on Christian Reconstruction was "Democracy as Heresy," published in *Christianity Today*.[21] I have seen its conclusions repeated in numerous articles critical of Christian Reconstruction. In many cases this is a subsequent article's *only* source of information for its critique. Are the author's conclusions reliable and his assessments fair? In most cases they are not, and there is no way that they could be, since Mr. Clapp stated that "he had not had time to read our books in detail, for the Reconstructionists publish too much."[22] There seems to be a pattern here. Self-proclaimed heresy hunters have become "experts" without reading an adequate number of the published works of Reconstructionists, and their false reporting gets picked up by others who fail to check the reliability of their sources. While Reconstructionists certainly do publish quite a few books each year, they are all indexed! There is no excuse for sloppy scholarship.

The misrepresentations of the "Democracy as Heresy" article are too numerous to list. A single example, however, will give you some idea how bad this article really is. On the first page of

---

20. Bob and Gretchen Passantino, *Witch Hunt* (Nashville, TN: Thomas Nelson, 1990).
21. Rodney Clapp, "Democracy as Heresy," *Christianity Today* (February 20, 1987), pp. 17-23.
22. Gary North, "Honest Reporting as Heresy: My Response to *Christianity Today*" (Tyler, TX: Institute for Christian Economics, 1987), p. 3.

"Democracy as Heresy" the author asserts that Reconstruction-ists would abolish democracy and reinstitute slavery.[23] But no-where does the author define democracy[24] for his readers, and it is only later in the article that slavery is defined, not as "chat-tel slavery," as was practiced in the United States, but as "bibli-cal slavery" (Exodus 22:3b).[25] "Biblical slavery," more appro-priately described as "indentured servitude," would "allow im-poverished persons to labor away their indebtedness, or crimi-nals to make restitution."[26] The Thirteenth Amendment to the Constitution supports "involuntary servitude . . . as a punish-ment for crime whereof the party shall have been duly convict-ed" (Section 1). This is the Reconstructionist position. It is also the position of Prison Fellowship president Charles Colson, a strong advocate of biblical restitution. As one letter to the editor in response to "Democracy of Heresy" stated: "[T]o claim that a major proposal of the Reconstructionists is the reinstitution of slavery, only later clarifying that this means a form of inden-tured servanthood, is misleading and prejudicial."[27] We agree.

Categorizing the Critics

After reading every supposed refutation that has come across my desk, I have been able to put them into one of five catego-ries: (1) Gross Misrepresentation, (2) Eschatology as the Test of Orthodoxy, (3) Anti-Biblical Culture, (4) A Combination of Gross Misrepresentation and No Alternative, and (5) Honest Disagreement but Appreciation and Benefit.

1. Gross Misrepresentation

The first category of critics so misrepresents Christian Recon-struction that the authors either have not read what we have

23. Clapp, "Democracy as Heresy," p. 17.
24. For a biblical and historical understanding of democracy, see Gary DeMar, "Vox Populi, Vox Dei?," *The Biblical Worldview* (February 1990).
25. For a comprehensive study of slavery, see Gary North, *Tools of Dominion: The Case Laws of Exodus* (Tyler, TX: Institute for Christian Economics, 1990), pp. 111-206.
26. Clapp, "Democracy as Heresy," p. 20.
27. *Christianity Today* (April 3, 1987), p. 8.

written or they have purposely distorted our position. Hal Lindsey's *The Road to Holocaust* is in this category, although he is not alone. There are so many factual errors, logical fallacies, chopped quotations, and blatant misrepresentations that one wonders if Lindsey read any of the books written by Reconstructionist authors.[28]

In doing further research on Lindsey's critical analysis of Christian Reconstruction, after the publication of *The Legacy of Hatred Continues*, I came across an issue of *Passport Magazine* (January-February 1988). After reading its critique of Christian Reconstruction, I noticed that it contained many of the same errors I found in Lindsey's *The Road to Holocaust*. For example, Rousas John Rushdoony is listed in the footnotes of both the *Passport* article and *The Road to Holocaust* as John Rousas Rushdoony. Obviously, neither critic has read Rushdoony's books.

There are more serious errors than a reversal of first and middle names. Lindsey writes of Rushdoony's view of the law (the only quotation from Rushdoony's 849 pages of *The Institutes of Biblical Law*): "The love affair the Reconstructionists have with the Law permeates their writings. Rushdoony adds, 'So central is the Law of God, that the demands of the law are fulfilled as the necessary condition of grace.' In other words, we earn grace by keeping the Law."[29] But Lindsey only quotes half of Rushdoony's sentence. Here is Rushdoony's *full* statement with the missing section in italics: "So central is the Law of God, that the demands of the law are fulfilled as the necessary condition of grace, *and God fulfills the demands of the law on Jesus Christ*."[30] This same chopped quotation can be found on page 4 of the *Passport* article, footnote number 14.

Either the author of *Passport* copied Lindsey's errors from a previous article written by Lindsey or another unnamed source, or else Lindsey copied the *Passport* material, errors and all.

---

28. For an analysis of *The Road to Holocaust*, see Gary DeMar and Peter Leithart, *The Legacy of Hatred Continues: A Response to Hal Lindsey's The Road to Holocaust* (Tyler, TX: Institute for Christian Economics, 1989).

29. Hal Lindsey, *The Road to Holocaust* (New York: Bantam Books, 1989), p. 157.

30. Rousas John Rushdoony, *The Institutes of Biblical Law* (Phillipsburg, NJ: Presbyterian and Reformed, 1973), p. 75.

Either way, the errors are identical and teach the opposite of what Rushdoony actually wrote and still believes. This type of "scholarship" is not uncommon. Numerous errors of this variety were pointed out to Mr. Lindsey soon after the publication of *The Road to Holocaust*; therefore, it is inexcusable that a reprint edition was issued in 1990 with *none* of the errors corrected. But it is also typical.

2. Eschatology as the Test of Orthodoxy

The second group of criticisms falls into the category of making a single eschatological position a test of orthodoxy. Dave Hunt's books fit into this category, especially his *Whatever Happened to Heaven?* Hunt is a dispensational premillennialist who believes that the pre-trib rapture is imminent. In addition, he teaches that a regard for the earth and the biblical evaluation and rescue of institutions of law, economics, education, and civil government are a denial of the Christian's sole task to preach the gospel and proclaim that the rapture is near. Our hope is heaven, Hunt says, not earth.

There isn't a Christian alive who would disagree that heaven is the Christian's hope and home. But the Reconstructionist asks, as did Francis Schaeffer and many others before him: "How should we then live prior to our being taken to heaven either in death or at the return of Christ?"[31] Hunt offers little that would satisfy the millions of Christians who believe that God has called His redeemed people to be stewards of the world, whether He comes tomorrow or in a thousand years.

The imminent return of Christ has captivated Hunt, as it has countless others before him, always to the detriment of God's kingdom work and for the advance of humanism.

> The effect of the teachings rising out of these years was a drastic pessimism which precluded the courage to face liberal defections (indeed, such defections were expected and inevitable) or to under-

---

31. Francis A. Schaeffer, *How Should We Then Live?* in *The Complete Works of Francis A. Schaeffer: A Christian Worldview*, 5 vols. (Westchester, IL: Crossway Books, [1976] 1982), vol. 5., pp. 83-277.

take long-term projects for the church. For example, F. W. Newton declared that the imminent return of Christ "totally forbids all working for earthly projects distant in time." Social and political endeavor was no longer seen as legitimate.[32]

Should a single eschatological position, especially dispensational premillennialism, which had its beginnings in the late 1820s, be used as a test for orthodoxy? This would mean that the church was ill-informed on eschatological issues for over 1800 years until J. N. Darby (or possibly Margaret Macdonald) came on the scene with the pre-tribulational rapture doctrine! As even dispensational scholars admit, the church knew nothing of this doctrine until its advocacy by Darby. While history is not authoritative, it can teach us some valuable lessons. Reformed scholar R. C. Sproul writes:

> Although tradition [or history] does not rule our interpretation, it does guide it. If, upon reading a particular passage, you have come up with an interpretation that has escaped the notice of every other Christian for two thousand years, or that has been championed by universally recognized heretics, chances are pretty good that you had better abandon your interpretation.[33]

Reconstructionists are not the only ones who believe Hunt's dispensationalism is not taught in Scripture and has not been taught in the church until the early nineteenth century. Dispensational premillennialism has always been thought of as aberrational if not "heretical." Amillennialist scholar R. B. Kuiper, a professor at Westminster Theological Seminary, wrote in 1936 that two grievous errors were "prevalent among American fundamentalists, Arminianism and the Dispensationalism of the Scofield Bible." The General Assembly of the Orthodox Presbyterian Church described Arminianism and Dispensationalism as "anti-reformed heresies."[34]

---

32. Greg L. Bahnsen, "The *Prima Facie* Acceptability of Postmillennialism," Symposium on the Millennium, *The Journal of Christian Reconstruction*, ed. Gary North, III:2 (Winter 1976-77), pp. 51-52.

33. R. C. Sproul, "A Serious Charge," *The Agony of Deceit: What Some TV Preachers are Really Teaching*, ed. Michael Horton (Chicago, IL: Moody Press, 1990), p. 35.

34. R. B. Kuiper, *The Presbyterian Guardian* (September 12, 1936), pp. 225-27. Quoted

John Murray, also of Westminster Seminary, wrote that the " 'Dispensationalism' of which we speak as heterodox from the standpoint of the Reformed Faith is that form of interpretation, widely popular at the present time, which discovers in the several dispensations of God's redemptive revelation distinct and even contrary principles of divine procedure and thus destroys the unity of God's dealings with fallen mankind."[35]

Premillennialism of the covenantal variety was not under attack by these men. Kuiper made this crystal clear:

> It is a matter of common knowledge that there is ever so much more to the dispensationalism of the Scofield Bible than the mere teaching of Premillennialism. Nor do the two stand and fall together. There are premillennarians who have never heard of Scofield's dispensations. More important than that, there are serious students of God's Word who hold to the Premillennial return of Christ and emphatically reject Scofield's system of dispensations as fraught with grave error.[36]

How can we avoid the pitfalls of "orthodoxy by eschatology," especially when that eschatology is the aberrational dispensationalism? If we all stick with the historic creedal formulation that Jesus will "come again to judge the quick and the dead" a lot more understanding will take place among those who differ on eschatological systems of interpretation.[37] Christian Reconstructionists have been unjustly criticized by a novel millennial view for holding an eschatological position that has both scriptural and historical support.

---

in Edwin H. Rian, *The Presbyterian Conflict* (Grand Rapids, MI: Eerdmans, 1940), p. 101.

35. *The Presbyterian Guardian* (February 3, 1936), p. 143. Quoted in *ibid.*, pp. 236-7.
36. *The Presbyterian Guardian* (November 14, 1936), p. 54. Quoted in *ibid.*, p. 31.
37. Carl Henry wrote the following in 1947:

> Furthermore, there is a noticeable shift in eschatological thinking. On the one hand, there appears a return to a more conservative type of pre-millennialism, such as that of Alford and Trench, with an accompanying tendency to discard dogmatism on details; if this continues, the eschatological preaching of next generation Fundamentalists will concentrate on the proclamation of the kingdom, the second coming, the bodily resurrection of the dead, and the future judgment, and will not concern itself too much with lesser events (*The Uneasy Conscience of Modern Fundamentalism* [Grand Rapids, Eerdmans, 1947], p. 51).

3. Anti-Biblical Culture

Even a cursory reading of historical records will show that for many centuries, the church, both individually and corporately, has been involved in applying the Bible to society. Take the United States as a singular example. The first colleges in America were started by Christians — Harvard, Yale, and Princeton being the most well known. Our nation's political system cannot be understood without an understanding of the Bible. State constitutions were explicitly Christian. Our nation's laws presuppose the Christian religion. In 1892, the United States Supreme Court determined, in the case of *The Church of the Holy Trinity vs. United States*, that America was a Christian nation from its earliest days. The court opinion was an exhaustive study of the historical and legal evidence for America's Christian heritage. After examining hundreds of court cases, state constitutions, and other historical documents, Justice Josiah Brewer, who delivered the opinion of the Court, concluded with these words:

> This is a religious people. This is historically true. From the discovery of this continent to the present hour, there is a single voice making this affirmation. . . . These and many other matters which might be noticed, add a volume of unofficial declarations to the mass of organic utterances that this is a Christian nation.[38]

The list could go on. These facts have been documented so many times that there is no need to chronicle them here.[39]

Since the rise of dispensational premillennialism in the mid-nineteenth century — which is Hunt's operating interpretive methodology — the church has steadily turned the culture over

---

38. Decision of the Supreme Court of the United States in the case of *The Church of the Holy Trinity v. The United States* (143 United States 457 [1892]).

39. Gary DeMar, *God and Government*, 3 vols. (Brentwood, TN: Wolgemuth & Hyatt, 1990); *Ruler of the Nations: Biblical Blueprints for Government* (Ft. Worth, TX: Dominion Press, 1987), pp. 225-40; "The Theonomic Response to National Confessionalism," *God and Politics: Four Views on the Reformation of Civil Government*, ed. Gary Scott Smith (Phillipsburg, NJ: Presbyterian and Reformed, 1989), pp. 200-12; Gary North, *Political Polytheism: The Myth of Pluralism* (Tyler, TX: Institute for Christian Economics, 1989), pp. 383-97.

to those who deny Christ and His law. Society has become progressively worse because Christians have abandoned culture. The resultant decline of culture has added further fuel to the heightened millennial fires of a near-return of our Lord.

4. A Combination of Gross Misrepresentation and No Alternative

The fourth group of critiques is a combination of the first category (Gross Misrepresentation) and the lack of a specific biblical alternative. This category differs from that of eschatological critiques because the rapture does not play a role in the evaluation. Although there are disagreements over eschatology, they usually focus on the nature of the kingdom of God and not the timing of the rapture.

Reconstructionists are easy targets for this category of criticism because we attempt to offer *specific*, Bible-based answers to today's *specific* problems. We take God and His law seriously. This irritates our critics. Consider this summary of what Rodney Clapp perceives is wrong with Reconstructionist distinctives:

> Is God really nothing more than the abstract, impersonal dispenser of equally abstract and impersonal laws? And is the objective of the Christian church, and its hope for the world to concentrate on the Law itself — or to come to know the Lawgiver?[40]

This is nonsense — an egregious example of a false dilemma. The laws that Reconstructionists turn to as the standard for righteousness for self-government, family government, church government, and civil government are the same laws given by Noah (Genesis 9:6-7), Abraham (18:19; 26:5), Moses (e.g. Exodus 21-23), Jesus (e.g., Matthew 5-7; 28:18-20), and Paul (Romans 13:9). Was God "nothing more than the abstract, impersonal dispenser of equally abstract and impersonal laws" to these men? Of course not. Did their love for God's law (Psalm 119:97a, 113b, 119b) mean that they did not "come to know the Lawgiver"? Read Psalm 119 and try to separate the Psalmist's love for God from his love for God's law. Jesus said that if we

---

40. Clapp, "Democracy as Heresy," p. 23.

truly love Him we will keep His commandments (John 14:15). Paul writes that loving one's neighbor is the fulfillment of the law. But Paul does not allow us to define love in our own way. He cites the law: "You shall not commit adultery [Exodus 20:-14], You shall not murder [20:13], You shall not steal, You shall not covet [20:17]" (Romans 13:9).

My files are filled with numerous other attempts at refutation of the distinctives known as Christian Reconstruction. None of the critics offers what I would call a comprehensive, worked-out alternative social theory. The closest anyone comes is Norman L. Geisler. His answer is a variant of Greek natural law theory. Geisler maintains that the Bible cannot and should not be used by the nations as a blueprint for living.[41]

Others such as Charles Colson are a bit schizophrenic in their rejection of Christian Reconstruction. For example, Colson says that Reconstructionists are wrong in their application of the Mosaic law to contemporary society. But it is Colson who turns to the Mosaic law (Exodus 22) as the only hope to resolve our nation's crime problem. He asserts that the only solution to the crime problem is "to take nonviolent criminals out of our prisons and make them pay back their victims with restitution. This is how we can solve the prison crowding problem."[42] Richard Chewning, a sometime critic of Christian Reconstruction, discusses some of the advantages of a seven-year limit on debt as set forth in Deuteronomy 15:1-5.[43] Why can Colson and Chewning legitimately go to the Old Testament for instruction while Reconstructionists cannot? Is it because these men pick and choose what they like and ignore what they don't like? This is convenient, but it is hardly a biblical approach.

The debate is over how the Christian should live and by what standard he should govern his life. Should the Christian turn to

---

41. Norman L. Geisler, "Natural Law and Business Ethics," *Biblical Principles and Business: The Foundations*, ed. Richard C. Chewning (Colorado Springs, CO: NavPress, 1989), pp. 157-78.

42. Charles Colson, "The Kingdom of God and Human Kingdoms," *Transforming Our World: A Call to Action*, ed. James M. Boice (Portland, OR: Multnomah, 1988), pp. 154-55.

43. Richard C. Chewning, "Editor's Perspective," *Biblical Principles & Business: The Practice* (Colorado Springs, CO: NavPress, 1990), pp. 247-48.

the Bible as his rule book? Should the world look to the Ten Commandments as laws or "suggestions"? It seems that most of our critics view God's laws as "mere suggestions." Ted Koppel, host of "Night Line," has a better handle on the nature of God's law than do many Christians:

> What Moses brought down from Mt. Sinai were not the Ten Suggestions. They are commandments. *Are*, not *were*. The sheer brilliance of the Ten Commandments is that they codify in a handful of words acceptable human behavior, not just for then or now, but for all time. Language evolves. Power shifts from one nation to another. Messages are transmitted with the speed of light. Man erases one frontier after another. And yet we and our behavior and the commandments governing that behavior remain the same.[44]

Reconstructionists say that the Bible is the standard, both for salvation and holy living. Most of our critics say that while the Bible is our standard, it does not give us specific guidelines on economics, law, politics, and other secular matters, although few are ever consistent on this point. It does not offer "blueprints." For example, Christians protest abortion and the legalization of homosexuality because the Bible is against these practices. As we saw above, Charles Colson believes the Bible is the only solution to prison reform: restitution in place of imprisonment. Who among us would support bestiality? The New Testament does not have a law against bestiality.[45]

For years conservatives have been opposing those who claim that while the Bible may be authoritative on matters regarding salvation, it is not necessarily inerrant and infallible on matters of science and history. The battle within the Southern Baptist Convention is over this very point.

---

44. Ted Koppel, Commencement Address at Duke University, Durham, North Carolina (May 10, 1987). Emphasis added. Quoted in Robert H. Bork, *The Tempting of America: The Political Seduction of Law* (New York: The Free Press, 1990), p. 164.

45. A noted dispensational professor and author stated that bestiality should not be considered either a sin or a crime because the New Testament does not condemn it. For the consistent dispensationalist, only those Old Testament laws *repeated* in the New Testament are valid. You can read more about this in Kenneth L. Gentry, Jr., "Must God Stutter?," *Dispensationalism in Transition*, III:5 (May 1990).

"Conservatives" and "moderates" within the SBC part paths essentially on their fundamental views of Scripture. Both sides believe the Bible as originally written was infallible insofar as it tells the story of salvation. Conservatives maintain additionally that the original autographs were inerrant in all matters, including history and science.[46]

If conservatives want to maintain that the Bible is authoritative "in all matters, including history and science," then why not economics, law, and civil government? All talk about an inerrant and infallible Bible goes down the drain if these so-called secular disciplines are categorized along with the liberal assessment of "history and science."

5. Honest Disagreement but Appreciation and Benefit

A fifth category of criticisms has done a fair job in evaluating Christian Reconstruction and has found the position helpful and insightful, although there are still disagreements on a number of issues. Keep in mind, however, that no two theologians agree on every point of any doctrine. This is why we have Baptists, Presbyterians, Methodists, Pentecostals, and numerous other theological traditions.

John Frame, a professor at Westminster Theological Seminary in Escondido, California, writes that it is "necessary for us to do careful exegetical study in the law itself in order to determine its applications, rather than simply trying to make deductions from broad theological principles." He writes the following about Reconstructionists and others who are attempting to do the necessary exegetical and applicational work:

> A number of writers have made good beginnings in this direction. See James B. Jordan, *The Law of the Covenant* (Tyler, Texas: Institute for Christian Economics, 1984); Gary North, *Economic Commentary on the Bible*, so far in three volumes: *The Dominion Covenant: Genesis; Moses and Pharaoh*; and *The Sinai Strategy* [and the most recent *Tools of Dominion*] (Tyler, Texas: Institute for Christian Economics, 1982, 1985, 1986, [1990]); [Vern Poythress], *Understanding [the Law of Mo-*

---

46. "Southern Baptist Schism: Just a Matter of Time?," *Christianity Today* (May 14, 1990), p. 47.

ses]; Rousas John Rushdoony, *Institutes [of Biblical Law]*; Gordon Wenham, *The Book of Leviticus* (Grand Rapids, MI: Eerdmans, 1979). The conclusions of these books are not always consistent with one another, and the authors' exegesis is of uneven quality. But they are attempting to do what most needs to be done in this area.[47]

Not all of the writers listed in the above quotation would call themselves Reconstructionists, but they are wrestling with the same issues. While a dispensationalist would dismiss the Mosaic law in its entirety — it's Jewish law — theologians guided by the distinctives of the Reformation believe that all of God's law, even those laws given specifically to Israel, have some application for today.

In the same issue of *The Westminster Theological Journal*, another author acknowledges the contributions made by Reconstructionists in the area of biblical ethics.

> One positive contribution of theonomy[48] is a renewed interest in the validity of God's law as an ethical standard. The question of the continuity of the Mosaic law as a binding code for Christians is receiving attention from a growing segment of the evangelical community. This increased concern for God's revealed moral standards is a healthy sign, much in need during these times.[49]

John Jefferson Davis acknowledges that the "theonomy movement has generated a good deal of discussion and controversy" and that "some of the initial criticism appears based on a misreading of the true intent of the position."[50] He specifically mentions the charge of "legalism" as a common misrepresentation. Davis lists a number of positive contributions: "Theonomy certainly represents a significant attempt in the contemporary

47. John M. Frame, "Toward a Theology of the State," *The Westminster Theological Journal*, 51:2 (Fall 1989), p. 204, note 11.

48. "Theonomy" (God's law) is often used as a synonym for Christian Reconstruction. In reality, however, theonomy, the application of God's law to all aspects of society, is simply one pillar of the system.

49. Douglas O. Oss, "The Influence of Hermeneutical Frameworks in the Theonomy Debate," *ibid.*, p. 228.

50. John Jefferson Davis, *Foundations of Evangelical Theology* (Grand Rapids, MI: Baker Book House, 1984), p. 267.

scene to apply a comprehensive biblical world view"; "Theonomy certainly represents a comprehensive challenge to secular humanism in American life today, on all fronts, on the basis of biblical theism and biblical authority"; "The theonomic movement also represents a call to the church to demonstrate principled, God-centered action in the midst of a decadent and permissive society. Not pietistic retreat but, a confident and aggressive attempt to extend[51] the kingdom of Christ in the world is the proper response to the social crises of the day"; "The theonomists have correctly seen that the humanistic faith at the foundation of Enlightenment culture is now in the process of crumbling, and must be replaced with biblical foundations"; "Even those who disagree with the details or even the central thesis of the theonomists can agree that our major institutions need to be reconstructed along more biblical lines."[52]

Cal Beisner in *Prosperity and Poverty* makes extensive use of Reconstructionist authors Bahnsen, Chilton, Grant, North, and Rushdoony, so much so that he has added an appendix to explain why he is *not* a Reconstructionist. He writes in an end note to the appendix "Methodological Note on the Use of Biblical Law": "While I quote some of these authors here, my doing so does not imply that I endorse their whole system of thought. While I disagree with them on some points, some of their exegetical and ethical arguments are persuasive on others. It would have been intellectually dishonest to have produced their ideas without giving them credit. Much criticism of their thought in mainstream evangelical circles is, I think, based on misunderstanding and caricature."[53]

Additional forms of appreciation can be found even in premillennial circles. Walter C. Kaiser quotes approvingly Reconstructionist author R. J. Rushdoony and his *Institutes of Biblical*

---

51. Notice that Dr. Davis does not charge Reconstructionists with trying to "bring in the kingdom." As a postmillennialist, Davis understands that the kingdom came at Christ's first coming. See John Jefferson Davis, *Christ's Victorious Kingdom: Postmillennialism Reconsidered* (Grand Rapids, MI: Baker Book House, 1986.

52. The above quotations can be found in Davis, *Foundations*, pp. 267-68.

53. E. Calvin Beisner, *Prosperity and Poverty: The Compassionate Use of Resources in a World of Scarcity* (Westchester, IL: Crossway Books, 1988), p. 277, note 4.

Law more than he quotes any other single author, including himself.[54] Even some dispensational writers cannot avoid Reconstructionist distinctives. J. Kerby Anderson edited a series of articles written by Christian leaders presently or formerly affiliated with Dallas Theological Seminary.[55] While the articles are a mixed bag, some of them would fit quite easily into the Reconstructionist mold. One article in particular caught my attention: "The Purpose of Penology in the Mosaic Law and Today." Keep in mind that the title of the book is *Living Ethically in the '90s*, not Living Ethically under the Old Covenant 3,400 Years Ago. The author, Gary R. Williams, writes:

> It is the purpose of this chapter to compare the objectives of modern penology with those of the God-given Mosaic Law in order to shed some light on the direction in which penological philosophy should be moving to solve some of its current conundrums.[56]

His article could have been written by a Reconstructionist. Since it was written by a dispensationalist, no one bats an eye, except maybe those authors in this same book who espouse a different position. I have in mind Robert P. Lightner's "Theonomy and Dispensationalism" and Norman L. Geisler's "A Dispensational Premillennial View of Law and Government."

Conclusion

Being a good critic of contemporary religious movements is a risky business, especially a "movement" like Christian Reconstruction. For example, the sheer volume of material put out by Reconstructionists necessitates at least a few years of study and interviews. There are additional pitfalls in being a critic. Since a number of people have taken it upon themselves to be judges of Christian Reconstruction, they should be reminded what

---

54. Walter C. Kaiser, Jr., *Toward Old Testament Ethics* (Grand Rapids, MI: Zondervan, 1983), pp. 73, 88, 117, 144, 145, 147, 148, 149, 154, 155, 157, 164, 165, 169, 196, 198, 199, 213, 229, 231, 256.

55. J. Kerby Anderson, ed., *Living Ethically in the '90s* (Wheaton, IL: Victor Books, 1990).

56. *Ibid.*, p. 124.

Scripture says: "Do not judge lest you be judged yourselves. For in the way you judge, you will be judged; and by your standard of measure, it shall be measured to you" (Matthew 7:1-2, NASB, which I use throughout my essays).

Jesus is not telling us to refrain from evaluating a theological position held by Christians who are making an impact in the Christian world. Jesus was in the business of evaluating the thoughts, words, and actions of His critics. In another place we are warned not to "believe every spirit"; instead, we are to "test the spirits to see whether they are from God; because many false prophets have gone out into the world" (1 John 4:1). The warning in Matthew 7:1-2 is designed to make the judge aware of a possible counter judgment that might prove damaging. The passage is not a command to remain silent when error is perceived to be rampant in the church.

Our criticism is not with our critics' attempts to deal with a view that they disagree with. Our argument is with the poorly reasoned approach and the failure to study the existing material.

The critic opens himself to a counter critique by those he criticizes. This was Jesus' warning to those who set themselves up as judges. In the case of our critics: How does *their* theology compare to the Bible and any other criteria they have used to call a rival theological position like Christian Reconstruction aberrational? The assumption of every critic is that his belief system is orthodox while the position he is examining is unorthodox. His methodology is equally on the line. It is indeed possible that Reconstructionists have theological "specks" in their eyes, but it may be equally true that after careful scrutiny we might find a few theological "logs" in the eyes of our critics (Matthew 7:3-5).

PART I

GOD'S COVENANTAL KINGDOM

Gary North

Chapter 1

THE NATURE OF GOD'S KINGDOM

Jesus answered, "My kingdom is not of this world. If My kingdom were of this world, My servants would fight, so that I should not be delivered to the Jews; but now My kingdom is not from here" (John 18:36; New King James Version).

Few passages in the Bible are misinterpreted in our day as often as this one. The only other one that seems to rival it is the favorite verse of the people who resent all church discipline (or any other kind of discipline imposed in the name of God): "Judge not, that you be not judged" (Matthew 7:1). (Can you imagine a police department that went by this rule?) We will consider the interpretation of this passage in Chapter 2. But before we do, we need to know exactly what Jesus meant by the word, "kingdom."

What about the kingdom of God? Does it have any jurisdiction or manifestation on earth, or is it strictly heavenly and limited to the human heart? Whenever a Christian argues that Christians have a God-given responsibility to work today to build God's kingdom on earth, unless he is referring only to personal evangelism or missions, someone will object. "Jesus wasn't building a political kingdom. He was only building His church. The church isn't an earthly kingdom. After all, His kingdom is not of this world."

Notice the implicit argument. First, Jesus was (and is) building His church (true). Second, Jesus was (and is) also building His kingdom (true). Third, the church is not supposed to be political (true). Fourth, His kingdom therefore is not political (true only if His kingdom is identical to His church).

Question: Is His kingdom identical with His church?

Protestants and Catholics

It always astounds me when I hear Protestants cite John 18:36 in order to defend a narrow definition of God's kingdom in history. Four centuries ago, this narrow definition was the Roman Catholic view of the kingdom. Roman Catholics equated the kingdom with the church, meaning the church of Rome. The world is outside the church, they said, and it is therefore doomed. The institutional church is all that matters as far as eternity is concerned, they argued. The world was contrasted with the kingdom ("church"), and the church could never encompass the world.

In sharp contrast, the Protestant Reformation was based on the idea that the *institutional* church must be defined much more narrowly than God's world-encompassing kingdom. Protestants always argued that God's kingdom is far wider in scope than the institutional church. So, from the Protestant viewpoint:

1. The kingdom is more than the church.
2. The church is less than the kingdom.

The Protestant doctrine, "every man a priest" — as Protestant an idea as there is — rests on the assumption that each Christian's service is a holy calling, not just the ordained priest's calling. Each Christian is supposed to serve as a full-time worker in God's kingdom (Romans 12:1). What is this kingdom? *It is the whole world of Christian service,* and not just the institutional church.

What we find today is that fundamentalist Protestants have unknowingly adopted the older Roman Catholic view of church and kingdom. Writes Peter Masters of Spurgeon's Metropolitan Tabernacle: "Reconstructionist writers all scorn the attitude of traditional evangelicals who see the church as something so completely distinct and separate from the world that they seek no 'authority' over the affairs of the world."[1] We do not argue, as this critic argues to defend his own position of cultural isolation, that "The kingdom of God is the church, small as it may sometimes appear, not the world. . . ."[2]

This definition of *the kingdom of God as the institutional church* is the traditional Roman Catholic definition of the kingdom, and it has led in the past to ecclesiocracy. It places everything under the institutional church. The church in principle absorbs everything.

This same definition of the church can also lead to the ghetto mentality and cultural isolation: it places nothing under Christianity, because the kingdom is narrowly defined as merely the institutional church. Because the institutional church is not authorized to control the State (correct), and because the kingdom is said to be identical to the church (incorrect), the kingdom of God is then redefined as having nothing to do with anything that is not strictly ecclesiastical. This is our critic's view of the kingdom.

So, pietists have sharply separated the kingdom of God (narrowly defined) from the world. Separating the institutional church from the world is necessary, but *separating God's kingdom from this world leads to the surrender of the world to **Satan's** kingdom.* Thus, it is never a question of "earthly kingdom vs. no earthly kingdom"; it is always a question of *whose* earthly kingdom, God's or Satan's? To deny that God's kingdom extends to the earth in history — the here and now — is necessarily to assert that Satan's kingdom is legitimate, at least until Jesus comes again. But Satan's kingdom is not legitimate, and Christians should do whatever they can to roll it back. *Rolling back Satan's earthly kingdom means rolling forward Christ's earthly kingdom.*

What Christian Reconstructionists argue is that this originally Protestant view of the kingdom of God in history has been steadily abandoned by Protestants since at least 1660, to the detriment of the gospel in general and Protestantism specific-

---

1. Peter Masters, "World Dominion: The High Ambition of Reconstructionism," *Sword & Trowel* (May 24, 1990), p. 18.

2. *Idem.*

ally. They call for the recovery and implementation of the older Protestant view of God's kingdom. This is what has made Christian Reconstructionists so controversial. Today's Protestants do not want to give up their medieval Roman Catholic definition of the kingdom of God, and they deeply resent anyone who asks them to adopt the original Protestant view. Their followers are totally unaware of the origins of what they are being taught by their leaders.

The Kingdom of God

There are a lot of definitions of the kingdom of God. Mine is simultaneously the simplest and the broadest: the *civilization* of God. It is the creation — the entire area under the King of Heaven's lawful dominion. It is the area that fell under Satan's reign in history as a result of Adam's rebellion. When man fell, he brought the whole world under God's curse (Genesis 3:17-19). The curse extended as far as the reign of sin did. This meant everything under man's dominion. This is what it still means. The laws of the kingdom of God extend just as far as sin does. This means every area of life.

God owns the whole world: "The earth is the LORD'S, and the fulness thereof; the world, and they that dwell therein" (Psalm 24:1). Jesus Christ, as God's Son and therefore legal heir, owns the whole earth. He has leased it out to His people to develop progressively over time, just as Adam was supposed to have served as a faithful leaseholder before his fall, bringing the world under dominion (Genesis 1:26-28). Because of Jesus' triumph over Satan at Calvary, God is now bringing under judgment every area of life. How? Through the preaching of the gospel, His two-edged sword of judgment (Revelation 19:15).

Reform and Restoration

The kingdom of God is the arena of God's redemption. Jesus Christ *redeemed* the whole world — that is, He *bought it back*. He did this by paying the ultimate price for man's sin: His death on the cross. *The whole earth has now been judicially redeemed.* It has been given "a new lease on life." The lease that Satan gained from Adam has been revoked. The Second Adam (Jesus Christ) holds lawful title.

The world has not been fully restored in history, nor can it be; sin still has its effects, and will until the day of final judgment. But progressively over time, it is possible for the gospel to have its restorative effects. Through the empowering of God's Holy Spirit, redeemed people are able to extend the principles of healing to all areas under their jurisdiction in life: church, family, and State.

All Christians admit that God's principles can be used to reform the individual. They also understand that if this is the case, then the family can be reformed according to God's Word. Next, the church is capable of restoration. But then they stop. Mention the State, and they say, "No; nothing can be done to restore the State. The State is inherently, permanently satanic. It is a waste of time to work to heal the State." The Christian Reconstructionist asks: Why not?

They never tell you why not. They never point to a passage in the Bible that tells you why the church and family can be healed by God's Word and Spirit, but the State can't be. Today, it is the unique message of Christian Reconstruction that civil government, like family government and church government, is under the Bible-revealed law of God and therefore is capable in principle of being reformed according to God's law.

This means that God has given to the *Christian community as a whole* enormous responsibility throughout history. This God-given responsibility is far greater than merely preaching a gospel of exclusively personal salvation. The gospel we preach must apply to every area of life that has been fouled by sin and its effects. The church and individual Christian evangelists must preach the biblical gospel of *comprehensive redemption*, not just personal soul-winning.[5] Wherever sin reigns, there the gospel must be at work, transforming and restoring. The only area of

---

3. Gary North, "Comprehensive Redemption: A Theology for Social Action" (1981), reprinted in North, *Is the World Running Down? Crisis in the Christian Worldview* (Tyler, Texas: Institute for Christian Economics, 1988), Appendix C.

life outside of the reach of Spirit-empowered restoration is an area that was not affected by the fall of man. This, of course, means no area at all.

Denying Responsibility

There are millions of Christians today (and in the past) who have denied the obvious implications of such a view of God's earthly kingdom. Nevertheless, very few of them have been ready to deny its theological premises. If you ask them this question — "What area of life today is not under the effects of sin?" — they give the proper answer: *none*. They give the same answer to the next question: "What area of sin-filled life will be outside of the comprehensive judgment of God at the final judgment?"

But when you ask them the obvious third question, they start squirming: "What area of life today is outside of the legitimate effects of the gospel in transforming evil into good, or spiritual death into life?" The answer is obviously the same — *none* — but to admit this, modern pietistic Christians would have to abandon their pietism.

What is pietism? Pietism preaches a limited salvation: "individual soul-only, family-only, church-only." It rejects the very idea of the comprehensive redeeming power of the gospel, the transforming power of the Holy Spirit, and the comprehensive responsibility of Christians in history. In this rejection of the gospel's political and judicial effects in history, the pietists agree entirely with modern humanists. There is a secret alliance between them. Christian Reconstruction challenges this alliance. This is why both Christians and humanists despise it.

Chapter 2

THE PIETIST-HUMANIST KINGDOM

Jesus answered, "My kingdom is not of this world. If My kingdom were of this world, My servants would fight, so that I should not be delivered to the Jews; but now My kingdom is not from here" (John 18:36; New King James Version).

The standard, run-of-the-mill response to the message of Christian political responsibility rests on a faulty reading of Jesus' words to Pilate regarding His kingdom. What was really involved? Jesus was explaining to Pontius Pilate how He could be a king, yet also be standing before Pilate to be judged. Pilate was implicitly asking: How could Jesus be a king? Where were His defenders? Where were His troops?

Jesus' point was clear: the *source* of His kingly authority is not earthly. His kingdom is not *of* this world. The source of His authority as king is from far *above* this world. His is a *transcendent* kingdom.

Nevertheless, this kingdom also has earthly manifestations. Rahab, a former pagan harlot, understood this much, for she confessed to the Hebrew spies, "The Lord your God, He is God in heaven above and on earth beneath" (Joshua 2:11b). She understood that God's kingdom was about to replace Jericho's kingdom. She understood that God's kingdom does have earthly manifestations politically. There are millions of Christians today who have yet to come to grips with Rahab's confession of faith.

At the time of His crucifixion, Jesus said that His kingdom

was not then geographically "from here." That is, it did not yet have institutional, visible power on earth. "But *now* My kingdom is not from here." Nevertheless, His words implied that *at some time in the future*, His kingdom would indeed possess institutional power. He would then have His defenders.

Three centuries later, Christians took over the administration of the shattered remains of the Roman Empire. God's kingdom by then was visible in a way that Pilate could not have foreseen or foretold. Christ had visibly defeated Caesar, not in the sense of being physically on the same throne that the Caesars had occupied, but through His people. His people now brought judicial sanctions in history.

"Politics Fourth!"

This brief chapter uses politics as a launching pad for a discussion of Christian Reconstruction, yet Christian Reconstruction is only peripherally related to politics. As the co-founder of the Christian Reconstruction movement, my political slogan is: "Politics fourth!" Concern about politics should come only after one's personal conversion to Jesus Christ. Politics is an aspect of evangelism — *comprehensive evangelism* — but it should never be allowed to become a substitute for personal evangelism. Political reform should come only after the reform of the church and the reform of the family, in this order.[1]

The modern church hates the very thought of comprehensive evangelism. It hates the greatness of the Great Commission.[2] Christians want to narrowly define evangelism in order to reduce their comprehensive responsibility before God. Writes Peter Masters, heir of Spurgeon's pulpit at the Metropolitan Tabernacle in London: "Reconstructionists teach that the great commission of Christ to His disciples goes beyond the work of evangelism. In their view it includes this quest for the social-political dominion of the world; the persuading of all nations to

---

1. Gary North, *Political Polytheism: The Myth of Pluralism* (Tyler, Texas: Institute for Christian Economics, 1989), p. 559.

2. Kenneth L. Gentry, Jr., *The Greatness of the Great Commission* (Tyler, Texas: Institute for Christian Economics, 1990).

submit to the rule of Israel's ancient laws."[3]

Notice his phrase, "beyond the work of evangelism." Into this brief phrase is packed an entire worldview, the worldview of Christian pietism. Evangelism is narrow, he presumes. To discuss men's requirements to obey the laws set forth in the Old Testament is necessarily to discuss social transformation. These laws deal with all aspects of society. In Masters' view, all such discussions are peripheral to evangelism.

God has set forth requirements to His people concerning their earthly responsibilities for constructing His comprehensive kingdom. Christians are required by God to become active in building God's visible kingdom. But most people today think "politics" when they hear the word "activism." Such a conclusion is incorrect. This formula, "*politics = activism*," is the error of the modern humanist and the ancient pagan; it should not be the error of the Christian. Society is far broader than mere politics. Social transformation involves far more than politics. It involves personal and institutional regeneration.

Salvation by Grace, Not Law

The message of the Bible is clear: we are saved by grace through faith in the atoning work of Jesus Christ at Calvary. "For by grace are ye saved through faith; and that not of yourselves: it is the gift of God: Not of works, lest any man should boast" (Ephesians 2:8-9). Yet the very next verse reminds us that we are given eternal life so that we might perform *good works* in history: "For we are his workmanship, created in Christ Jesus unto good works, which God hath before ordained that we should walk in them" (Ephesians 2:10).

This was the message of the Old Testament, too. The prophet Habakkuk said: "Behold, his soul which is lifted up is not upright in him: but the just shall live by his faith" (Habakkuk 2:4). God is more interested in righteousness than in precise ritual. The prophet Micah said: "Wherewith shall I come before the LORD, and bow myself before the high God? shall I come

---

3. Masters, "World Dominion: The High Ambition of Reconstructionism," *Sword & Trowel* (May 24, 1990), p. 13.

before him with burnt offerings, with calves of a year old? Will the LORD be pleased with thousands of rams, or with ten thousands of rivers of oil? shall I give my firstborn for my transgression, the fruit of my body for the sin of my soul? He hath shewed thee, O man, what is good; and what doth the LORD require of thee, but to do justly, and to love mercy, and to walk humbly with thy God?" (Micah 6:6-8). This message has not changed.

Christian Reconstructionists are falsely accused of saying that men are saved in some way through political activism. This is utter nonsense. Men are saved by grace through faith, and nothing else. R. J. Rushdoony, who was the primary early developer of the Christian Reconstruction viewpoint (1963-73), made this plain in 1973. He had this to say about social and political progress: "The key is regeneration, propagation of the gospel, and the conversion of men and nations to God's law-word."[4] Again, "The key to social renewal is individual regeneration."[5] Critics who accuse Christian Reconstructionists of teaching a doctrine of political salvation are spreading a grotesque falsehood. If they had read our materials — and very few of the published critics have — they would know better. They are bearing false witness, long after we have published detailed clarifications of a position that was already clarified in numerous other works.[6]

Judicial Evangelism

Nevertheless, political activism is one of the ways that righteousness is expressed in history. Why should Christians deny this? Surely, one of the factors that led to the anti-Communist upheavals in Eastern Europe in late 1989 was the self-conscious

4. R. J. Rushdoony, *The Institutes of Biblical Law* (Nutley, New Jersey: Craig Press, 1973), p. 113.

3. *Ibid.*, p. 122.

6. Gary DeMar and Peter Leithart, *The Reduction of Christianity: A Biblical Response to Dave Hunt* (Ft. Worth, Texas: Dominion Press, 1988); Gary DeMar, *The Debate Over Christian Reconstruction* (Ft. Worth, Texas: Dominion Press, 1988); Greg L. Bahnsen and Kenneth L. Gentry, Jr., *House Divided: The Break-Up of Dispensational Theology* (Tyler, Texas: Institute for Christian Economics, 1989).

stand taken by church members in many of the satellite nations. What are we to say, that the courageous stand taken by those pastors and churches in several denominations was totally misguided, "getting religion mixed up with politics," and an improper application of biblical principles to history? Rev. Laszlo Tokes, the Hungarian pastor who sparked the Romanian Revolution, "put God at the head of Europe's liberation movement: 'Eastern Europe is not just in a political revolution but a religious renaissance.' "[7]

Yet this is what all those who oppose Christian Reconstructionism's view of biblical responsibility do implicitly deny. They have forgotten that *righteous civil government is a legitimate means of evangelism,* a testimony to the spiritually lost of the greatness of God's deliverance in history:

> Behold, I have taught you statutes and judgments, even as the LORD my God commanded me, that ye should do so in the land whither ye go to possess it. Keep therefore and do them; for this is your wisdom and your understanding in the sight of the nations, which shall hear all these statutes, and say, Surely this great nation is a wise and understanding people. For what nation is there so great, who hath God so nigh unto them, as the LORD our God is in all things that we call upon him for? And what nation is there so great, that hath statutes and judgments so righteous as all this law, which I set before you this day? (Deuteronomy 4:5-8).

Contemporary Christianity has long forgotten about this tradition of *evangelism through law.* It has therefore forfeited politics to the enemies of Christ, especially the modern humanists, who see no salvation outside the true "church" of politics — the same way that the residents of the ancient Greek *polis* (city-state) viewed salvation. Contemporary humanists do understand the implications of evangelism through law, and like the humanists of ancient Rome, they despise it. It threatens their control in history.

---

7. Barbara Reynolds, "Religion is Greatest Story Ever Missed," *USA Today* (March 16, 1990), p. 13A.

Chapter 3

HUMANISM AND POLITICS

Now if ye be ready that at what time ye hear the sound of the cornet, flute, harp, sackbut, psaltery, and dulcimer, and all kinds of music, ye fall down and worship the image which I have made; well: but if ye worship not, ye shall be cast the same hour into the midst of a burning fiery furnace; and who is that God that shall deliver you out of my hands? (Daniel 3:15).

Then shall they deliver you up to be afflicted, and shall kill you: and ye shall be hated of all nations for my name's sake (Matthew 24:9).

Humanism is an old religion. It is with us still. We live in an era of humanism. Humanism is a simple enough religion. The humanist believes the following:

1. Man, not God, owns the earth. Original ownership, meaning the original title to the earth, belongs to man. Man is sovereign.

2. Man the creature rules over God the Creator. In fact, man *is* the creator, for he alone understands and controls nature. Man represents only man.

3. Man, therefore, makes the rules, which means that an elite group of men make the rules for everyone else.

4. "Man proposes, and man disposes." He takes an oath only to himself. He answers only to man, which means of course that the vast majority of men answer to a handful of other men. Man is the sovereign judge of the universe.

5. The future belongs to autonomous (self-law) man, meaning to

those who worship man as God.

Christians disagree with each of the above humanist assertions.

1. Original ownership belongs to God. God, not man, created, owns, and controls the earth. God is sovereign.

2. The Creator rules the creature, but God has delegated subordinate ownership to mankind. God is in charge; man is fully responsible to God.

3. God has made the rules (laws). The Ten Commandments express the fundamental principles of God's law.

4. Men are responsible before God to abide by the rules. Man proposes and disposes only within the eternal decree and plan of God. God judges man in terms of His law.

5. The future belongs to God and God's people.

Here we have it: two rival religions based on two rival views of God. This earth is the battlefield in this war of ideas. The two religions are locked in deadly combat. *This conflict takes place in history.* The humanists have had a much clearer view of the true nature of this historical battle than the Christians have. They have planned for it far longer than the Christians have.

Politics is a major part of this battlefield. "Not the only one," the Christian hastens to add. "On the contrary," the humanist immediately replies, "politics is by far the most important part." Even here, the two religions disagree.

We must not make the mistake that the humanists have so often made: identifying politics as the heart of the battle. This war is taking place on all fronts: church, State, education, art, economics, and all the areas of life that are engulfed in sin and in need of revival and reform. Politics is one aspect of this fight, but it is not the central aspect, for politics itself is not central. *The worship of God is central.* The central issue therefore is this: Which God should mankind worship? The God of the Bible or a god of man's imagination?

The Power Religion

Most humanists see the State as man's most powerful institution. Theirs is a religion of power, so they make the State the central institution. They make the State their church.[1] What Christians say is that *the church, as the institution entrusted by God with His Word and His sacraments, is the central institution.* Neither the family nor the State is of equal importance to the church in history or eternity. The Bible teaches that the gates of hell will not stand against the onslaught of the church.

Because the prevailing humanist tradition from the Greeks to the present has made the State into man's primary agency of earthly salvation, Christians in self-defense need to focus their attention on this battlefield. We must remember, however, that this battle over politics is important today primarily because our opponents have chosen to make their stand on the political battlefield. Christians need to understand what the humanists seldom if ever understand, namely, that *the battle for political dominion will **not** be won primarily through political action.* Politics is the working out of religious first principles in the civil realm (covenant). It is a battle over the true nature of God, man, law, and time.[2]

Only recently have both the humanists and the Christians begun to understand clearly that Christianity must either be subdued by the humanists or else it will subdue them. *There is no neutrality.* So, the battle intensifies. The humanists and the Christians can agree on only two things: first, there is an earth, and second, somebody owns it and therefore controls it. The question is: Which God? Another question is: Who speaks in the name of this God?

A comprehensive war over these explicitly theological issues has been fought throughout history. Part of this battle is political, but only part. There will be political winners and political losers in history.

---

1. This is not true of anarchists and libertarians.
2. Gary North, *Unconditional Surrender: God's Program for Victory* (3rd ed.; Tyler, Texas: Institute for Christian Economics, 1988), Part I.

Who Wins, Who Loses?

Thirty years ago, I took a university course in the history of political theory. It was taught by a graduate student who had studied political philosophy under Sheldon Wolin. Some eight years later, when I was a graduate student in history, I had the opportunity to attend a lecture by Professor Wolin. I had no idea what he would be discussing, but I decided to attend. Wolin, then of the University of California, Berkeley, later a professor at Princeton University, gave a one-hour speech to a small group of graduate students. Most of the others had never heard of him.

It was the most important academic lecture I ever heard. He introduced us to Thomas Kuhn's crucial book, *The Structure of Scientific Revolutions*,[1] one of the most important books of the 1960's. That book became extremely important for me, as it did for thousands of other young scholars in that era. Wolin argued that many of the major concepts of political philosophy were not discovered in some rational, academic manner, but have in fact been formed during periods of religious and political conflict.[2] We live in such an era.

Finally, a quarter century after I took that undergraduate class, I read Professor Wolin's textbook in political theory. It is far more than a textbook. It is a brilliant humanist defense of political participation as something remarkably close institutionally and psychologically to the sacrament of the Lord's Supper. He traces the history of political theory as something bordering on being a secular substitute for worship. This was what I had not understood so many years before: *the history of humanism is the history of man's attempt to achieve secular salvation through politics.*

Early in his book, he makes a very important observation. I believe the phenomena described by this observation will become increasingly important to Christians over the next few

---

1. University of Chicago Press, 1962.
2. Sheldon S. Wolin, "Paradigms and Political Theories," in Preston King and B. C. Parekh (eds.), *Politics and Experience* (Cambridge, England: At the University Press, 1968), pp. 147-48.

decades. Wolin writes:

> . . . most of the great statements of political philosophy have been
> put forward in times of crisis; that is, when political phenomena are
> less effectively integrated by institutional forms. Institutional break-
> down releases phenomena, so to speak, causing political behavior
> and events to take on something of a random quality, and destroy-
> ing customary meanings that had been part of the old political
> world.[3]

This is fancy academic language for a simple idea: when
things blow up politically, new people pick up the pieces, and
then other bright new people start rethinking the proper ar-
rangement of the theoretical puzzle of politics and government.
The theoretical puzzle gets put back together very differently,
just as the various institutional puzzles get put back together
differently, and new words and concepts are developed that
help justify (and even actively promote) the new arrangements.
In short, some groups win, while others lose. Most people don't
care who wins one way or the other, if they are left alone — if
they are *allowed* to be left alone.

In the revolutionary political changes of the last two centuries, almost nobody has been allowed to be left alone. It is this
fact of political life that Christians in the United States have
only begun to recognize since about 1980: *the humanist State is
not going to leave Christians alone.* Furthermore, it never intended
to leave them alone; and this disturbing realization on the part
of American Christians is part of the present political transformation.

The non-neutrality of the modern humanist State has been
readily apparent to anyone living in Communist-dominated
nations, but Americans have naively imagined otherwise for
over two centuries. They have imagined that atheist tyranny
was Eastern Europe's problem, or Communist China's problem,
but not their problem. Slowly and painfully, they are learning
the truth. Every time a church is sued in civil court for disci-

---

3. Sheldon Wolin, *Politics and Vision: Continuity and Innovation in Western Political
Thought* (Boston: Little, Brown, 1960), p. 8.

plining or excommunicating someone, or a Christian school is attacked by some state Superintendent of Public Instruction, they learn. Unfortunately, they learn incredibly slowly.

Changing Opinions

As American Protestant Christians have begun to rethink their political vulnerability, something unique has been taking place in their thinking. They are at last becoming aware that they are biblically responsible for participating in politics, not just as citizens but as self-conscious Christians. They have repeated the slogan, "The Bible has answers for every area of life," and now they are being called upon publicly to articulate these answers in such controversial areas as politics.

Christians have had very few specific answers. Why? Because we must go to the Old Testament to find specific, authoritative, *Bible-revealed* social and political answers, and Christians have been taught for over three centuries that the Old Testament is "off limits" judicially to Christians in the New Testament era. Only the Christian Reconstructionists today affirm the continuing validity of Old Testament law. They alone insist that the civil laws of the Old Testament commonwealth also applied to all nations of the earth, not just to Israel. The coming of Jesus Christ in history did not alter these laws.[4] These same civil laws apply today, unless overturned by New Testament revelation.

Christian Reconstructionists offer specific solutions to the social problems of our time, specifics based explicitly on biblical revelation. Our critics offer no explicitly Bible-based alternatives. Christians today are beginning to turn to the Bible for answers. This is why Christian Reconstructionism has been winning the intellectual battle by default. Reconstructionists alone honor the implications of an old political slogan: "You can't beat something with nothing."

---

4. Greg L. Bahnsen, *By This Standard: The Authority of God's Law Today* (Tyler, Texas: Institute for Christian Economics, 1985).

Chapter 4

GOD AND GOVERNMENT

*Let every soul be subject unto the higher powers. For there is no power but of God: the powers that be are ordained of God. Whosoever therefore resisteth the power, resisteth the ordinance of God: and they that resist shall receive to themselves damnation. For rulers are not a terror to good works, but to the evil. Wilt thou then not be afraid of the power? do that which is good, and thou shalt have praise of the same: For he is the minister of God to thee for good. But if thou do that which is evil, be afraid; for he beareth not the sword in vain: for **he is the minister of God**, a revenger to execute wrath upon him that doeth evil (Romans 13:1-4).* (emphasis added)

Politics is a ministry of God. It is not the only ministry, but it is one. The civil magistrate brings God's negative sanctions in history. In a democratic society, voters bring negative sanctions against civil magistrates. Thus, politics begins with the *individual citizen*, who is covenanted in a civil order under God. He governs himself, and then he executes judgment through politics.

Politics is the means of establishing and controlling civil government. *This does **not** mean that politics is central to government.* It is one of the great heresies of our era that only civil government is "government," and that the other, lawful, God-ordained governments are something less than government. There is self-government, church government, and family government. It is this monopolizing of the concept of government by the State that is at the heart of the loss of liberty in the twentieth century.

My former instructor, the conservative sociologist and historian Robert Nisbet, has written in his classic book, *The Quest for Community* (1952), that "The argument of this book is that the single most decisive influence upon Western social organization has been the rise and development of the centralized territorial State."[1]

Politics has therefore become central to modern man. It derives its importance from the State. Nisbet continues: "Unlike either kinship or capitalism, the State has become, in the contemporary world, the supreme allegiance of men and, in most recent times, the greatest refuge from the insecurities of and frustrations of other spheres of life. . . . [T]he State has risen as the dominant institutional force in our society and the most evocative symbol of cultural unity and purpose."[2] He is correct when he says that this modern faith in the State as the supreme manifestation of man's unity, purpose, and power "makes control of the State the greatest single goal, or prize, in modern struggles for power."[3]

It is this struggle for control over the State that is the equivalent of medieval man's quest for salvation. What Professor Wolin wishes to accelerate — political participation as the primary means of social transformation — his former faculty colleague at Berkeley, Professor Nisbet, wishes to reverse. What Wolin says is the great evil of modern political philosophy — the separation of State and society[4] — Nisbet says has gone way too far, and therefore he wants to reaffirm the moral and institutional legitimacy of this very separation.[5]

Society is far more than the State, Nisbet insists, following Edmund Burke, the late eighteenth-century English politician and social philosopher. Society is a complex of lawful institutions — families, churches, businesses, and many voluntary associations and memberships. A denial of the distinction between society and State is, Nisbet argues, the first step toward totalitarianism. The West has long since taken this step.

---

1. Nisbet, *The Quest for Community* (New York: Oxford University Press, 1952), p. 98.
2. *Ibid.*, p. 99.
3. *Ibid.*, p. 103.
4. Sheldon Wolin, *Politics and Vision: Continuity and Innovation in Western Political Thought* (Boston: Little, Brown, 1960), ch. 10.
5. Nisbet, *Quest for Community*, ch. 5.

Rushing Toward the Year 2000

The authors who are part of the Christian Reconstruction movement are convinced that we are now moving into a period of great turmoil historically — not just U.S. history, but world history. Every inhabited continent is being plowed up institutionally and religiously by God. This process is unquestionably worldwide in scope. Telecommunications now link the whole world, and so does the New York Stock Exchange. For the first time in human history, the whole world is operating with the same science, technology, and mathematics. It is also struggling with the same fundamental philosophical questions. The whole world is experiencing the same breakdown in man's ability to understand and govern God's world. *God is plowing it up.*

We are rapidly approaching the year 2000, an apocalyptic-sounding year if there ever was one. The sense of urgency will only increase from this point forward. The visible collapse of Communism in Eastern Europe, the possible break-up of the Soviet Empire, the threat of a military *coup* in the U.S.S.R., the disarming of the West, the neutralization of Germany, the rise of a "green" politics based on supposed ecological terrors and the quest for political solutions to modern economic and environmental problems, and the attempt to create a politically unified Western Europe all point to enormous dislocations.

The New World Order (Again)

The humanists are at last proclaiming the advent of their long-promised *New World Order*. In the midst of an unprecedented budget crisis and political deadlock, and in the midst of a military confrontation between the U.S. and Iraq, President Bush announced to Congress:

> A new partnership of nations has begun. We stand today at a unique and extraordinary moment. The crisis in the Persian Gulf, as grave as it is, also offers a rare opportunity to move toward an historic period of cooperation. Out of these troubled times, our fifth objective — a new world order — can emerge: a new era, freer from the threat of terror, stronger in the pursuit of justice, and more secure in the quest for peace. An era in which the nations of the

world, east and west, north and south, can prosper and live in harmony.

A hundred generations have searched for this elusive path to peace, while a thousand wars raged across the span of human endeavor. Today that new world is struggling to be born. A world quite different from the one we've known. A world in which the rule of law supplants the rule of the jungle. A world in which nations recognize the shared responsibility for freedom and justice. A world where the strong respect the rights of the weak.

This is the vision I shared with President Gorbachev in Helsinki. He, and other leaders from Europe, the gulf and around the world, understand how we manage this crisis today could shape the future for generations to come.[6]

He speaks of a hundred generations. This takes us back to the era of Abraham or thereabouts, in the days when Egypt rocked the cradle of civilization. From Egypt to 1990: a lengthy gestation period. I think Mr. Bush was not deliberately exaggerating, as messianic as his extended timetable may initially appear. The model of Egypt is always the covenant-breaker's preferred alternative to decentralized biblical civilization. It is time to recall the words of the great German sociologist Max Weber, in a speech he delivered in 1909:

> To this day there has never existed a bureaucracy which could compare with that of Egypt. This is known to everyone who knows the social history of ancient times; and it is equally apparent that today we are proceeding towards an evolution which resembles that system in every detail, except that it is built on other foundations, on technically more perfect, more rationalized, and therefore more mechanical foundations. The problem which besets us now is not: how can this evolution be changed? – for that is impossible, but: what is to come of it?[7]

---

6. "Text of President Bush's Address to Joint Session of Congress," *New York Times* (Sept. 12, 1990).

7. Max Weber, "Speech to the *Verein für Sozialpolitik*" (1909); reprinted in J. P. Meyer, *Max Weber and German Politics* (London: Faber & Faber, 1956), p. 127. Cf. Gary North, "Max Weber: Rationalism, Irrationalism, and the Bureaucratic Cage," in North (ed.), *Foundations of Christian Scholarship: Essays in the Van Til Perspective* (Vallecito, California: Ross House Books, 1976), ch. 8.

48CHRISTIAN RECONSTRUCTION

Our generation is about to get the answer to Weber's question. We now face the looming threat of Egypt revisited. This is far more of a threat to the enemies of Christ than to the Church. "Thus saith the LORD; They also that uphold Egypt shall fall; and the pride of her power shall come down: from the tower of Syene shall they fall in it by the sword, saith the Lord GOD" (Ezek. 30:6). The towers of this world shall crumble, and those who trust in them shall fall.

But there is already a New World Order. It was announced by Jesus to His disciples:

> And Jesus came and spake unto them, saying, All power is given unto me in heaven and in earth. Go ye therefore, and teach all nations, baptizing them in the name of the Father, and of the Son, and of the Holy Ghost: Teaching them to observe all things whatsoever I have commanded you: and, lo, I am with you alway, even unto the end of the world. Amen (Matthew 28:18-20).

It is this world order – the fifth and final kingdom – that alone will expand to fill the earth:

> Thou sawest till that a stone was cut out without hands, which smote the image upon his feet that were of iron and clay, and brake them to pieces. Then was the iron, the clay, the brass, the silver, and the gold, broken to pieces together, and became like the chaff of the summer threshingfloors; and the wind carried them away, that no place was found for them: and the stone that smote the image became a great mountain, and filled the whole earth (Daniel 2:34-35).

We are witnessing a world revolution. It is an ancient revolution. It is the advent of a new quest for empire. It will inevitably fail. But it is a revolution. When we hear the word "revolution," we usually think politics and bombs. But revolutions do not spring up full grown overnight. They do not take place in historical vacuums. They take a lot of planning. Revolutions are always preceded by major shifts in people's thinking, especially the thinking of the intellectual elite. This is taking place now. The various humanist intellectual elites are visibly in philosophical retreat. The moral and political leaders have lost confidence in the existing liberal worldview. They talk tough, but their economies are being threatened by massive debt. They talk tough, but international terrorism now raises its ugly head, against which the politicians can do next to nothing. There are no more self-attesting truths in the world of humanism, except one: that the God of the Bible isn't possible.

It is this deeply religious presupposition that Christians necessarily reject. It is this rejection that enrages the humanists. Christianity, in its orthodox form, challenges all forms of the power religion. Christianity is the religion of Christ's kingdom (civilization). It offers a better way of life and temporal death, for it offers the only path to eternal life. It offers comprehensive redemption – the healing of international civilization.[8] It is the dominion religion.[9]

When Christianity departs from its heritage of preaching the progressive sanctification of men and institutions, it abandons the idea of Christ's progressively revealed kingdom (civilization) on earth in history. It then departs into another religion, the escape religion. This leaves the battle for civilization in the hands of the various power religionists. Russia saw the defeat of the visible national Church when the theology of mysticism and suffering (kenotic theology) at last brought paralysis to the Russian Orthodox Church. It had been infiltrated by people holding pagan and humanistic views of many varieties.[10] The Church was incapable of dealing with the power religion of

---

8. Gary North, *Is the World Running Down? Crisis in the Christian Worldview* (Tyler, Texas: Institute for Christian Economics, 1988), Appendix C: "Comprehensive Redemption: A Theology for Social Action."

9. On escape religion, power religion, and dominion religion, see my analysis in *Moses and Pharaoh: Dominion Religion vs. Power Religion* (Tyler, Texas: Institute for Christian Economics, 1985), pp. 2-5.

10. Ellen Myers, "Uncertain Trumpet: The Russian Orthodox Church and Russian Religious Thought, 1900-1917," *Journal of Christian Reconstruction*, XI (1985), pp. 77-110. She writes: "Russian pre-revolutionary religious thought was thus generally suspended between the poles of materialist-Marxist and mystic-idealist monism. It partook of fundamentally anarchist Marxist and also Buddhist-style withdrawal from reality; an infatuation with hedonistic classical paganism over against Christian supposedly joyless morality; a 'promethean' desire to raise mankind to godlike superman status; and, concomitant to all three, an 'apocalyptic,' nihilist rejection of the entire existing order in Russia in anticipation of an imminent new, other, and better utopian state of affairs." *Ibid.*, p. 93.

Lenin, and especially Lenin's successor, the former seminary student, Joseph Stalin.

We are seeing today a replay of those years written large. The war for the hearts and minds of men continues to escalate internationally. The technology of nuclear destruction competes with the technology of economic healing and the mass communication of the gospel. But, contrary to Marx, it is not the substructure of the mode of production that determines the superstructure of religious faith; the contrary is the case. The battle is over covenants and ethics, not economics.

Chapter 5

THE MYTH OF NEUTRALITY

After this manner therefore pray ye: Our Father which art in heaven, Hallowed be thy name. Thy kingdom come. Thy will be done in earth, as it is in heaven (Matthew 6:9-10).

Christians are praying for a worldwide revival. If such a revival comes, that last humanist truth will be abandoned. People will believe that the God of the Bible is not only possible, He has in fact entered into their lives personally.

But when this revolutionary shift of faith comes, what will Christians recommend in place of today's collapsing humanist culture? That's what the biblical law is all about: building a new world by means of: (1) God's permanent moral and institutional blueprints; (2) the empowering of the Holy Spirit. Society is required to manifest progressively in history what Jesus announced after His resurrection: the discipling of the nations. Whole nations must be *disciplined* by Christ. How? Through the imposition of sanctions by Christians in terms of God's Bible-revealed law — not just in politics, but in every area of life.

Pietists cringe in horror at such a thought. Sanctions? Imposed by Christians? Before Jesus comes again bodily to impose His international bureaucracy? They shudder at the very thought of Bible-based sanctions in the "Church Age." (Yes, even local church sanctions on church members. When was the last time you witnessed a public excommunication? Nobody is ever removed from the churches' rolls today except by death or by voluntary transfer of membership.)

This widespread hostility to biblical civil sanctions necessarily forces Christians to accept the legitimacy of non-biblical civil sanctions. There will always be civil sanctions in history. The question is: *Whose sanctions?* God's or Satan's? There is no neutrality. Only the legalization of abortion on demand has at last forced a comparative handful of Christians to face the truth about the myth of neutrality. There can be no neutrality for the aborted baby. There is no neutrality in the abortionist's office. There is either life or death.

We need to begin to train ourselves to make a transition: *the transition from humanism's sanctions to the Bible's sanctions, in every area of life.* This includes politics. God has given His people major political responsibilities that they have neglected for at least fifty years, and more like a century. Christians are being challenged by God to reclaim the political realm for Jesus Christ. We must publicly declare the crown rights of King Jesus.

New Sanctions, New Covenant

Christians today have a golden opportunity — an opportunity that doesn't come even as often as once in a lifetime. It comes about once every 250 years. The last time it came for Christians was during the American Revolution era (1776-1789). The revolutionary humanists who created and ran the French Revolution (1789-95) created a satanic alternative, one which is with us still in the demonic empire of Communism. But that empire has now begun to crumble visibly.[1]

A showdown is coming, in time and on earth: Christ vs. Satan, Christianity vs. humanism, the dominion religion vs. the power religion. *You are being called by God to take up a position of judicial responsibility on the side of Christ.* One aspect of this responsibility is to render biblical political judgments.[2]

It is time to begin to prepare ourselves for an unprecedented

---

1. This economic and also ideological crumbling is real, but not necessarily irreversible militarily. The killing power of the weaponry still in the hands of Soviet generals and admirals dwarfs anything possessed by the West.

2. George Grant, *The Changing of the Guard: Biblical Blueprints for Political Action* (Ft. Worth, Texas: Dominion Press, 1987).

revival. It is time to prepare ourselves for a "changing of the guard" — in every area of life, all over the world. Our preparation must help us to answer the hoped-for question of God-fearing new converts to Christ: "I'm saved; what now?"

The Covenant Structure

To get the correct answers, we need first to ask the right questions. For a long, long time, Christians and Jews have had the right questions right under their noses, but no one paid any attention. The questions concerning lawful government are organized in the Bible around a single theme: *the covenant.*

Most Christians and Jews have heard the biblical word, "covenant." They regard themselves (and occasionally even each other) as covenant people. They are taught from their youth about God's covenant with Israel, and how this covenant extends (or doesn't) to the Christian church. Yet hardly anyone can define the word. If you go to a Christian or a Jew and ask him to outline the basic features of the biblical covenant, he will not be able to do it rapidly or perhaps even believably. Ask two Jews or two Christians to explain the covenant, and compare their answers. The answers will not fit very well.

For over four centuries, Calvinists have talked about the covenant. They are known as *covenant theologians.* The Puritans wrote seemingly endless numbers of books about it. The problem is, nobody until 1985 had ever been able to come up with "the" covenant model in the writings of Calvin, nor in the writings of all his followers. The Calvinists had always hung their theological hats on the covenant, yet they had never put down on paper precisely what it is, what it involves, and how it works — in the Bible or in church history.

The Five-Point Covenant Model

In late 1985, Pastor Ray Sutton made an astounding discovery. He was thinking about biblical symbols, and he raised the question of two New Testament covenant symbols, baptism and communion. This raised the question of the Old Testament's covenant symbols, circumcision and passover. What did they have in common? Obviously, the covenant. But what, precisely, is the covenant? Is it the same in both Testaments (Covenants)?

He began rereading some books by Calvinist theologian Meredith G. Kline. In several books (collections of essays), Kline mentioned the structure of the Book of Deuteronomy. He argued that the book's structure in fact parallels the ancient pagan world's special documents that are known as the suzerain (king-vassal) treaties.

That triggered something in Sutton's mind. Kline discusses the outline of these treaties in several places. In some places, he says they have five sections; in other places, he indicates that they may have had six or even seven. It was all somewhat vague. So Sutton sat down with Deuteronomy to see what the structure is. He found five parts.

Then he looked at other books of the Bible that are known to be divided into five parts: Psalms and Matthew. He believed that he found the same structure. Then he went to other books, including some Pauline epistles. He found it there, too. When he discussed his findings in a Wednesday evening Bible study, David Chilton instantly recognized the same structure in the Book of Revelation. He had been working on this manuscript for well over a year, and he had it divided into four parts. Immediately he went back to his computer and shifted around the manuscript's sections electronically. The results of his restructuring can be read in his marvelous commentary on Revelation, *The Days of Vengeance*.[3]

Here, then, is the five-point structure of the biblical covenant, as developed by Sutton in his excellent book, *That You May Prosper: Dominion By Covenant*.[4]

1. Transcendence/presence of God
2. Hierarchy/authority/deliverance
3. Ethics/law/dominion
4. Oath/sanctions: blessings and cursings
5. Succession/inheritance/continuity

---

3. Ft. Worth, Texas: Dominion Press, 1987.
4. Tyler, Texas: Institute for Christian Economics, 1987.

The acronym is **THEOS**. Simple, isn't it? Yet this view of the covenant structure has implications beyond what even covenant theologians have been preaching for over four centuries. Here is the key that unlocks the structure of human government, and not just civil government. Here is the structure that Christians can use to analyze church, State, family, as well as all other non-covenantal but contractual institutions.

Perhaps you can better understand its importance by considering the five basic questions a person needs to ask before joining any institution:

1. Who's in charge here?
2. To whom do I report?
3. What are the rules?
4. What happens to me if I obey (disobey)?
5. Does this outfit have a future?

God gives us the answers in His Bible. (1) He is in charge; there are no other Gods before Him. (2) All men are to serve Him, worship Him, and rely on Him. Covenantally faithful people do this by becoming members of His church. (3) They show their loyalty by obeying His commandments. (4) If they do obey these commandments, He will (a) protect them and (b) dismay their enemies because they are also His enemies. (5) They and their spiritual heirs will inherit the earth. "His soul shall dwell at ease; and his seed shall inherit the earth" (Psalm 25:13). "For evildoers shall be cut off: but those that wait upon the LORD, they shall inherit the earth" (Psalm 37:9). "For such as be blessed of him shall inherit the earth; and they that be cursed of him shall be cut off" (Psalm 37:22).[5]

---

5. Gary North, *Inherit the Earth* (Ft. Worth, Texas: Dominion Press, 1987).

Chapter 6

THE FOUR COVENANTS OF GOD

That at that time ye were without Christ, being aliens from the commonwealth of Israel, and strangers from the covenants of promise, having no hope, and without God in the world (Ephesians 2:12).

We examine our condition in life not simply by our present outward condition, but by the Word of God, the Bible. History is governed by God in terms of His eternal standards. Through Adam, God placed all mankind under a covenant, *the dominion covenant.*[1] He told Adam that he must subdue the earth (Genesis 1:28).

What is a covenant? God comes before man and "lays down the law" — His law. Man must either conform to God by obeying His law or else be destroyed. As He told Adam, "Eat of the tree of the knowledge of good and evil, and you will die." God deals with men as a king deals with his subjects. His covenant is to prosper us when we obey and curse us when we rebel.

First, God makes a personal covenant with man. A man's eternal destiny depends on how he responds to God's covenant. God also makes institutional covenants with men. There are three of these: family, church, and State. Each has an appropriate oath. Each has laws. Each has penalties for disobedience.

As I wrote in Chapter 5, a biblical covenant has five sections:

---

1. Gary North, *The Dominion Covenant: Genesis* (2nd ed.; Tyler, Texas: Institute for Christian Economics, 1987).

1. An announcement that God is *transcendent* – the supreme Creator and deliverer of mankind. God is completely superior to and different from men and the world He created. Yet He is also present with it: *immanent*.

2. The establishment of a *hierarchy* to enforce God's authority on earth.

3. A set of *ethical rules* or laws man must follow in exercising his dominion over the earth. God will judge man by how well he follows these rules.

4. A list of *judgments* that will be imposed by God, who blesses man for obedience and curses man for disobedience.

5. A program of *inheritance* – a lawful transition that mortal men need in order to extend their dominion over creation.

We examine the laws of God, and we evaluate how well we are following them personally and with our own families. Then we compare the requirements of God's laws with institutions in our own nation: church, State, and family. If we find that society is disobeying God's covenantal principles, then we can conclude that *judgment is coming*. The curses of God will fall on those who rebel against Him.

These five points are *inescapable concepts*. We never face the question of "covenant or no covenant." We face the question: "*Whose* covenant?" It is a choice between God's covenant or man's covenant, a covenant with the Creator or a covenant with Satan. There are no other choices available. There is no covenantal neutrality.

Christians are called by God to exercise dominion in every area of life. God has transferred the ownership of the world to Christians, just as He transferred it to Adam before Adam rebelled. We now are called to take possession of the world in terms of God's covenantal principles, and by means of God's sovereign grace.

Christians must begin immediately to reconstruct their own lives, families, and churches before God's judgment on society begins. We must prove ourselves ready to lead. We must do this by following God now, *before* His judgment begins. Obedience to God's principles produces leadership. Disobedience to God's principles produces His judgment: man's disinheritance from God's riches, both in history and eternity.

If you don't want to be disinherited, either eternally or on earth, then start obeying God. Jesus said: "If ye love me, keep my commandments" (John 14:15). This is a basic theme of the New Testament:

> But whoso keepeth his word, in him verily is the love of God perfected: hereby know we that we are in him (I John 2:5).

> Beloved, if our heart condemn us not, then have we confidence toward God. And whatsoever we ask, we receive of him, because we keep his commandments, and do those things that are pleasing in his sight. And this is his commandment, That we should believe on the name of his Son Jesus Christ, and love one another, as he gave us commandment. And he that keepeth his commandments dwelleth in him, and he in him. And hereby we know that he abideth in us, by the Spirit which he hath given us (I John 3:21-24).

> For this is the love of God, that we keep his commandments: and his commandments are not grievous (I John 5:3).

> Blessed are they that do his commandments, that they may have right to the tree of life, and may enter in through the gates into the city (Revelation 22:14).

The Lord of the Covenant

Jesus Christ is Lord of the covenant. He sits at the right hand of God, governing history. He ascended to this lofty position at His ascension, which occurred forty days after His resurrection from the grave. This was Peter's message on the day of Pentecost:

> This Jesus hath God raised up, whereof we all are witnesses. Therefore being by the right hand of God exalted, and having received of the Father the promise of the Holy Ghost, he hath shed forth this, which ye now see and hear. For David is not ascended into the heavens: but he saith himself, The Lord said unto my Lord, Sit thou on my right hand, Until I make thy foes thy footstool.

Therefore let all the house of Israel know assuredly, that God hath made that same Jesus, whom ye have crucified, both Lord and Christ (Acts 2:32-36).

This eschatological passage is a development of the great promise of Psalm 110:

A Psalm of David. The LORD said unto my Lord, Sit thou at my right hand, until I make thine enemies thy footstool. The LORD shall send the rod of thy strength out of Zion: rule thou in the midst of thine enemies. Thy people shall be willing in the day of thy power, in the beauties of holiness from the womb of the morning: thou hast the dew of thy youth. The LORD hath sworn, and will not repent, Thou art a priest for ever after the order of Melchizedek. The Lord at thy right hand shall strike through kings in the day of his wrath. He shall judge among the heathen, he shall fill the places with the dead bodies; he shall wound the heads over many countries. He shall drink of the brook in the way: therefore shall he lift up the head.

Jesus Christ, the great high priest, is the Lord over history, the King of kings. He alone possesses both offices of high priest and King. This is why there must be separate institutional authorities on earth: priests and magistrates, both lawful rulers, but each with his own office and sphere of legitimate authority. Each is under God and therefore under obligation to proclaim and enforce God's law. The church is not under the State; neither is the State under the church. Both are under God.

Where does Jesus sit? At the right hand of God. Where is this? In heaven. Does this mean that Jesus will not return to earth to sit on an earthly throne in Jerusalem or some other city? Yes. He reigns in history from on high. To leave His throne in heaven, He would have to give up power and authority, unless that heavenly throne were also to come to earth, along with His Father, next to Whom He sits. But this transfer of God's throne of judgment to earth will happen only at the resurrection of the dead and the final judgment.

The Coming of the Kingdom

Much of modern evangelical Christianity believes that

Christ's kingdom cannot and will not come until He returns physically to reign over saints and sinners during a thousand-year future period. This is not what He said about the arrival of His kingdom; it is already here: "But if I cast out devils by the Spirit of God, then the kingdom of God is come unto you" (Matthew 12:28). He cast them out, and His kingdom came — not in its historic fullness, but it came judicially (by law).

It is today the God-assigned task of all Christians to work out in history the fullness of His kingdom's principles, to manifest it to all the world. This is the Great Commission (Matthew 28:18-20). The Holy Spirit enables Christ's people to achieve this goal progressively in history, before Jesus comes again to judge the world.

It is no more necessary that Jesus sit on a physical throne in a literal Jerusalem in order for His kingdom on earth to be present in history than it is for Satan physically to sit on a throne in some earthly location — New York City, perhaps? — in order for his kingdom to be present in history. No Christian teaches that Satan's kingdom is unreal in history just because Satan is not here on earth physically. Yet all premillennialists are forced by their eschatology to insist that Christ's earthly Kingdom is not yet real in history, since He is on His throne in heaven. This is totally inconsistent with what they believe about Satan's kingdom.

Empowering by the Holy Spirit

Because Jesus Christ is not physically present with His church in history, the church has greater power. This was the explicit teaching of Christ:

> These things have I spoken unto you, being yet present with you. But the Comforter, which is the Holy Ghost, whom the Father will send in my name, he shall teach you all things, and bring all things to your remembrance, whatsoever I have said unto you. Peace I leave with you, my peace I give unto you: not as the world giveth, give I unto you. Let not your heart be troubled, neither let it be afraid (John 14:25-27).

Jesus made it plain that His disciples were better off with Him physically absent from them. "Nevertheless I tell you the truth; It is expedient for you that I go away: for if I go not away, the Comforter will not come unto you; but if I depart, I will send him unto you" (John 16:7).

The Ascension

The modern church has all but ignored the doctrine of Christ's ascension. The modern church does not see the ascension in terms of His definitive triumph in history over Satan and his forces. His blood was shed at Calvary. The bodily ascension of Jesus Christ was the historical event through which His church has been empowered for world dominion by the Holy Spirit. The world will be progressively transformed through the work of the Holy Spirit on the hearts of individuals, and also through the efforts of His people to proclaim biblical law and obey it in history.

Those who deny this — and millions of Christians do deny it — are simply unimpressed by the power of the Holy Spirit and the efficacy of biblical law. They believe that Satan, acting through the hearts and actions of covenantally rebellious people, possesses far more power in history than God exercises through His Spirit-empowered people. Christians today seem more impressed with the power of humanism than with the transforming power of the Holy Spirit. In this, they share a fundamental principle with the humanists.

Nevertheless, critics publicly insist that because Christian Reconstructionists proclaim the heart-transforming, world-transforming power of the Holy Spirit in history, Reconstructionists are therefore humanistic. Most incredible of all, there are Christians who actually believe this preposterous accusation.

Chapter 7

POSTMILLENNIALISM'S "FAITH IN MAN"

*Uphold me according unto thy word, that I may live: and let me not be ashamed of my hope. Hold **thou** me up, and I shall be safe: and I will have respect unto thy statutes continually. **Thou** hast trodden down all them that err from thy statutes: for their deceit is falsehood. **Thou** puttest away all the wicked of the earth like dross: therefore I love thy testimonies (Psalm 119:116-19).* (emphasis added)

Again and again, premillennialists and amillennialists accuse postmillennial Christian Reconstructionists of having too much faith in man. This is somewhat amusing to Christian Reconstructionists, since the founders and present leaders of the movement are all Calvinists. They believe in the traditional Calvinist doctrine of the total depravity of man — a doctrine denied by all Arminians ("free will religion"), which the vast majority of premillennialists and amillennialists are. The Calvinist believes that there is nothing innately good in fallen man:

> But we are all as an unclean thing, and all our righteousnesses are as filthy rags; and we all do fade as a leaf; and our iniquities, like the wind, have taken us away (Isaiah 64:6).

> The heart is deceitful above all things, and desperately wicked: who can know it? (Jeremiah 17:9)

> For I know that in me (that is, in my flesh) dwelleth no good thing: for to will is present with me; but how to perform that which is good I find not (Romans 7:18).

What Christian Reconstructionists believe in is *the effective empowering by the Holy Spirit in history*. They know that no person is ever brought to saving faith in Jesus Christ except by the work of the Holy Spirit. They know that the natural man does not otherwise receive the things of the Spirit (I Corinthians 2:14). They know that it is no more difficult for the Holy Spirit to bring five billion people to saving faith than it is for Him to bring one lost sheep back into the fold.

Here is the great irony of the debate over the Reconstructionists' "faith in man." It is the Reconstructionists' Arminian critics who believe that unsaved man is inherently autonomous and therefore possesses the power to resist the Holy Spirit's decision to save him. They believe that a postmillennial revival is inherently impossible because of the power of rebellious autonomous men. They have great faith in man – autonomous, unsaved man. He can thwart the plan of God. Autonomous man says "no" to God, and God supposedly chooses never to overcome this "no."

So, it is in fact the critic of postmillennialism who has faith in autonomous man. He believes that the unsaved mankind has such enormous power to do evil that God cannot or will not overcome evil in history by the Spirit-empowered gospel. God has decided to let the earth go to hell, historically speaking (amillennialism), or else restore it by the exercise of political power (premillennialism): the bodily return of Jesus Christ, who will set up a political kingdom and rule from a literal throne on earth.

It is never a biblical question of "faith in man" vs. "faith in God." It is rather a question of faith in God's willingness and ability to manifest His plan for history: (1) by the historical triumph of covenant-breaking men, or (2) by the historical triumph of covenant-keeping men. The question is this: Should we have greater faith in the future success of God's human representatives in history or Satan's human representatives? The humanists, amillennialists, and premillennialists vote for the second group. The postmillennialists do not. This is why they are so deeply resented. They are challenging the pietist-humanist agreement.

Rushdoony has said it well: "Fundamentalists believe in God but not in history. Humanists believe in history but not in God. Postmillennialists believe in both God and history." History is therefore not a threat to Christianity; it is an inescapable threat to anti-Christianity. Only postmillennialists can consistently say this.

A Shift in Premillennial Rhetoric

Nevertheless, these days we find that many fundamentalist activists are saying things very much in line with postmillennialism's vision of the church's historical victory, which shows how far they have departed from traditional premillennialism. The inherent pessimism of the premillennial position disturbs the activists, who tend to be heavy donors to the major fundamentalist ministries. This is why the premillennial leaders no longer say very much about eschatology. Eschatology has therefore very nearly become a dead issue among major premillennial leaders.

This shift in emphasis is evidence of the rapid fading of the old dispensational premillennial position.[1] There are today very few dispensationalist seminary professors who are willing to go into print about the details of premillennial eschatology, let alone its cultural implications. Their silence is revealing.

The last two major television evangelists who prominently preached traditional pietistic premillennialism were Jim Bakker and Jimmy Swaggart. Both of them suffered public humiliation. Swaggart attacked Bakker publicly when he got caught in sexual sin, and then fell himself when another of his pastoral victims who had been caught and exposed by Swaggart, losing his ministry as a result, hired a private investigator to catch his tormenter — just one big, happy, dispensational family, all under grace and not law.

Swaggart said repeatedly before the cameras that he was the last of the dispensational position's prominent defenders. Just before his front-page crisis over his visits to a prostitute, he was

---

1. Greg L. Bahnsen and Kenneth L. Gentry, Jr., *House Divided: The Break-Up of Dispensational Theology* (Tyler, Texas: Institute for Christian Economics, 1989)

preaching weekly against "dominion theology." I journeyed to Baton Rouge in the fall of 1986 and had a meeting with him and several of his Bible college instructors over this issue. I feared that he would begin to single out Christian Reconstructionists as examples of "dominion theology."[2] He did agree to read some Reconstructionist books before attacking us publicly. He never got around to us in time — prime time, anyway.

The traditional premillennialist insists that he does have faith in history, but only in the historical period after Christ returns to set up His international bureaucratic Kingdom. Only when the present world order is replaced by Christ's bureaucratic order, they insist, will history cease to be a threat to Christians and the church. (The amillennialist does not even have this post-rapture hope, which is why Rushdoony once called them premillennialists without earthly hope.)

---

2. The Library of Congress has added "dominion theology" to its catalogue reference guidelines, but not Christian Reconstruction. Thus, my books are listed under this broader identification.

Chapter 8

PREMILLENNIALISM'S FAITH IN BUREAUCRACY

Our hope is not in taking over this world, but in being taken to heaven by our Lord, to be married to Him in glory and then to return with Him as part of the armies of heaven to rescue Israel, destroy His enemies and participate in the Millennial reign.

Dave Hunt[1]

Hunt makes it clear: when Christians are in complete charge, "Justice will be meted out swiftly."[2] Premillennialism's promised New World Millennial Order will by governed by the most powerful bureaucracy in the history of man. Premillennialism is a religion of millennial bureaucracy. It implies that only a top-down bureaucracy run at the top personally by Jesus (and by Christians in all lower levels, of course) can restore justice to mankind.

Premillennialism is therefore an eschatology based on faith in total bureaucracy. Its appeal today is based on the presupposition that God-fearing Christian people, by preaching the gospel and obeying God's law, are doomed to failure in history until Jesus comes bodily to set up a reign of terror against evildoers. The key to social regeneration, the premillennialist says, is a bureaucracy personally administered by Christ. Until then, nothing significant can be done to heal this world.

---

1. Dave Hunt, "Looking for that Blessed Hope," *Omega Letter* (Feb. 1989), p. 15.
2. Dave Hunt, *Beyond Seduction: A Return to Biblical Christianity* (Eugene, Oregon: Harvest House, 1987), p. 250.

This means that nothing positive that Christians do today will survive the Great Tribulation. All our good works will inevitably be destroyed, either pre-tribulationally (historic premillennialism) or post-tribulationally (conventional dispensationalism). There will be no institutional continuity between today's church with the church of the future millennium. *This is a denial of history*, for "history" in premillennial theology gets broken; there can be no historical continuity with the millennium. The Great Tribulation will intervene.[3] Everything Christians leave behind will be swallowed up. This is great news, not tribulation news, Dave Hunt tells us.

> While the Rapture is similar to death in that both serve to end one's earthly life, the Rapture does something else as well: it signals the climax of history and opens the curtain upon its final drama. It thus ends, in a way that death does not, all human stake in continuing earthly developments, such as the lives of the children left behind, the growth of or the dispersion of the fortune accumulated, the protection of one's reputation, the success of whatever earthly causes one has espoused, and so forth.[4]

This is why premillennialism is inherently, inescapably pessimistic with regard to efforts of social reform.

Only Christ's millennial bureaucracy can bring peace and freedom in history, we are told. We Reconstructionists ask: How can any bureaucracy make men or societies righteous? How can a top-down bureaucratic order change the nature of man? It cannot. Premillennialists would obviously admit this. So, the premillennialist is left with this defense of the millennial bureaucracy: men will be so afraid of the consequences of doing evil that they will obey God's law. (Question: Did Adam obey?)

(Side question: Where will people learn about the details of this Kingdom law? The answer is obvious — in the Old Testament, just as the Reconstructionists assert — but this answer sounds so theonomic that they never mention it.)

---

3. The Great Tribulation actually took place at the fall of Jerusalem in A.D. 70. See David Chilton, *The Great Tribulation* (Ft. Worth, Texas: Dominion Press, 1987).
4. Dave Hunt, "Looking for that Blessed Hope," *Omega Letter* (Feb. 1989), p. 14.

A Distant Supreme Judge

Then why aren't people today afraid of disobeying God? Apparently only because Jesus is not bodily present on earth. But in a world of billions of people, He will be as good as invisible for most people most of the time. (Will His throne of judgment be televised? Will anyone watch?) What about the long lines in front of Jesus' court of final appeal? Why will it be any shorter than the line was in Moses' day, when Jethro advised Moses to set up a hierarchical appeals court (Exodus 18)? It will be a lot longer: He will have billions of people to judge, not just the 1.2 million adults who left Egypt with Moses.

What about the quality of judgments from millennial judges? Why will they be superior to judgments rendered today? In what way? How? Just because only Christians will be empowered to render civil judgment? But this points directly to theocracy — a theonomic ideal. What will happen to the modern ideal of democracy during the millennium? Why is democracy the premillennialists' political ideal today and theocracy the ideal for the coming millennium? Why should theocracy work better then than now? After all, Jesus will be busy rendering judgments, day and night. He can't do it all by Himself. What makes the human judges' judgment better in the future millennium than it is today?

I can see only one possible answer: *a belief that Christians during the millennium will be in some way supernaturally transformed.* They will get new wisdom. But where in the Bible does it even hint that Jesus' mere bodily presence can in some way, in and of itself, change His people into competent judges? Yet if this belief in near-magical transformation is not the unstated heart and soul of premillennial-dispensational political theory — as I argue that it is — then what difference in 99.99% of the court cases will it make that Jesus is bodily present thousands of miles away? Not very much.

This is why I say that premillennialism is a social theory based on faith in bureaucracy. A similar faith in the transforming power of bureaucracy is the essence of the power religion, i.e., the religion of secular humanism. Premillennialists share with liberal humanists the basic outlook of this faith with respect to the question of social transformation. They are power religionists with respect to the coming millennium. They think they or their spiritual heirs will bash heads for Jesus, bringing swift justice for all.

This view of the future implies (though never admits publicly) that political freedom is morally corrupt. Why is political freedom corrupt in such a worldview? Because political freedom, contrary to secular humanists, is impossible under extensive bureaucracy. This would be as true with a bureaucracy ruled by Jesus as it is under any other bureaucracy. The reliability of Jesus' handful of daily judgments would not automatically transform the character or the competence of the earthly judges under Him. Men and civil judges would still need to turn to the Bible in search of justice, just as they need to do now.

What men need is freedom under Bible-revealed law, not more bureaucracy. What they need is the Holy Spirit, not more bureaucracy. What they need is a theonomic revival, not more bureaucracy. What they need is a Bible-based social theory that teaches that covenant-keepers can successfully transform institutions today, including the State, for the glory of God.

The pro-bureaucracy, premillennial view of civil government is one more element in the traditional pietist-humanist agreement. It goes back to 1660 in England – the restoration of King Charles II after the death of Oliver Cromwell – and much farther back on the continent of Europe.

The Christian Reconstructionist rejects such a view of the Kingdom of God in history. He argues that it is the presence of Jesus Christ at the right hand of God – the traditional creed of orthodox Christianity – that alone makes possible the transformation of men and covenantal associations. Because Jesus reigns from on high, He and His Father have sent the Holy Spirit to bring men to saving faith in Christ. It is this Holy Spirit-directed transformation, rather than the establishment of a future international bureaucracy, that is the only legitimate biblical basis of comprehensive social transformation.

Chapter 9

THE PIETIST-HUMANIST ALLIANCE

And they met Moses and Aaron, who stood in the way, as they came forth from Pharaoh: And they said unto them, The LORD look upon you, and judge; because ye have made our savour to be abhorred in the eyes of Pharaoh, and in the eyes of his servants, to put a sword in their hand to slay us (Exodus 5:20-21).

Premillennialists preach escape for today — escape from involvement in politics, plus the inevitable cultural retreat and defeat of the church on this side of the Second Coming. They also preach the wonders of bureaucratic power for the far side of the Second Coming. What they mean by today's escape is today's subordination to the culture of "Egypt."

They resent anyone who would make their humanist taskmasters angry. What frightens some of the dispensational critics is their fear of persecution. David Allen Lewis warns in his book, *Prophecy 2000*, that "as the secular, humanistic, demonically-dominated world system becomes more and more aware that the Dominionists and Reconstructionists are a real political threat, they will sponsor more and more concerted efforts to destroy the Evangelical church. Unnecessary persecution could be stirred up."[1] In short, because politics is supposedly humanistic by nature, any attempt by Christians to speak to political issues as people — or worse, as *a* people — who possess an explicitly biblical agenda will invite "unnecessary persecution."

---

1. Lewis, *Prophecy 2000* (Green Forest, Arkansas: New Leaf Press, 1990), p. 277.

Question: On what philosophical basis can they legitimately challenge the many modern humanistic versions of the power religion, which also have great faith in the transforming power of bureaucracy? Only on this basis: The humanists do not allow the Christians to run the show, whereas Christ will allow this during the millennium. In short, Premillennialists are merely preaching a "new, improved" version of bureaucracy in the future.

For today, however, they preach that "you shouldn't polish brass on a sinking ship." They preach that the ship of State cannot be saved on this side of the rapture, and any attempt to save it is a waste of time and money. If they are consistent with their premillennial faith, they have to agree with Professor Harold Hoehner of Dallas Theological Seminary when he says: "I think the whole thing is wrong-headed. I just can't buy their basic presupposition that we can do anything significant to change the world. And you can waste a lot of time trying."[2]

Only inconsistent premillennialists disagree with this outlook – the people who have been deeply influenced by Reconstructionism's this-world agenda, despite their loud protests to the contrary. These are the people, praise God, whose calls for Christian activism are steadily softening up the resistance to Christian Reconstructionism's message within premillennial circles.

The number of these inconsistent premillennial activists is growing rapidly. Members of the older school of premillennialism see exactly where their social activist colleagues are headed theologically, but the activists are sick and tired of sitting passively in the back of humanism's bus. They want to protest against their status as second-class citizens, even though they also believe that Christians will never get into the driver's seat this side of the rapture.

What they do not want to admit yet is that biblical law provides the only valid road map. We Christian Reconstructionists believe that they will eventually change their minds, or at least

---

2. "Is Christ or Satan the Ruler of This World?" *Christianity Today* (March 5, 1990), p. 43.

their brightest younger followers will. So do the traditional premillennialists, but there is little that they can do about it.

Isaiah's Millennial Vision

Autonomous man, the traditional, consistent premillennialist says, is more powerful in history than the Spirit-empowered gospel. Then premillennialists accuse Christian Reconstructionists of having too much faith in man. But is it "faith in man" to preach that the Holy Spirit will change the hearts of many men in history? Is it "faith in man" to preach, with Isaiah, that a better day is coming? "Behold, a king shall reign in righteousness, and princes shall rule in judgment. And a man shall be as an hiding place from the wind, and a covert from the tempest; as rivers of water in a dry place, as the shadow of a great rock in a weary land. And the eyes of them that see shall not be dim, and the ears of them that hear shall hearken. The heart also of the rash shall understand knowledge, and the tongue of the stammerers shall be ready to speak plainly. The vile person shall be no more called liberal, nor the churl said to be bountiful. For the vile person will speak villany, and his heart will work iniquity, to practise hypocrisy, and to utter error against the LORD, to make empty the soul of the hungry, and he will cause the drink of the thirsty to fail. The instruments also of the churl are evil: he deviseth wicked devices to destroy the poor with lying words, even when the needy speaketh right. But the liberal deviseth liberal things; and by liberal things shall he stand" (Isaiah 32:1-8).

Must this king reign from some future earthly throne in order for this prophecy to be fulfilled? Why? Why can't He reign from on high, at the right hand of God? Why can't He reign through the Holy Spirit and His holy people? Theologically speaking, *why not*?

The Reign of Jesus Christ

What kind of religion is premillennialism? What kind of ethical system does it teach? The same as amillennialism teaches: the defeat of Christian civilization in history. Evil men will triumph culturally in history. The church's gospel of salvation will never transform the world. It will at best produce besieged little groups of Christians, vainly struggling to keep from being overwhelmed.

But why should evil men get more powerful as time goes on, while righteous men get less powerful over time? Both the amillennialist and the premillennialist insist that this is the case in the era of the church in history. But why should this be the case? Do unbelievers have the principles of success? Does evil produce good fruit in history, and righteousness produce bad fruit? Does God in the long run in history reward the unjust and curse the just?[3] Jesus taught the opposite: "Even so every good tree bringeth forth good fruit; but a corrupt tree bringeth forth evil fruit. A good tree cannot bring forth evil fruit, neither can a corrupt tree bring forth good fruit. Every tree that bringeth not forth good fruit is hewn down, and cast into the fire" (Matthew 7:17-19).

The premillennialist has to argue that Jesus Christ's earthly millennial reign will alone bring righteousness the way that Isaiah describes. This ethical transformation somehow cannot (or will not) be achieved from on high. This means that Jesus Christ's physical presence at the head of an international bureaucracy will alone make possible Isaiah's scenario — a heart and mind kind of change — but Jesus cannot (or refuses to) achieve this transformation from on high. This means that Jesus can more efficiently change men's actions through the power of an earth-based bureaucracy than the Holy Spirit can by changing people's hearts through the power of the gospel. Premillennialists do not put it this way, of course, since it sounds terrible, but this is what they implicitly teach.

Premillennialists do not discuss the nature of the millennial bureaucracy, just as Marx refused to discuss the details of his post-revolution millennial world. You cannot find detailed premillennial discussions of this absolutely crucial question:

---

3. For a detailed refutation of this view of ethical cause and effect in history, see Gary North, *Dominion and Common Grace: The Biblical Basis of Progress* (Tyler, Texas: Institute for Christian Economics, 1987).

What will be fundamentally different about the future millennial era?

Why will people be more obedient to God during the earthly millennial rule of Christ? Why will an international bureaucracy be able to make men behave according to God's law (or will)? Why will Christ's mere physical presence 10,000+ miles away make mankind significantly more obedient, when they refuse to obey Him as God today? What will make the bureaucrats in the justice system any more reliable today than those in the Exodus wilderness under Moses?

Obviously, the premillennialist cannot answer that more people will be converted to saving faith merely because of the bodily presence of Christ on earth. This would make the saving work of the Holy Spirit today into little more than an after-thought.

There may be premillennialists who do not hold such a view of the future. If there are, they have an obligation to explain their views in print, where their arguments can be scrutinized by the rest of us. They need to explain precisely what will be different about civil justice in the future millennium. Why should Christ's bodily presence make any fundamental differ-ence in history except for the handful of people whose court cases actually reach His supreme world court in Jerusalem (or wherever His throne will be)? Why should Jesus' perfect judicial decisions achieve anything fundamentally different than Moses' perfect judgments achieved in the wilderness (Exodus 18)?

Saving Faith

The reason why I emphasize the judicial character of the millennium is that this is the only world-transforming change that traditional dispensationalism asserts for the bodily return of Christ during the millennium. Orthodox premillennialists know that Jesus' bodily presence will, in and of itself, be able to con-vert no more people to saving faith than His bodily presence did two millennia ago. It is the Holy Spirit who converts men to saving faith, and He will not be "more present" then than He is now. Indeed, if we are to take seriously Jesus' comments in John 16, the Holy Spirit will be in some way less present. Jesus had to leave the earth in order for the Spirit to come in full power.

Premillennialism is a very strange Christian outlook. It implicitly denies what it explicitly preaches: the heart-transforming power of the gospel in history. The premillennialist looks forward to the justice of the coming earthly millennium, with its bureaucratic order, yet he also proclaims the blessings of spiritual conversion today. Will men be better off eternally because of Jesus' judicial bureaucracy than they are today under the Holy Spirit's soul-saving power? In what way?

It is odd that premillennialists should accuse postmillennialists of having too much faith in man, when their own vision of the healing power of international bureaucracy dwarfs anything that the socialists or Communists have ever taught about social salvation through power. Christian Reconstructionists have little faith in bureaucracy, either now or in the future. Our faith in the transforming power of the Holy Spirit is the basis of our confidence in a bottom-up, freedom-based transformation of society. If this is "faith in man," make the best of it!

Meanwhile, the pietist-humanist alliance continues: a rejection of the idea of Christian social transformation based on a return to biblical law. The Christians of our day do not want deliverance from Egypt. They prefer slavery to freedom, if this freedom means that they must challenge the rulers of our day in the name of God.

The humanists want Christians to stay out of politics as Christians. The pietists agree. The humanists deny that there are valid biblical blueprints that apply to this world. The pietists agree. The humanists argue that Old Testament laws, if applied today, would produce tyranny. The pietists agree. The humanists say that the civil government should be run in terms of religiously neutral laws. The pietists agree. The humanists deny that the God of the Bible brings predictable sanctions in history against societies that do not obey His law. The pietists agree. The humanists deny that the preaching of the gospel will ever fundamentally change the way the world operates. The pietists agree. The humanists say that Christians should sit in the back of cultural bus. The pietists agree. This is why both sides hate the message of Christian Reconstruction.

CONCLUSION, PART I

Let us hear the conclusion of the whole matter: Fear God, and keep his commandments: for this is the whole duty of man. For God shall bring every work into judgment, with every secret thing, whether it be good, or whether it be evil (Ecclesiastes 12:13-14).

God will bring all of man's works into judgment. Thus, we are to fear Him and keep His commandments. You might not initially imagine that these words of Solomon would be highly controversial, but they are, *if* a Christian Reconstructionist cites them as authoritative.

The Christian Reconstructionist believes that God's judgments, like His free gift of sanctification to men and institutions, are threefold: definitive, progressive, and final. God brought definitive judgment against Adam in the garden and against Jesus Christ on Calvary. He also brings progressive judgments in history against individuals and societies that rebel against Him: against the generation of Noah, the generation of the Tower of Babel, and Old Covenant Israel in 70 A.D. Babylon, Medo-Persia, Alexander's empire, and Rome also fell. He will bring final judgment at the end of history. *So, a basic aspect of evangelism is calling upon God to bring His negative sanctions against His enemies in history.* Having churches pray the imprecatory psalms (e.g., Psalm 83) is an important and neglected aspect of evangelism. This means confrontation with God's enemies and also with all those inside the camp of the saints who maintain a permanent cease-fire with humanism. We must work to break up the alliance before God's judgments in history escalate.

The Alliance

The modern church does not believe that Solomon's words apply to the New Testament era. They apply only to the final judgment. Non-Christians do not believe that the words will ever apply to man. Here we see the heart of the problem of both the modern church and modern humanism. Neither side takes Solomon's words seriously. The humanist denies that God will bring anyone into judgment, either in time or eternity. Christians believe in God's final judgment, but they are far less confident about His judgments in history.[1] They are also unwilling to say which commandments are still binding today, let alone in what specific ways.

So, *there is today an operational alliance between the pietist churches and the humanists' world order.* Both sides implicitly agree not to raise the question of God's commandments in public debate. Both sides are happy to debate the issues of the day apart from any reference to God's law.[2]

This cozy alliance is today being challenged at every point by two developments: (1) the growing awareness in the thinking of a minority of Christian leaders and a majority of humanist leaders that there is an inevitable war between two New World Orders: Christ's and autonomous man's; (2) the theological system known as Christian Reconstruction, which for the first time in church history offers the biblical foundations of a comprehensive alternative to humanist civilization. I say "at every point" in order to make clear that I am not limiting my discussion to politics. The challenge of Christian Reconstructionism is much broader and far deeper than mere politics. Our concern is *government*, but not simply civil government. We begin our call for reconstruction with *self-government under God*. From there we go to church government, family government, and only then to civil government. My slogan is "politics fourth!"[3]

---

1. Gary North, *Millennialism and Social Theory* (Tyler, Texas: Institute for Christian Economics, 1990).

2. See Chapter 9, above.

3. Gary North, *Political Polytheism: The Myth of Pluralism* (Tyler, Texas: Institute for Christian Economics, 1989), p. 559.

The Biblical Alternative

Christian Reconstruction is a relatively small Christian intellectual movement which is now beginning to influence Christian activists. While it began in the United States in the late 1960's, it is self-consciously internationalist in perspective, for its members believe that God calls the whole world to repentance.[1] Its theology provides the biblical support for the idea of Christian activism, political and otherwise. It teaches that every area of life apart from God's healing grace is in sin, under Satan's covenant, and therefore under God's judgment, in history and eternity. Christian Reconstructionists therefore insist that the gospel of Christ's salvation is comprehensive in scope.

The legal and moral principles of the gospel must be applied plainly and specifically to every area of life; the church must therefore speak prophetically. Just as the prophets of old came to the kings and people of ancient Israel, so do Christian Reconstructionists come to Christians today and non-Christians: to remind them of the four covenants of God. We are inescapably under God's comprehensive covenant sanctions. Better to be under His positive sanctions than His negative sanctions, both in history and in eternity.

We Christians must proclaim this message of comprehensive redemption to the whole world. The whole creation longs to be released from the curse of sin (Romans 8:22-23), and only the gospel can provide this progressive release from sin and its effects, until God's final judgment at last removes all curses from covenant-keepers and removes covenant-breakers from history, restoring His people and the creation to perfection.

No one individual and no institution can attain perfection in history, because of the effects of sin, but we are nevertheless required to work to achieve it. Perfection is our goal. "Be ye therefore perfect, even as your Father which is in heaven is perfect" (Matthew 5:48). This is a sufficiently large task to keep God's church busy for at least a thousand more years.

---

1. Gary North, *Healer of the Nations: Biblical Blueprints for International Relations* (Ft. Worth, Texas: Dominion Press, 1987).

PART II

QUESTIONS FREQUENTLY ASKED ABOUT CHRISTIAN RECONSTRUCTION

Gary DeMar

Question No. 1

WHAT IS CHRISTIAN RECONSTRUCTION?

And they shall build the old wastes, they shall raise up the former desolations, and they shall repair the waste cities, the desolations of many generations. And strangers shall stand and feed your flocks, and the sons of the alien shall be your plowmen and your vinedressers. But ye shall be named the Priests of the LORD: men shall call you the Ministers of our God: ye shall eat the riches of the Gentiles, and in their glory shall ye boast yourselves (Isaiah 61:4-6; King James Version).

Christian Reconstruction, unlike Christian "movements" in general, has no central director, no overall, tightly controlled strategy. What unites Reconstructionists is their commitment to certain distinctive biblical doctrines that are fundamental to the Christian faith and have been supported by the church for centuries. In particular, Reconstructionists espouse the following distinctives:

1. Regeneration – salvation by grace through faith – is man's only hope both in this age and in the age to come. Only new men who reflect the image of God in Christ can bring about any significant social change since social change follows personal change, and personal change can only come through regeneration. God's sovereignty as it relates to personal salvation and limited institutional authority is foundational for the salvation of man and the abolition of tyranny.

2. The continuing validity and applicability of the whole law of God, including, but not limited to, the Mosaic case laws is the standard by which individuals, families, churches, and civil governments should conduct their affairs.

3. A victorious view of the future progress of the kingdom of God prior to the return of Christ is foundational for the building of a Christian civilization.

4. Presuppositional apologetics as opposed to evidentialism establishes that God's Word is self-authenticating and is the judge of all other supposed authorities, human reason included.

5. A decentralized social order where civil government is only one legitimate government among many other governments, including family government and ecclesiastical (church) government, is the basis for a free and orderly society.

One does not have to hold to all of these distinctives to be thought of as a Reconstructionist, although the belief that personal regeneration precedes family, church, civil, and societal regeneration is foundational to all theories of social reform. (The rejection of this premise was the fatal flaw among those who advocated a "social gospel.") God has not prescribed either anarchy or revolution as ways to change our world. (This is the error of "liberation theology.")

As the informed Christian will quickly realize, each of the above distinctives has a great deal of biblical support as well as having formed the foundation of orthodox (conservative) Christianity for centuries. In a word, Christian Reconstructionist distinctives are nothing new to the church. The same cannot be said for Christian Reconstructionism's most ardent critic, dispensational premillennialism, which had its beginnings in the early nineteenth century and has been denounced as aberrant since its inception.

In simple terms, however, a Reconstructionist is anyone who believes that the Bible applies in some way to issues beyond personal salvation. Do you believe that the Bible has some very direct instructions on how a pre-born baby ought to be treated and that civil government has a role in prohibiting abortion? (Exodus 21:22-25). If you do, then you are a Reconstructionist to some degree. Do you believe that the Bible is a blueprint for prison reform? (Exodus 22:1-9; Ephesians 4:28). If you do, then you are a Reconstructionist to some degree. Read, for example, what Charles Colson, president of Prison Fellowship, writes about prison reform:

> Recently I addressed the Texas legislature. . . . I told them that the
> only answer to the crime problem is to take nonviolent criminals out
> of our prisons and make them pay back their victims with restitution.
> This is how we can solve the prison crowding problem.
> The amazing thing was that afterwards they came up to me one
> after another and said things like, "That's a tremendous idea. Why
> hasn't anyone thought of that?" I had the privilege of saying to them,
> "Read Exodus 22. It is only what God said to Moses on Mount Sinai
> thousands of years ago."[1]

This is the essence of Christian Reconstruction. The Bible's
laws, including, but not limited to, the case laws of the Old
Testament, are applicable today, and, in Colson's words, are
"the only answer to the crime problem." Of course, a Reconstructionist would say that these laws are an answer for our
crime problem and much more, including, but not limited to
economics, education, law, politics, business, ecology, journalism,
and medicine.

The above five distinctives are the most debated features of
Christian Reconstruction. One might be able to find other distinctives held by people who call themselves Reconstructionists,
but these five are usually the ones that come up in discussions
over the topic.

Regeneration

Regeneration is the starting point for Reconstructionists, as it
should be for all Christians. Little can change for good in the
broader culture unless man changes. The only way man can
change is through the regenerating work of the Holy Spirit.
Those "dead in trespasses and sins" (Ephesians 2:1) must have
a "new heart" and a "new spirit." The "heart of stone" must be
removed and a "heart of flesh" substituted. This is God's work.
God's Spirit must be in us before we can "walk in" His "statutes." The result will be that we "will be careful to observe" His

---

1. Charles Colson, "The Kingdom of God and Human Kingdoms," *Transforming Our World: A Call to Action*, ed. James M. Boice (Portland, OR: Multnomah, 1988), pp. 154-55.

dinances" (Ezekiel 36:26-27). The New Testament summarizes it this way: "If any man is in Christ, he is a new creature; the old things passed away; behold, new things have come" (2 Corinthians 5:17, NASB). All of this requires a belief in the sovereignty of God. Only God can make dead men live. Only God can make a dead culture thrive. Noted Reconstructionist scholar Rousas J. Rushdoony summarizes it this way:

> The key to remedying the [modern] situation is *not* revolution, nor any kind of resistance that works to subvert law and order. The New Testament abounds in warnings against disobedience and in summons to peace. *The key is regeneration, propagation of the gospel, and the conversion of men and nations to God's law-word.*[2]
> Clearly, there is no hope for man except in regeneration.[3]

Politics, a conservative economic policy, and other social-oriented agendas are not the ultimate answers to man's dilemma. Man is a sinner in need of salvation. He can not make proper evaluations of how he ought to live in the world until he has a new heart that guides a new mind.

If any critic of Christian Reconstruction fails to recognize this distinctive, then that critic has not done his homework. He has not read what Reconstructionist authors have written over and over again: personal regeneration is essential before any appreciable change will occur in the broader culture.

Keep in mind that we espouse *Christian* Reconstruction. There will be no reconstruction unless there are Christians. While unbelievers can follow the Word of God and benefit by its wisdom, it is only the Christian who can fully understand the full implications of what God's Word is all about. The non-Christian has the *work* of the law written in his heart (Romans 2:15), but not the law itself (Hebrews 8:9-13).[4]

---

2. Rousas J. Rushdoony, *The Institutes of Biblical Law* (Phillipsburg, NJ: Presbyterian and Reformed, 1973), p. 113.

3. *Ibid.*, p. 449.

4. John Murray, *The Epistle to the Romans*, 2 vols. (Grand Rapids, Michigan: Eerdmans, 1959), I, pp. 72-76.

Biblical Law

Civil governors, legislators, and judges are just as responsible to keep God's law as any individual is in his family, school, business, church, and civic duties. Many Christians want to deny that God's law is applicable today, especially in the area of civil government. These Christians cut themselves off from the Old Testament in spite of the New Testament's own validation of it. Paul says the Old Testament is "inspired by God [God-breathed] and profitable for teaching, for reproof, for correction, for training in righteousness; that the man of God may be adequate, equipped for every good work" (2 Timothy 3:16-17).

Consider for a moment what options we have if the Old Testament laws, especially the case laws of Exodus, no longer apply. We are left with either a New Testament-only ethic, natural law, general revelation, or some form of moral relativism (typically described as "pluralism"). But all Ten Commandments from Exodus 20 and Deuteronomy 5 are repeated or alluded to in the New Testament, including the Sabbath rest law.[5] Since these laws *summarize* all of the laws found in the Bible, we can conclude that it is proper to look to the Old Testament for legal instruction for individual morality, church law, and civil law. Jesus and the New Testament writers certainly do not hesitate in applying certain laws from the Old Testament to New Testa-

---

5. Richard A. Fowler and H. Wayne House, *Civilization in Crisis: A Christian Response to Homosexuality, Feminism, Euthanasia, and Abortion*, 2nd ed. (Grand Rapids, MI: Baker Book House, [1983] 1988), p. 131. Norman Geisler dismisses Old Testament law because, offering one reason, "only nine of the Ten Commandments are restated in any form in the New Testament. The command to worship on Saturday is not repeated for obvious reasons: Jesus rose, appeared to his disciples, ascended into heaven, and sent the Holy Spirit on Sunday." Norman L. Geisler, *Christian Ethics: Options and Issues* (Grand Rapids, MI: Baker Book House, 1989), p. 203.

There is no "command to worship on Saturday" found in the fourth commandment, only to cease from doing "any work" (Exodus 20:10). This is why Jesus said that the Sabbath was "made for man," thus, upholding the sanctity of the seventh day for man to cease from his labor (Mark 2:27-28). It would seem that a restatement of "only nine of the Ten Commandments . . . in the New Testament" supports the Reconstructionists' claims more than it does Geisler's. Anyway, who says a law must be repeated in the New Testament before it becomes obligatory for Christians to obey? Does Geisler realize that Exodus 21:17 and Leviticus 20:9 are repeated in the New Testament (Mark 7:10), but Leviticus 18:23 and Deuteronomy 27:21 (laws prohibiting bestiality) are not? See Kenneth L. Gentry, Jr., "Must God Stutter?," *Dispensationalism in Transition* (May 1990).

ment situations. Here's a *sample* of Mosaic laws reaffirmed and applied in the New Testament:

Old Testament Reference	New Testament Reference
• Deuteronomy 8:3	• Matthew 4:4
• Deuteronomy 6:16	• Matthew 4:7
• Deuteronomy 6:13	• Matthew 4:10
• Exodus 20:12; 21:17; Leviticus 20:9; Deuteronomy 5:16	• Matthew 15:4
• Deuteronomy 19:15	• Matthew 18:16; 1 Timothy 5:19
• Exodus 20:12; Deuteronomy 5:16-20; Leviticus 19:18	• Matthew 19:18-19; 22:39; Romans 13:9
• Exodus 20:13; Leviticus 19:18; Deuteronomy 5:17	• Romans 13:9
• Deuteronomy 25:4	• 1 Corinthians 9:9
• Leviticus 19:18	• Galatians 5:14
• Deuteronomy 25:4	• 1 Timothy 5:18

But let's suppose that only those laws *repeated* in the New Testament from the Old Testament are valid. Of course, there is no such principle of interpretation found in the Bible. And we might go even further by stating, as the dispensationalist does, that the church age did not begin until after Acts 2. This would mean that laws found in the gospels would be relegated to the Old Covenant era. They cannot be made to apply during the "church age," the dispensationalist wants us to believe, since Jesus was addressing Israel, not the Gentile nations.

There was a time in dispensational theology when even the Sermon on the Mount could not be adopted by the church as an ethical code. It could only be applied in the future millennium. The Sermon was described as "kingdom law," and since the kingdom (millennium) had not come, these laws had to await a future application. With all of this in mind, the church is now left with a Bible from Acts 3 through Revelation 3 from which he can formulate a law code.[6] This would mean, for example,

---

6. According to dispensationalists, the "rapture" occurs at Revelation 4:1. After the church is gone, God once again deals with His earthly people, Israel. Jewish time begins

no specific prohibitions against abortion and bestiality since there is nothing in the New Testament that would prohibit their practice. But even if the case could be made that prohibitions against abortion and bestiality can be deduced from the New Testament prohibition against fornication (and they can), these prohibitions would apply only to the church since fornication must be defined in Old Testament terms as they relate to the people of Israel! The State could then decriminalize abortion and homosexuality (as it has done) because, as noted dispensational advocate Norman Geisler maintains, the "Mosaic legislation" is no longer "binding on human governments today."[7]

The only consistently biblical position is that the precepts of God's law (prior to Moses, the Mosaic legislation, the wisdom literature, the prophets, the ministry of Christ in the gospels, and the remainder of the New Testament) are "morally obligatory for all men in all ages to obey."[8] Since the New Testament supports this thesis, the New Testament is the interpretative guide in determining how all of God's law should apply.

Postmillennialism

Postmillennialism[9] is the belief that God's kingdom will advance throughout history, that all authority in "heaven and in *earth*" has been given to Jesus, that God's kingdom is represented by the stone that is cut without hands and becomes a mountain that fills the whole earth (Daniel 2:34, 44-45). Premillennialists assert that these promises are reserved for a future "millennium" where Jesus Christ will be physically present on earth.

---

at this point.

7. Geisler, *Christian Ethics*, p. 202.

8. Greg L. Bahnsen, Kenneth L. Gentry, Jr., *House Divided: The Break-Up of Dispensational Theology* (Tyler, TX: Institute for Christian Economics, 1989), p. 132.

9. The term *post*millennialism has reference to the timing of Jesus' return. Jesus will return *after* (post) the thousand year period of Revelation 20 which is a symbolic period of the reign of Christ. Premillennialists believe that Jesus will return *before* (pre) the thousand years to set up an earthly kingdom. The amillennialist, like the postmillennialist believes that the thousand year period is symbolic and that Jesus will return after the thousand years are ended. Unlike the postmillennialist but like the premillennialist, the amillennialist does not see a period of gospel prosperity prior to Jesus' return. Thus, the prefix *a* tells us that there is no "millennium."

Postmillennialists believe the Bible teaches that the stone cut without hands immediately follows the destruction of the fourth kingdom of Nebuchadnezzar's dream: First-century Rome. The dispensational premillennialist must create a future fifth kingdom made up of the ten toes of Nebuchadnezzar's statue (a resurrected Roman Empire) in order for this yet future kingdom to be realized.

Clearly, the Bible tells us that "the kingdom of God has come upon" us (Matthew 12:28). How do we know this? Because Jesus cast out demons: "But if I cast out demons by the finger of God, the *kingdom of God has come upon you*" (Luke 11:20).

Those who believe that the kingdom promises are relegated to a millennium yet to come, also believe that little if anything can be done to change this world. Societal destruction is inevitable under both amillennialism and all varieties of premillennialism, especially *dispensational* premillennialism. Prominent dispensational writers have created a theology that discounts a future earthly perspective that could lead to any success prior to an earthly millennium. Consider these examples:

> This world is not going to get any easier to live in. Almost unbelievably hard times lie ahead. Indeed, Jesus said that these coming days will be uniquely terrible. Nothing in all the previous history of the world can compare with what lies in store for mankind.[10]

> What a way to live! With optimism, with anticipation, with excitement. We should be living like persons who don't expect to be around much longer.[11]

> I don't like cliches but I've heard it said, "God didn't send me to clean the fish bowl, he sent me to fish." In a way there's a truth in that.[12]

Ted Peters writes of dispensationalism that "it functions to

---

10. Charles C. Ryrie, *The Living End* (Old Tappan, NJ: Revell, 1976), p. 21.

11. Hal Lindsey, *The Late Great Planet Earth* (Grand Rapids, MI: Zondervan, 1970), p. 145.

12. Hal Lindsey, "The Great Cosmic Countdown," *Eternity* (January 1977), p. 21. Consider what happens to fish if the bowl is not cleaned. They die!

justify social irresponsibility," and many "find this doctrine a comfort in their lethargy."[13] Ideas, especially eschatological ideas, have consequences. Harold Hoehner of Dallas Theological Seminary, the current bastion of dispensational theology, considers involvement in societal issues as "wrong-headed." What does he say of those who are working to apply the Bible to issues beyond personal piety?: "I just can't buy their basic presupposition that we can do anything significant to change the world. And you can waste an awful lot of time trying."[14]

There is no neutrality. If you believe that the Bible applies to issues beyond personal salvation, then you are a Reconstructionist in some sense. If you do not believe that the Bible applies to issues beyond personal salvation, then you are not a Reconstructionist.

Presuppositionalism

As presuppositionalists, Reconstructionists hold that there is no neutrality, that the only common ground between believer and unbeliever is that both know that God exists. The unbeliever, however, suppresses the truth of his knowledge of God in unrighteousness (Romans 1:18-32). He knows God and what God requires of him, but he chooses to reject God. The unbeliever, because he rejects both God and His Word, seeks to build a worldview independent of God. As the unbeliever becomes more consistent with His anti-God position, his worldview self-destructs. God is not mocked.

The successful aspects of non-Christian philosophies are the result of borrowing from the biblical worldview. The scientist who holds to the evolutionary theory of chance occurrence does not believe in chance occurrence when he works within the framework of the scientific model where chance is not a consideration. Here he borrows biblical presuppositions to make his experiment work, all the time developing theories that hope to

---

13. Ted Peters, *Futures: Human and Divine* (Atlanta, GA: John Knox, 1978), pp. 28, 29.

14. Cited in "Is Christ or Satan Ruler of This World?," *Christianity Today* (March 5, 1990), p. 43.

show that there is no need for God.

There is a tendency among evangelicals to assume (1) that there is an area of philosophical neutrality in the areas of law, education, politics, and economics; (2) that knowledge is somehow "neutral," (3) that facts can be interpreted without any prior presuppositions, and (4) that the facts "speak for themselves. This is an untenable position. All facts are interpreted facts. It is a mistake, therefore, to believe that the world of unbelieving thought has anything to contribute to the Christian worldview when it is based on unbelieving presuppositions.

Humanistic theories of law, politics, education, and economics survive because they draw on the fruit of the Christian religion, although they deny the root, Jesus Christ. This can be seen in the current attempts of the humanists to derive an ethic antithetical to Christianity. Christian concepts like virtue, freedom, compassion, and honesty are given humanistic content. But these ideals do not exist in an evolutionary worldview without God. Therefore, if humanism has any life in itself, it is only because it still operates within a Christian context. Strip humanism of its Christian categories and it would, if it were consistent with its man-centered presuppositions, lead to heinous results.

Norman Geisler claims in his book *Is Man the Measure?* that "Secular humanism has made many positive contributions to human life."[15] One "positive contribution" of humanism, Geisler says, is the recognition of "the need for freedom of the individual. In 'Humanist Manifesto II' they declare, 'To enhance freedom and dignity the individual must experience a full range of *civil liberties* in all societies.'"[16] But civil liberties without a biblical context can lead to death. Abortion is claimed to be a fundamental "right" by those who believe in "a full range of civil liberties. Homosexuality is also touted as a "right."

Centuries ago the following question was asked: What does Jerusalem have to do with Athens? Jerusalem represents Christ, His Word, and revelation-driven Christian thought. Athens was

---

15. Norman L. Geisler, *Is Man the Measure?* (Grand Rapids, MI: Baker Book House, 1983), p. 123.

16. *Ibid.*, p. 124.

the epitome of a man-centered philosophy committed to the "Academy" of humanistic learning. Tertullian asked it this way:

> What indeed has Athens to do with Jerusalem? What concord is there between the Academy and the Church? What between heretics and Christians? Our instructions come from the "porch of Solomon" [Acts 3:11], who had himself taught that "the Lord should be sought in simplicity of heart." Away with all attempts to produce a mottled Christianity of Stoic, Platonic, and dialectic composition! We want no curious disputation after possessing Christ Jesus, no inquisition after enjoying the gospel! With our faith, we desire no further belief. For this is our palmary faith, that there is nothing which we ought to believe besides.[17]

Tertullian writes in the same context that "heresies are themselves instigated by philosophy." But it was a certain kind of philosophy that he had in mind, what the Bible describes as "deceitful spirits and doctrines of demons" (1 Timothy 4:1), produced for itching ears of the spirit of this world's wisdom to hear anything but the truth of the gospel (Acts 7:57). Paul had been at Athens, and had become acquainted with their supposed wisdom which pretends to be sent from heaven (Acts 17:16-34). "He did not attempt to find common beliefs which would serve as starting points for an uncommitted search for 'whatever gods there may be.'"[18]

> Paul was well aware of the philosophical climate of his day. Accordingly he did *not* attempt to use premises agreed upon with the philosophers, and then pursue a "neutral" method of argumentation to move them from the circle of their beliefs into the circle of his own convictions. When he disputed with the philosophers *they* did not find any grounds for agreement with Paul at any level of their conversations. Rather, they utterly disdained him as a "seed picker," a slang term (originally applied to gutter-sparrows) for a peddler of second-hand bits of pseudo-philosophy – an intellectual scavenger (v. 18). The word of the cross was to them foolish (I Cor. 1:18), and in their pseudo-wisdom they knew not God (I Cor. 1:20-21). Hence Paul

---

17. Tertullian (A.D. 145-220), *The Prescription Against Heretics*, VII.
18. Greg L. Bahnsen, "The Encounter of Jerusalem with Athens," *Ashland Theological Bulletin*, Vol. XIII, No. 1 (Spring 1980), p. 15.

would not consent to use their verbal "wisdom" in his apologetic, lest the cross of Christ be made void (I Cor. 1:17).[19]

If Paul did not compromise the gospel in his discussions with these pagan philosophers over the nature of religion, then why do some Christian scholars maintain that it is permissible to compromise in the area of law, politics, economics, and education to develop an ethical system without regard to the Bible?

Decentralized Social Order

Reconstructionists believe in a "minimal state." The purpose of getting involved in politics, as Reconstructionists see it, is to *reduce* the power of the State. Reconstructionists are not calling on the State to mandate prayer and Bible reading in the public (government) schools, as most fundamentalists advocate. Neither do we advocate teaching "Creation Science."[20] It is the non-Reconstructionists who petition the State for greater influence of the Christian worldview areas over which the Bible gives the state no jurisdiction. Reconstructionists do not believe that the State has the God-given authority to educate our children.

Because of our belief in a minimal State, taxes would be lowered for every citizen. This would encourage savings, reduce interest rates, and spur investment in high-risk technological ventures for the long-term betterment of the citizenry. Caring for the poor, as outlined by a book first published by American Vision in 1985 (*Bringing in the Sheaves*), is not the domain of the State. In fact, George Grant sees the State as a hindrance when it develops policies designed to "help the poor." Of course, Reconstructionists are not alone in this assessment.[21]

Reconstructionists believe in the political process. We also

---

19. *Ibid.*, pp. 14-15.

20. Norman L. Geisler, an ardent critic of Christian Reconstruction, supports the teaching of "Creation Science" in government schools. Geisler, *The Creator in the Courtroom: The Controversial Arkansas Creation-Evolution Trial* (Milford, MI: Mott Media, 1982). Isn't this mandating that the State involve itself in religion?

21. See the books by non-Christians such as Charles Murray, Thomas Sowell, Walter E. Williams, and by Christian author E. Calvin Beisner: *Prosperity and Poverty: The Compassionate Use of Resources in a World of Scarcity* (Crossway Books, 1988).

believe in gradual, pervasive transformation of human institutions in the wake of worldwide conversion to orthodox Christianity. In the Reconstructionists' worldview, civil government at the top will change when government at the bottom changes: from self-government to civil governments at all levels. I've developed this concept in numerous books and articles. In fact, my first book, *God and Government: A Biblical and Historical Study* (1982), begins, not with politics and civil government, but with self-government, family government, church government, and various strata of civil government.[22] The same emphasis can be found in my *Ruler of the Nations* (1986). In *The Reduction of Christianity* I wrote the following:

> Politics is the "quick fix" approach to cultural transformation. "The next presidential election will turn the tide. A Change in the Supreme Court will bring our nation back to righteousness. If we could only get more conservatives elected to office." None of this will do it. Only a long-term effort to change all facets of society will bring about significant and lasting transformation. This means changing the hearts and minds of millions of people.[23]

R. J. Rushdoony's works express a similar theme.[24] The Reconstructionist view of social change, in the words of John Witherspoon, will result in "dominion by consent."[25]

Those who accuse Christian Reconstruction as advocating change through political processes are critiqued by me in a number of places. A cursory reading of *The Reduction of Christianity* will lead any reader to conclude that Reconstructionists believe just the opposite of what these critics assert that we say.

---

22. The three-volume *God and Government* series has been republished by Wolgemuth & Hyatt (1990).

23. Gary DeMar and Peter Leithart, *The Reduction of Christianity: A Biblical Response to Dave Hunt* (Ft. Worth, TX: Dominion Press, 1988), p. 297.

24. Rushdoony, *Law and Liberty* (Vallecito, CA: Ross House Books, [1971] 1986) and Rushdoony, *The Politics of Guilt and Pity* (Fairfax, VA: Thoburn Press, [1970] 1978).

25. "Dominion, it is plain from all that has been said, can be acquired only one way, viz. by consent. There are two other ways commonly mentioned, both of which are defective, inheritance and conquest." Quoted in *The Journal of Presbyterian History*: Presbyterian and the American Revolution: A Documentary Account, Vol. 52, No. 4 (Winter 1974), p. 356.

The Pyramid Society is a culture in which a majority of the people spend most of their time transforming the civil sphere of government to the near exclusion of themselves, their families, churches, schools, businesses, and local civil governments. By changing the powers at the top, we are led to believe that there will be a trickle-down effect of cultural transformation that will blossom into a better society. The problems that a nation faces, as this approach sees it, are solely political. Change the State, and all of society will change with it. This has been the vision of pagan empires since the building of the tower of Babel.[26]

The belief in a centralized political order that critics insist Christian Reconstructionists defend is described by me as "paganism." Instead of a Pyramid Society, Reconstructionists advocate a decentralized social order.

The Bible outlines a decentralized social order where power is diffused and the potential for corruption and tyranny are minimized. Freedom is enhanced because of the diluted strength of the one by the maintenance of the many.[27]

Gary North emphasizes a similar theme in the following quotation:

The biblical social order is utterly hostile to the pyramid society. The biblical social order is characterized by the following features. *First,* it is made up of multiple institutional arrangements, each with its own legitimate, limited, and derivative sovereignty under God's universal law. *Second,* each institution possesses a hierarchical chain of command, but these chains of command are essentially *appeals courts* – "bottom-up" institutions – with the primary duty of responsible action placed on people occupying the lower rungs of authority. *Third,* no single institution has absolute and final authority in any instance; appeal can be made to other sovereign agents of godly judgment. Since no society can attain perfection, there will be instances of injustice, but the social goal is harmony under biblical law, in terms of an orthodox creed. God will judge all men perfectly. The State need not seek perfect justice, nor should citizens be taxed at the astronomical

---

26. Gary DeMar and Peter Leithart, *The Reduction of Christianity: A Biblical Response to Dave Hunt* (Ft. Worth, TX: Dominion Press, 1988), p. 305.

27. *Ibid.,* p. 306.

rates necessary to sustain the quest for perfect justice.[28]

So then, the portrayal of Christian Reconstruction as wanting to establish a centralized political order is incorrect. We teach just the opposite. As I've shown, one does not need to search for very long to find these views expressed in our writings. They are prominent emphases.

---

28. Gary North, *Moses and Pharaoh: Dominion Religion Versus Power Religion* (Tyler, TX: Institute for Christian Economics, 1985), pp. 211-12.

Question 2

DO RECONSTRUCTIONISTS BELIEVE THAT
CHRISTIANS WILL BRING IN THE KINGDOM OF
GOD IN HISTORY?

Anyone familiar with the historic millennial positions (amillennialism, covenantal premillennialism, and postmillennialism) knows that each view teaches that the kingdom *has come* in some form and that it will be consummated only at Jesus' final coming when He delivers up the kingdom to His Father (1 Corinthians 15:23-24).

This "already—not yet" view of the kingdom is biblically sound and has been defended by numerous Bible-believing scholars from various millennial perspectives. Even dispensationalists are conceding that the kingdom has come in some way.

> The basic distinction here among dispensationalists is that older ones tended to see the kingdom relegated entirely to the future. More contemporary dispensationalists hold that the full realization of the kingdom for Israel and the world awaits the future, but certainly spiritual aspects of the kingdom are operational in the church.[1]

The Bible teaches the *nearness* of the kingdom in Jesus' day. This was the message of John the Baptist and Jesus (Matthew 3:2; 4:17, 23; Mark 1:14-15; Luke 4:16-30; 4:43; 8:1; 10:9; Colossians 1:13). The kingdom was also manifested through the

---

1. John S. Feinberg, ed., "Systems of Discontinuity," *Continuity and Discontinuity* (Westchester, IL: Crossway Books, 1988), p. 82

work of Christ (Matthew 11:2-6; Luke 4:21; 11:20; 17:21). The kingdom continually comes (Matthew 6:10) and progressively advances (Isaiah 9:1-7; Daniel 2:31-34, 44-45; 1 Corinthians 15:24; Matthew 13:31-33). In addition, Jesus tells the Pharisees that the kingdom has actually come. The sign that demons are cast out is *prima facie* evidence that the kingdom has come upon us: "But if I cast out demons by the Spirit of God, then the kingdom of God *has come upon you*" (Matthew 12:28).[2] How can Reconstructionists be accused of "bringing in the kingdom" when Jesus plainly states that the kingdom had come upon His first-century hearers?

In another place, Jesus tells the Pharisees that the kingdom is among them or in their midst.[3] While Paul was consistently "preaching the kingdom of God" (Acts 28:30-31), modern-day kingdom critics preach the rapture and an exclusively future kingdom (millennium). Reconstructionists as postmillennialists do not teach that we "bring in the kingdom." The kingdom has come, is coming, will come, and one day will be delivered up to God the Father, when "He has abolished all rule and all authority and power. For He must reign until He has put all His enemies under His feet" (1 Corinthians 15:24-25). The Bible clearly tells us that Jesus' reign is a *present* reality. He is sitting on David's throne (Acts 2:22-36); He has been seated at the Father's "right hand in the heavenly places" (Ephesians 1:20); all things have been put under Jesus' feet by His Father (v. 22); and "He delivered *us* from the domain of darkness, and transferred *us* to the kingdom of His beloved Son" (Colossians 1:13).

A good number of critics of Christian Reconstruction want to maintain that the kingdom is not a reality because Jesus' kingdom is "not of this world" (John 18:36). But if they mean by

---

2. In the only full length critique of Christian Reconstruction, authors H. Wayne House and Thomas Ice do not even reference this verse. See *Dominion Theology: Blessing or Curse? A Critique of Christian Reconstructionism* (Portland, OR: Multnomah Press, 1988).

3. Should the text read, "The kingdom is within you," or "the kingdom of God is in your midst"? Both translations are possible. But since Jesus was speaking to the unbelieving Pharisees, the kingdom could not have been within *them*. Rather, they were in the midst of the kingdom but could not "see the kingdom" (John 3:3) because they had not undergone the new birth.

this that the kingdom cannot manifest itself on this earth, then it can never be manifested on this earth. This includes the millennium, the seventh dispensation called "the kingdom age" by dispensational theology. "Of this world" does not have reference to *where* Jesus' kingdom operates but only the source of His kingdom's power. His kingdom is "of heaven" — this is why it is described as the "kingdom *of heaven*" — but it affects this world. "Thy kingdom come. Thy will be done on *earth* as it is in *heaven*" (Matthew 6:10).

Why do so many dispensationalists misrepresent Reconstructionists on this issue? I believe the following will help shed some light on those dispensationalists who want no part of a theology that stipulates that the kingdom is a present reality. Dispensationalists view anyone who works for social change as trying to "bring in the kingdom" since only Jesus can accomplish this with His *physical* presence. Since Jesus is not physically present, the kingdom is not present; it is *exclusively* future and millennial in character. They then impose this (false) definition of a future kingdom run by Jesus from Jerusalem who dispenses punishment for the least infraction on a present-kingdom definition that must operate by less than perfect sinners without Jesus being present. They suppose if the true kingdom means Jesus will punish *any* and *all* outward acts of disobedience, then anyone who claims that the kingdom is a present reality must be advocating the same type of kingdom but without the presence of Jesus. This is an improper understanding of Christ's kingdom. When a dispensationalist hears the word "kingdom," he thinks of its governmental characteristics in *earthly* terms. The following is a typical example:

> The second important characteristic of the millennial rule of Christ is that His government will be absolute in its authority and power. This is demonstrated in His destruction of all who oppose Him (cf. Ps. 2:9; 72:9-11; Isa. 11:4). . . . The wicked are warned to serve the Lord lest they feel His wrath (Ps. 2:10-12). It seems evident from many passages that no open sin will go unpunished. . . . [T]hose who merely profess to follow the King without actually being saints . . . are forced to obey the King or be subject to the

penalty of death or other chastisement.[4]

The above passages are taken by Walvoord to refer to the rule of Christ *on* earth rather than the rule of Christ from heaven *over* the earth. There is no indication in the context where these passages are found that an earthly, bodily kingship is in mind. God is presently judging the earth through various means, not all of which are political or immediate. With dispensationalism, there seems to be less grace during the millennium than there is now.

For the dispensationalist, the millennium's social order is centralized around the *earthly* rule of Christ. Reconstructionists view the present-operating kingdom as a *decentralized* social order where no individual or group of individuals has absolute power. Jesus rules from heaven and delegates *limited* authority to individuals and institutional governments such as families, churches, and civil governments. Reconstructionists maintain that evidence will still be required to convict any person of criminal behavior. Society will not be structured along some type of "Big Brother" concept. The power of civil government at all levels will be decreased considerably. This will mean a great reduction in taxation of all citizens. All the laws set forth in the Bible to protect those accused of crimes will be applied and enforced. Laws protecting life and property will receive strong advocation.

The dispensationalist sees the kingdom coming as a cataclysm at the end of what they propose is a future seven year tribulation period that the church will never experience. The Reconstructionist views the kingdom as a present reality that manifests itself as sinners embrace the gospel and live out their new lives in conformity to the Bible. There is no kingdom to bring in, since we are living in the kingdom. A millennial era of blessings will be produced by the covenantal obedience of Christians, coupled with the saving work of the Holy Spirit.

---

4. John F. Walvoord, *The Millennial Kingdom* (Grand Rapids, MI: Dunham Publishing Company, [1959] 1967), pp. 301-2. Dave Hunt writes that "Justice will be meted out swiftly" during the millennium. *Beyond Seduction: A Return to Biblical Christianity* (Eugene, OR: Harvest House, 1987), p. 250.

Question 3

DO CHRISTIAN RECONSTRUCTIONISTS BELIEVE THAT CHRISTIANS ARE STILL UNDER THE LAW?

James tells us that "for whoever keeps the whole law and yet stumbles in one point, he has become guilty of all" (James 2:10). One sin, one transgression of the law, is enough to condemn any person to eternal judgment. Only Jesus kept the law perfectly. God "made Him [Jesus] *who knew no sin* to be sin on our behalf, that we might become the righteousness of God in Him" (2 Corinthians 5:21). Jesus "redeemed us from the curse of the Law, having become a curse for us" (Galatians 3:13). Salvation is by grace through faith (Ephesians 2:8-10). In this sense, we are not under law but under grace (Romans 6:14). In fact, the Bible teaches that the church since Adam has always been under grace and not law! The New Testament did not set forth any new way to be saved (Romans 4; Galatians 3:6).

But does salvation by grace through faith mean that Christians are free to live any way they please since they are "redeemed from the curse of the law"? Paul asks it this way: "Do we then nullify the Law through faith? May it never be! On the contrary, we establish the Law" (Romans 3:31). In another place Paul tells us that "the Law is good, if one uses it lawfully" (1 Timothy 1:8). So then, even our use of the law should be governed by the law.

Why, then, did the early church have so much trouble with the Judaizers if the Bible says that the law is "good"? J. Gresham Machen, a staunch early twentieth-century defender of the faith, explains what the issues were regarding the proper understanding and application of the law for believers.

Paul as well as the Judaizers believed that the keeping of the law of God, in its deepest import, is inseparably connected with faith. The difference concerned only the logical — not even, perhaps, the temporal — order of three steps. Paul said that a man (1) first believes on Christ, (2) then is justified before God, (3) then immediately proceeds to keep God's law. The Judaizers said that a man (1) believes on Christ and (2) keeps the law of God the best he can, and then (3) is justified.[1]

A Pharisee believes that following a man-made tradition saves a person (Mark 7:9). A Judaizer is someone who believes that salvation is by grace through faith *plus* keeping the law, this included laws regulating diet, blood sacrifice, and circumcision. A Christian is someone who believes that a person is saved by grace through faith *apart from* the law or any supposed "good works."

No one can be saved by keeping the law. This is the Bible's point when Romans 6:14 says that the Christian is not under the law. This is far different from saying that the Christian is not obligated to obey the law as a standard of righteousness. Prior to regeneration, a person is unable to keep the law and is condemned for his "lawlessness." After a person comes to Christ the curse of the law is lifted. Jesus became a curse for us and suffered the penalty for broken law (Isaiah 53). But now, through the agency of the Holy Spirit, the redeemed sinner is willing and enabled to keep the law, although not perfectly (Ezekiel 36:26-27). This imperfect law keeping, however, does not condemn the Christian as it did prior to being saved by grace, although there may be temporal ramifications for disobedience.

Christians are not left helpless when they do sin, however: "If anyone sins, we have an Advocate with the Father, Jesus Christ the righteous" (1 John 2:1). But sin is still "*law*lessness" (1 John 3:4). Obviously some law is still in force or there would be no sin, and if there is no sin then we do not need an Advocate with the Father. In addition, "if we confess our sins [*law*-

---

1. J. Gresham Machen, *Christianity and Liberalism* (Grand Rapids, MI: Eerdmans, [1923] 1946), p. 24

lessness], He is faithful and just to forgive us our sins [*law*lessness] and to cleanse us from all unrighteousness" (1 John 1:9).

The real question is, What law are we bound to obey? Some objective *biblical* standard must be the sinner's guide. Our inability to obey the law set forth in Scripture, the same law that works on our heart to convict us of sin, drives us to Christ (Galatians 3:24). But there are other uses of the law. We can gauge our love for our neighbor by how well we keep the law (Romans 13:8-10). Our love for Jesus is expressed in terms of law-keeping. Jesus said, "If you love Me, you will keep My commandments" (John 14:15). Are Jesus' commandments different from those of His Father? No. He came to do the will of His Father and taught His disciples to do the same (Matthew 6:10; 7:21; Luke 22:42; John 4:34). Keeping God's law is God's will.

Question 4

DO CHRISTIAN RECONSTRUCTIONISTS BELIEVE THAT WE ARE SANCTIFIED BY THE LAW?

This question needs to be answered in a no/yes fashion. No, Christians are not sanctified by the law if one means that the law is *added* to faith to save someone (the Judaizing heresy). "I do not nullify the grace of God; *for if righteousness comes through the Law, then Christ died needlessly*" (Galatians 2:21). If there is anything that man can do to merit or retain his salvation, then there is room for boasting. The Bible says that rebellious sinners do not even add faith; it too is a "gift of God" (Ephesians 2:8).

> But now apart from the Law the righteousness of God has been manifested, being witnessed by the Law and the Prophets, even the righteousness of God through faith in Jesus Christ for all those who believe; for there is no distinction; for all have sinned and fall short of the glory of God, being justified as a gift by His grace through the redemption which is in Christ Jesus; whom God displayed publicly as a propitiation in His blood through faith. This was to demonstrate His righteousness, because in the forbearance of God He passed over the sins previously committed; for the demonstration, I say, of His righteousness at the present time, that He might be just and the justifier of the one who has faith in Jesus. *Where then is boasting? It is excluded. By what kind of law? Of works? No, but by a law of faith. For we maintain that a man is justified by faith apart from works of the Law* (Romans 3:21-28).

The Christian adds *nothing* to Jesus' finished work on the cross. Jesus paid it all. The debt is entirely the sinner's. The righteousness belongs entirely to Jesus. Jesus' righteousness is *imputed* or *credited* to those who are "dead in trespasses and sins," apart from any work of the law (Ephesians 2:1). This is called justification, a judicial act of God that happens only once, declaring sinners to be righteous based on the merits of Jesus Christ, His perfect obedience and His perfect sacrifice.

With justification comes definitive sanctification. A supporting text of Scripture for definitive sanctification is 1 Corinthians 1:2: "To the church of God which is at Corinth, *to those who have been sanctified in Christ Jesus*, saints by calling, with all who in every place call upon the name of our Lord Jesus Christ, their Lord and ours."

Scripture goes on to talk about *progressive* sanctification — spiritual growth — comparing it to natural growth: "Therefore, putting aside all malice and all guile and hypocrisy and envy and all slander, like newborn babes, long for the pure milk of the word, that by it you may *grow in respect to salvation*, if you have tasted the kindness of the Lord" (1 Peter 2:1-3). If justification is a point, then sanctification is a vector, starting at a point and then moving in one direction. Sanctification follows justification as growth follows birth. Paul says that "we are His workmanship, created in Christ Jesus for good works, which God prepared beforehand, that we should walk in them" (Ephesians 2:10). We were redeemed "from every lawless deed" so that we might be "zealous for good deeds" (Titus 2:14). No works or growth, no sanctification. No sanctification, no justification. Sanctification is evidence of justification.

Growth, however, depends on nourishment. The nourishment is "the pure milk of the word." Sanctification is not simply being "led by the Spirit." The Spirit uses the *word* to lead us into sanctification. Scripture is the *standard* for sanctification. How do we know when we are going through the process of sanctification? Feelings? Emotion? Personal opinion? Sentiment? Extra-biblical standards? The evaluation of others? Peter tells us that we are to "long for the pure milk of the *word*." This includes the law of God since it is part of God's word. In fact, a case could be made that the word of God and the law of God are one and the same, for all that proceeds out of the mouth of

God is the law-word of God (Matthew 4:4 quoting the law of Deuteronomy 8:3). Scripture is the very breath of God (2 Timothy 3:16). Whatever God says is law.

For if "everything created by God is good" when "sanctified by the word of God" (1 Timothy 4:5), then we ought to assume that we are sanctified by the word of God, the law included. The Spirit uses the Word of God in the sanctification process. "And the one who keeps His commandments abides in Him, and He in him. And we know by this that He abides in us, by the Spirit whom He has given us" (1 John 3:24). Notice that keeping the commandments and the Holy Spirit are not mutually exclusive. The Holy Spirit in us helps us keep the law of God and instructs us when we either keep or break His commandments. One way to tell if the Holy Spirit is in you is by the way you treat His commandments.

Take away the law of God and sanctification turns into subjectivism. It is no accident that Jesus said that a true disciple will be known by others by something external, since only God knows the heart: "You will know them by their *fruits*" (Matthew 7:20); "For we are His workmanship, created in Christ Jesus for good *works*" (Ephesians 2:10); "so faith, if it has no *works*, is dead" (James 2:17). We are saved by grace through faith, but saving faith always produces good works.

Question 5

AREN'T WE NOW UNDER THE "LAW OF CHRIST" RATHER THAN THE "LAW OF MOSES"?

Paul admonished the Corinthian church to depart from any doctrine that had the effect of dividing Christ (1 Corinthians 1:13). Many well meaning Christians maintain false divisions regarding the law which have the effect of dividing the Triune God. They want to make a radical distinction between the "law of God" and the "law of Christ" as if there are two law systems operating in the Bible. Using this methodology, Jesus of the New Testament is opposed to Jehovah of the Old Testament. Jesus is a God of love, while Jehovah is a God of wrath. Jesus is a God of grace, while Jehovah is a God of law. These are false distinctions.

In a similar way, the "law of Christ" is inappropriately pitted against both the "law of Moses" and the "law of God" as if there are three separate law systems, each in opposition to one another. Here's just one example of the way the "law of Christ" is made a separate body of laws superceding the "law of God."

> Currently, God has made a new covenant with his people – the church – and we live under the "law of Christ" (Galatians 6:2).[1]

What do these authors mean? Are we to assume that the "law of Christ" nullifies the "law of Moses" and the "law of God"? What is the "law of Christ"? The authors tell us that the "law of

---

1. H. Wayne House and Thomas D. Ice, *Dominion Theology: Blessing or Curse?* (Portland, OR: Multnomah Press, 1988), p. 262.

Christ is known by other names in other contexts: the perfect law, the law of liberty (James 1:25), the royal law (James 2:8), and the law of love (Romans 13:8-10)."[2] But can't these designations also be expressions for "God's law" in general? Why are they synonyms for the "law of Christ" but not for God's law, which would include the law of Christ since Jesus is God?

The Bible does not tell us that these are synonyms exclusively reserved for the "law of Christ." The Psalmist informs us that "the law of the LORD is perfect, restoring the soul" (Psalm 19:7). The law of Christ is also described as "perfect" (James 1:25). What law is then perfect: Both the "law of God" and the "law of Christ," because they are one and the same! "The Law of Moses is none other than the Law of Christ."[3] Remember, Moses is the agent of the law, not the author. "The law was given by him, or through him; the giver is God. Hence, before we begin to think poorly of Moses for the troubles he caused in giving Israel the law, we need to back up and remark, 'But the giver of *Torah* is God.' Law is a gift."[4]

House and Ice continue in vain to make a radical distinction between the "law of Christ" and the "law of Moses."

> Paul teaches that the essence of the law is "through love serve one another" ([Galatians] 5:13), and he echoes Christ's teaching when he says, "the whole law is fulfilled in one word, in the statement, 'You shall love your neighbor as yourself' " (5:14).[5]

But wait a minute! From what source does Jesus quote "You shall love your neighbor as yourself"? Let me quote it for you: "You shall not take vengeance, nor bear any grudge against the sons of your people, but *you shall love your neighbor as yourself*; I am the LORD" (Leviticus 19:18). Paul quotes Jesus. Jesus quotes the Mosaic law! The *law*, even the Mosaic law, tells us how "through love" we ought to "serve one another.

---

2. *Ibid.*, p. 179.

3. Ernest Kevan, *The Moral Law* (Jenkintown, PA: Sovereign Grace Publishers, 1963), p. 1.

4. Ronald B. Allen, "In His Law, the Surprise of His Grace," *Moody Monthly* (December 1989), p. 44.

5. House and Ice, *Dominion Theology*, p. 179.

Question No. 6

ISN'T NATURAL LAW RATHER THAN BIBLICAL LAW THE STANDARD OF RIGHTEOUSNESS FOR THE NATIONS?

Norman L. Geisler, an ardent opponent of Christian Reconstruction, wants us to believe that "Government is not based on special revelation, such as the Bible." Instead, he maintains, "it is based on God's general revelation to all men. . . . Thus, civil law, based as it is in the natural moral law, lays no specifically religious obligation on man."[1] According to Geisler, civil governments are obligated to follow only natural law.

What is natural law? As one might expect, there are numerous definitions of natural law depending on which tradition one turns to. Should we follow the natural law system advocated by Cicero, Plato, Sophocles, Aristotle, Aquinas, Montesquieu, Blackstone, Grotius, Pufendorf, or Locke? After taking all of the systems into account, the following definition adequately represents the many natural law theories: "Natural law theory rests on the assumption that man has an innate quality − reason − which enables him to perceive and live by natural laws which are 'self-evident truths' manifested in our natural surroundings."[2]

But there is a problem. While the above definition *might*

---

1. Geisler, "Dispensational Premillennial View of Law and Government," in J. Kerby Anderson, ed., *Living Ethically in the 90s* (Wheaton, IL: Victor Books, 1990), p. 157.

2. Rex Downie, "Natural Law and God's Law: An Antithesis," *The Christian Lawyer* IV, 4 (Winter 1973). Republished in *The Journal of Christian Reconstruction*, V, Symposium on Politics, ed. Gary North (Summer 1978), pp. 81-2.

work in a Christian context, where people generally understand (1) that rebellious man's autonomous reason should not be trusted, and (2) that there are certain absolute values. In non-Christian cultures, *righteous* natural law is an impossibility. The reason? As the late Chief Justice Fred M. Vinson declared, in expressing the implication of a consistent evolutionary theory of law and justice, "Nothing is more certain in modern society than the principle that there are no absolutes. . . ."[3] Natural law depends on an existing theological framework that takes into account God's sovereignty and ethical absolutes.

In addition there are several other problems with a natural law ethical position. First, how does one determine what laws found in general revelation are natural laws that conform to God's will? Is it possible that Christian natural law advocates are using the Bible as a grid in the construction of their natural law ethic? But what grid is being used by non-Christians? In a consistently evolutionary system, there can be no natural law, only evolving law determined by those presently in power, usually the State.

Second, how do we get people to agree on the content of "natural law" and how these laws should apply? Do we opt for a lowest common denominator type of law like "Do good to all men"? Should we agree that murder is wrong but not war and capital punishment since each of these would violate the general law of "do good to all men"? Does natural law, for example, tell us that abortion is wrong?

Third, what if we find a common set of laws in "nature" that contradict the Bible? As we will see below, polygamy can be supported as a natural law ethic, as can slavery, since most nations from time immemorial have practiced both. Would we, if we followed natural law, give up monogamy for polygamy?

---

3. *Dennis* v. *United States*, 341 U.S. 494 (1951) at 508 in Eugene C. Gerhart, *American Liberty and "Natural Law"* (Boston, MA: The Beacon Press, 1953), p. 17. *Time* magazine commented (July 23, 1951, pp. 67-68): "Whatever the explanation, Kentuckian Vinson's aside on morals drew no dissent from his brethren on the supreme bench. And no wonder. The doctrine he pronounced stems straight from the late Oliver Wendell Holmes, philosophical father of the present Supreme Court." Quoted in *ibid.*, p. 165, note 2.

Would we give up freedom for slavery?

Fourth, what if a "natural law" agrees specifically with a biblical law that is religious? For example, nearly all nations have some prohibition against worshipping other gods (e.g., Daniel 3:1-30). After Nebuchadnezzar realized the error of his ways in requiring the Israelites to bow down to a false god, he then made a law that prohibited anyone from speaking "anything offensive against the God of Shadrach, Meshach and Abednego" (v. 29). The penalty was pretty stiff: They "shall be torn limb from limb and their houses reduced to a rubbish heap" (v. 29). If Nebuchadnezzar turned to the Bible for the construction of this law, then his example would be proof that biblical law was applied to a non-Israelite nation. Since, as Geisler maintains, "civil law, based as it is in the natural moral law, lays no specifically religious obligation on man,"[4] Nebuchadnezzar must have been acting out the dictates of a natural law ethic. Therefore, magistrates, based on biblical law or natural law, could punish people for overtly religious crimes against Jehovah. But this is the one thing that natural law advocates do not want.

Fifth, natural law "does not furnish a specific consensus of ethical judgment."[5] Ultimately, it comes down to "what the individual conscience dictates; and consciences differ."[6] In order for natural law to function in any rational and workable way, there must be a generally held common belief system. When Catholic scholars, the foremost advocates of natural-law theory, made the State subject to natural law, there existed, in the words of Woodrow Wilson, a "common devotion to right."[7] But what is the source of that "common devotion to right"? What if that "common devotion to right" is no longer accepted by rulers and the courts?

Sixth, and finally, let us suppose that we can derive a body of

---

4. Geisler, "A Premillennial View of Law and Government," p. 157.

5. William Aylott Orton, *The Liberal Tradition* (New Haven, CT: Yale University Press, 1945), p. 95. Quoted in Gary North, *Political Polytheism: The Myth of Pluralism* (Tyler, TX: Institute for Christian Economics, 1989), p. 126.

6. *Idem.*

7. Quoted in Orton, *idem.*

law from nature. This would only tell us what the law *is*, or actually, what *might be*. Can we determine what we *ought to do* from what is or might be right?

Why have some Christians opposed biblical law in favor of "natural law"? Norman Geisler writes: "In brief, because not everyone accepts the Bible, but no one can avoid natural law, which is 'written on [the] hearts' of all men (Rom. 2:14-15). Only believers accept the Bible. But business must be done with unbelievers. Therefore, it is necessary for us to have some common ethical ground on which to engage in commercial transactions with them."[8] There are numerous unproven assumptions here, but the two most glaring ones are (1) "not everyone accepts the Bible" and (2) "but *no one* can avoid natural law." Does everyone have to accept a standard before it is legitimate or it can be enacted into law? What if the majority of the people do accept the Bible? Would this mean that a nation could then implement biblical laws over natural laws? Aren't Christians told to "disciple the nations," to teach the nations all that Jesus commanded? Instead of avoiding the Bible, why not make it a point of discussion, showing unbelievers that the Bible has answers to all of life's problems. We could just as easily assert that not everyone accepts natural law (which is true). Does this then nullify Geisler's natural law ethic?

Let us put Geisler's second assertion to the test. He would maintain that prohibitions against murder are natural laws. If "no one can avoid natural law," then why do people still murder? And when there was a prevailing *biblical* ethic in this nation, we had fewer murders, rapes, thefts, drug related crimes, illegitimate births, abortions, etc. People murder because they want to murder regardless what *any* law states, including biblical law and most certainly natural law. But because biblical law has sanctions attached to it — both temporal and eternal — there are more reasons not to murder under a system of biblical law than under natural law.

---

8. Norman L. Geisler, "Natural Law and Business Ethics," *Biblical Principles and Business: The Foundations*, ed. Richard C. Chewning (Colorado, CO: NavPress, 1989), p. 157.

If the natural law is a law in the legal sense, what are its sanctions? . . . [S]ince a law without punishment is vain, there must be another world to inflict it. Scholastics . . . appear to depend on the Christian commonwealth, whose civil law is bound to reflect the natural law, to punish overt breaches. This was not unrealistic as a theory among Christian states in the days when rulers and inhabitants alike were at least technically Christian, but difficulties occurred when it came to expecting pagan kings to punish breaches of the natural law. This problem confronted the sixteenth-century Spanish Thomists, who were most unwilling to grant Christian kings rights of intervention in pagan kingdoms to punish "crimes against nature", and found themselves reduced to hoping for native kings to act in their stead in suppressing long-standing customs like human sacrifice.[9]

So then, it was expected that a Christian commonwealth would be necessary before such a natural law ethic could actually be implemented. No such trust could be expected of pagan kings since human sacrifice might still be considered normative by them.

We have had in our nation a prominently displayed biblical ethic that gave guidance to all citizens, Christians and non-Christians alike. America was a beacon to the world because it had an operating biblical ethic: In theory, everyone was treated as equal before the law, and that law was essentially biblical. In fact, there has been a concerted effort to move our nation away from an explicitly biblical ethical system. Regularly biblical laws are overturned and replaced with atheistic laws. This is true with sodomy and abortion. Take abortion. The Supreme Court in *Roe* v. *Wade* rejected Christian teaching regarding abortion, and turned instead to "ancient attitudes." These "ancient traditions" were accepted over the "emerging teachings of Christianity," teachings that were thought to have influenced the adoption of the Hippocratic Oath. The Court surmised that the anti-abortion Hippocratic Oath would never have been adopted by the medical community if Christianity had not dominated the culture. Since "ancient religion did not bar abortion," as the

---

9. Bernice Hamilton, "Some Arguments Against Natural Law Theories," *Light on the Natural Law*, ed. Illtud Evans (Baltimore, MD: Helicon Press, 1965), pp. 44-45.

majority opinion in *Roe* determined, therefore, abortion would have to be legalized. And what were these "ancient traditions"?: Greek and Roman legal traditions that rested on *natural law*.[10]

Would our nation have Sunday as a day of rest and worship if we adopted natural law over biblical law? Even the Constitution follows biblical and not natural law in its regard for Sunday as a special *religious* day: "If any Bill shall not be returned by the President within ten Days (Sundays excepted) after it shall have been presented to him, the Same shall be a Law. . . ." (Article I, section 7). Would a natural law ethic permit religious oath-taking? No! Florida no longer requires Notaries to affirm "so help me God" on their written oath of office. The Rev. Gerard LaCerra, chancellor of the Archdiocese of Miami understands the implications of such an action: "What are we supposed to base our commitments on if something like this is removed? The State?"[11] This is where natural law leads us.

Some assert, using natural law as their operating principle, that the "celebration of Eros and the unlimited pleasure of the body should be elevated to constitutional principle."[12] Are any and all sexual practices legitimate under natural law? As nations become officially atheistic, a natural law ethic free from biblical influence becomes impossible to formulate, since natural law requires the existence of a Creator who has a law to deposit in the universe and in the heart of man. How can a natural law ethic be formulated when different traditions come to the formulating table with contrary presuppositions? Some are Christian, religious, agnostic, and atheistic. Those who believe in God at least have *some* common ground, although what god we have

---

10. Curt Young, *The Least of These: What Everyone Should Know about Abortion* (Chicago, IL: Moody Press, 1983), pp. 21-23.

11. " 'God' Removed from Notaries' Oath," *The Kansas City Star* (February 18, 1990), p. 2A. "The general situation in this country is that in all court proceedings witnesses may give testimony only after they have qualified themselves by taking an oath in the usual form ending with 'So help me God,' or by making an affirmation without that phrase. The provisions for witnesses generally apply also to jurors." Anson Phelps Stokes and Leo Pfeffer, *Church and State in the United States*, rev. one-vol. ed. (New York: Harper & Row, 1964), p. 490.

12. Robert H. Bork, *The Tempting of America: The Political Seduction of the Law* (Nw York: The Free Press, 1990), p. 210.

in common is another question altogether. When the agnostic and atheist come, the difficulties multiply in trying to prove a natural law theory, especially in the area of particulars.

> The reason for this difficulty seems to be that for those who really believe in creation and the supreme dominion of God, the principle is too obvious to need proof; whereas for those who do not believe in creation there is no basis on which to build proof.[13]

A natural law basis for moral behavior can be developed only when there is an already-operating biblical ethic. William Blackstone, the great English Jurist of the eighteenth century, wrote that natural law must be interpreted in terms of the revealed law, the Bible. "If we could be as certain of the latter [natural law] as we are of the former [revealed law], both would have an equal authority; but, till then, they can never be put in any competition together."[14] The Bible shaped Blackstone's conception of natural law, although he rarely referred to the Bible in his commentaries.[15] But this in itself might be indicative of how pervasively a biblical ethic influenced him.

Could there ever be a prohibition, for example, against polygamy based on natural law? While the Bible tolerated polygamy and established laws to govern it to protect the family unit, it never condoned it (Genesis 2:18-24; Leviticus 18:18; 1 Corinthians 7:2; 1 Timothy 3:2). Many in Israel, including such rulers as Gideon, David, and Solomon, adopted the polygamous practices of the surrounding nations. Of course, polygamy began soon after the fall (Genesis 4:19, 23; 26:34; 28:9; 29:15; 36:2; 1 Samuel 1:1-2). "Polygamy has always been odious among the northern and western nations of Europe, and, until the establishment of the Mormon Church, was almost exclusively a feature of the life of Asiatic and of African people. In common law, the second marriage was always void (2 Kent, Com.

---

13. Gerard Kelly, *Medico-Moral Problems* (Dublin: Clonmore and Reynolds, 1955), p. 167. Cited in Daniel Callahan, *Abortion: Law, Choice and Morality* (New York: Macmillan, 1970), pp. 310-11.

14. William Blackstone, *Commentaries on the Laws of England*, 4 vols. (Chicago, IL: University of Chicago Press [1765] 1979), vol. 1, p. 17.

15. North, *Political Polytheism*, pp. 322-24.

79), and from the earliest history of England polygamy has been treated as an offence against society."[16] Polygamy was denounced in Christian nations and practiced in non-Christian nations. Typically, "Asiatic" and "African" nations were non-Christian. Their practice of polygamy was "natural." With the advent of Christianity, monogamy was the practice and the Bible was the standard, not natural law.

The Supreme Court narrowly defined the legal protections of the First Amendment to exclude polygamy on the grounds that the practice was out of accord with the basic tenets of Christianity: "It is contrary to the spirit of Christianity and the civilization which Christianity has produced in the Western world."[17] A year earlier the Court declared that "Bigamy and polygamy are crimes by the laws of all civilized and Christian countries. . . . To call their advocacy a tenet of religion is to offend the common sense of mankind."[18]

So with the above in mind, what common ground do Christians and non-Christians have regarding the law? The evolutionist knows nothing of natural law. His system will not allow it. Law is an evolving principle like the universe itself. Roscoe Pound, a former Harvard law school dean, wrote "that 'nature' did not mean to antiquity what it means to us who are under the influence of evolution."[19] In "antiquity," nature was thought to have been created by God and thus ran according to certain "natural laws" (even though that god was a pagan deity). What many Christians regard as "natural laws" are in reality God's eternal decree.

The introduction of the concept of "Nature" and natural law, derived from Hellenic philosophy, led to a departure from biblical faith. Natural law spoke of a self-contained system of its own inher-

16. *Reynolds* v. *United States*, October 1878.
17. *Late Corporation of the Church of Jesus Christ of Latter Day Saints v. United States*, 136 U.S. 1 (1890).
18. *Davis v. Beason*, 133 U.S. 333, 341-342 (1890). Cited in John Eidsmoe, *The Christian Legal Advisor* (Milford, MI: Mott Media, 1984), p. 150.
19. Roscoe Pound, *Introduction to the Philosophy of Law* (New Haven, CT: Yale University Press, [1922] 1959), p. 31. Cited in John W. Whitehead, *The Second American Revolution* (Westchester, IL: Crossway Books, [1982] 1985, p. 48.

ent law. One of the products was Deism, which reduced God to the mechanic who had created "Nature," and now "Nature" functioned independently of God. The next step was to accept the ultimacy of "Nature" and to drop God entirely.[20]

There was predictability in the created order because God decreed all that comes to pass. The created order, what is erroneously described as "nature,"[21] was understood to be affected by the fall of man into sin. Special revelation was needed to correct the distortions of a creation disfigured by sin. With the advent of evolution, a new understanding of nature developed that supplanted the one of "antiquity." According to Roscoe Pound, "no current hypothesis is reliable, as ideas and legal philosophies change radically and frequently from time to time."[22]

In addition to natural law, Geisler writes that "most premillenarians recognize that God has not left Himself without a witness in that He has revealed a moral law in the hearts and consciences of all men (Rom. 2:14-15)."[23] Geisler asserts that the heart and conscience are repositories for an ethical code. But the heart of man "is more deceitful than all else and is desperately sick; who can understand it?" (Jeremiah 17:9; cf. Genesis 6:5; 8:21; Psalm 14:1; Proverbs 6:14; 12:20; 14:12). General revelation may give a very clear ethical system, but man suppresses "the truth" of general revelation "in unrighteousness" (Romans 1:18).

Since man's reason is imperfect, and may be swayed by his physical and social environment, the "truths" which men "know" have been various and self-contradictory. The law of nature has been quoted for every cause, from that of Negro slavery in the United States to that of red revolution in Paris. And it has often

---

20. Rousas J. Rushdoony, *The Mythology of Science* (Nutley, NJ: The Craig Press, 1967), p. 97.

21. Rousas J. Rushdoony writes that " 'Nature' is simply a collective name for an uncollectivized reality; the myth of nature is a product of Hellenic philosophy." *The Institutes of Biblical Law* (Phillipsburg, NJ: Presbyterian and Reformed, 1973), p. 608.

22. Rene A. Wormser, *The Story of the Law* (New York: Simon & Schuster, 1962), p. 485. Cited in Whitehead, *The Second American Revolution*, 48.

23. Geisler, "A Dispensational Premillennial View of Law and Government," p. 156.

shifted ground – or man's interpretation has shifted – on such thorny questions (for example) as private property.[24]

But isn't "the work of the Law written" on the heart actually *the law*? (Romans 2:15). "For when Gentiles who do not have the Law do instinctively the things of the Law, these, not having the Law, are a law to themselves, in that they show the work of the Law written in their hearts, their conscience bearing witness, and their thoughts alternately accusing or else defending them, on the day when, according to my gospel, God will judge the secrets of men through Christ Jesus" (Romans 2:14-16). The Gentiles, those without the written law found in the Bible, follow a law written on their hearts. It is the same law!

Second, general revelation contrary to Geisler, does lay a *specifically religious obligation on man*. According to Romans 1:18-32, which is the fullest biblical commentary on general revelation, men are guilty precisely because they "exchanged the glory of the incorruptible God for an image in the form of corruptible man and of birds and four-footed animals and crawling creatures" (v. 23). Where did they learn about "the incorruptible God"? "God made it evident to them. For since the creation of the world His invisible attributes, His eternal power and divine nature, have been clearly seen, being understood through what has been made, *so that they are without excuse*" (vv. 19-20).

Third, general or natural revelation and special revelation (Scripture) have the same moral content. But because of man's sinfulness and the deceitfulness of his heart, he needs an infallible guide to read natural revelation. The Bible is that infallible guide. The only safeguard that sinful man has in not misinterpreting and misapplying natural revelation "is to test his interpretations constantly by the principles of the written word."[25]

Paul says nothing to suggest that there is a difference in the

---

24. Herbert Agar, *A Declaration of Faith* (Boston, MA: Houghton Mifflin Company, 1952), p. 134.

25. Cornelius Van Til, "Nature and Scripture," in *The Infallible Word: A Symposium*, eds. Ned B. Stonehouse and Paul Wolley (Grand Rapids, MI: Eerdmans, 1953), p. 274.

moral content of these two revelations, written and natural. The written law is an advantage over natural revelation because the latter is suppressed and distorted in unrighteousness (Romans 1:18-25). But what pagans suppress is precisely the "work of *the law*" (2:14-15). Natural revelation communicates to them, as Paul says, "the *ordinance* of God" about "*all* unrighteousness" (1:29, 32). Because they "know" God's ordinance, they are "without excuse" for refusing to live in terms of it (1:20). What the law speaks, then, it speaks "in order that *all the world* may be brought under the judgment of God" (3:19). There is *one* law order to which all men are bound, whether they *learn* of it by means of natural revelation or by means of special revelation. God is no respecter of persons here (2:11). "*All* have sinned" (3:23) — thus violated that *common* standard for the "*knowledge of sin*" in all men, the law of God (3:20).[26]

Reconstructionists take God's revelation seriously: the law of God found in both Testaments *and* general revelation.

Did God, as Geisler maintains, place only the Israelites under obligation to the moral demands of those commandments specifically delivered to the nation through Moses? Are Gentile nations ever condemned for violating laws specifically given to Israel? If we can find just *one* law that fits into this category, then all nations are obligated to submit to God's special written revelation, the Bible. I will summarize the argument for you:

God gives a series of instructions to Moses for the people: "You shall not do what is done in the land of Egypt where you lived, nor are you to do what is done in the land of Canaan where I am bringing you; you shall not walk in their statutes. You are to perform my judgments and keep My statutes, to live in accord with them" (Leviticus 18:3-4). God then issues a list of Canaanite practices that were prohibited. He commands the Israelites not to engage in incest, polygamy, adultery, child sacrifice, profaning Jehovah's name, homosexuality, or bestiality (vv. 6-23). The Mosaic law outlawed all such behavior and severely punished it. Immediately following the long list of prohibitions, God's word describes what disobedience will bring: "Do not defile yourselves by any of these things; for by all these the nations which I am casting out before you have become defiled. For the land has become defiled, therefore I have visited its

---

26. Greg L. Bahnsen, "What Kind of Morality Should We Legislate?," *The Biblical Worldview* (October 1988), p. 9.

punishment upon it, so the land has spewed out its inhabitants. But as for you, you are to keep My statutes and My judgments, and shall not do any of these abominations, neither the native, nor the alien who sojourns among you; (for the men of the land who have been before you have done all these abominations, and the land has become defiled); so that the land may not spew you out, should you defile it, as it has spewed out the nation which has been before you" (Leviticus 18:24-28).

The transgression of the very law which God was revealing to Israel was *the same law* which brought divine punishment upon the Gentiles who occupied the land before them. "Israel and the Gentiles were under the same moral law, and they both would suffer the *same penalty* for the defilement which comes with violating it — eviction from the land."[27]

---

27. Greg L. Bahnsen, "For Whom Was God's Law Intended?," *The Biblical Worldview* (December 1988), p. 9.

Question No. 7

DO CHRISTIAN RECONSTRUCTIONISTS
REJECT DEMOCRACY?

Most Americans are under the impression that our nation is a democracy. To be sure, there are certainly democratic elements in our constitutional system. The First Amendment to the Constitution states that "the people" have the right "to petition the Government for a redress of grievances." The petition of the people, however, is only as good as the character of the people. Keeping in mind the biblical doctrine of the depravity of man, our constitutional framers steered clear of a pure democracy. Constitutional attorney John W. Whitehead writes:

> It must be remembered that the term *democratic* appears neither in the Declaration of Independence nor in the Constitution. Actually, when the Constitution is analyzed in its original form, the document is found to be a serious attempt to establish a government mixed with democratic, aristocratic, and monarchical elements – a government of checks and balances.[1]

A democracy places all power in the people. It is a government of the masses. Democratic law is based on the will of the majority. If the whims and fancies of the people change, the law changes.

John Winthrop declared democracy to be "the meanest and worst of all forms of government."[2] John Cotton wrote in 1636:

---

1. John Whitehead, *The Separation Illusion* (Milford, MI: Mott Media, 1977), p. 47.
2. Quoted in A. Marvyn Davies, *Foundation of American Freedom: Calvinism in the Development of Democratic Thought and Action* (Nashville, TN: Abingdon Press, 1955), p. 11.

"Democracy, I do not conceive that ever God did ordain as a fit government either for church or commonwealth. If the people be governors, who shall be governed?"[3] In the *Federalist Papers* (No. 10), Madison writes that democracies are "spectacles of turbulence and contention." Pure democracies are "incompatible with personal security or the rights of property. . . . In general [they] have been as short in their lives as they have been violent in their deaths."[4] Francis Schaeffer described law by majority opinion, certainly a definition of democracy, as "the dictatorship of the 51%, with no controls and nothing with which to challenge the majority."[5] Schaeffer deduces a simple implication of this definition of democracy: "It means that if Hitler was able to get a 51% vote of the Germans, he had a right to kill the Jews."[6]

Democracies degenerate into exploitation because some voters discover that they can vote themselves political and financial favors out of the public treasury. Those seeking power through majority rule always vote for the candidate promising the most benefits. The results are certain: democracies collapse because the public treasury is milked dry, due to greater voter demand. A dictatorship normally follows.

Actually, our constitutional government is a "republic," a system in which the law, not the majority, is supreme. Democracies can degenerate into what Francis Schaeffer called the "tyranny of the 51%." If whatever the majority wants becomes law, then a government will become oppressive of its minorities. If the will of the majority is the law, then an old majority can be overturned by a new majority. Hitler, it should be recalled, was elected to public office. Reconstructionists, on the contrary, press for the enforcement of God's law, which requires just

---

3. Letter to Lord Say and Seal, *The Puritans: A Sourcebook of Their Writings*, 2 vols., eds. Perry Miller and Thomas H. Johnson (New York: Harper and Row, [1938] 1963), Vol. 1, pp. 209-10.

4. Alexander Hamilton, James Madison, and John Jay, *The Federalist*, ed. Jacob E. Cooke (Middletown, CT: Wesleyan University Press, 1961), p. 61.

5. Francis A. Schaeffer, *The Church at the End of the Twentieth Century* (Downers Grove, IL: InterVarsity Press, 1970), pp. 33f.

6. *Idem.*

treatment of both the citizen and the "stranger," the majority and the minority, because God has given *one* law for the people (e.g., Exodus 22:21; 23:9).

Finally, as Gary North has recently pointed out, *"Christian reconstruction depends on majority rule."*[7] God uses lawful historical means to extend His earthly kingdom. Reconstructionists thus affirm that God's laws should be passed and enforced according to the rules of the democratic process. Reconstructionists do not preach revolution or a top-down bureaucratic take-over. But Reconstructionists also do not believe that the will of the political majority is the final law in society. If this were the final law, then the will of the political majority would be the will of God. The democratic majority would then be God. What Christian could believe such a doctrine?

---

7. Gary North, *Political Polytheism: The Myth of Pluralism* (Tyler, Texas: Institute for Christian Economics, 1989), p. 586.

Question 8

DO CHRISTIAN RECONSTRUCTIONISTS BELIEVE IN "SALVATION BY POLITICS"?

One of the most persistent myths about Christian Reconstruction is that it advocates "salvation by legislation." This was the charge levelled against Christian Reconstruction by Prison Fellowship founder Charles Colson on the Bill Moyers special about Christian Reconstruction. Colson insisted that Christian Reconstruction is

> part of the political illusion of our day, the idea that there's a political solution to every problem, and we can't solve things quickly enough, so let's get to Washington and let's get a law passed, and see if we can't get revival through Congress. Well, that's just not the way God works.[1]

With all due respect for Mr. Colson's ministry and achievements, it needs to be said that that's not the way Reconstructionists work either.[2] In fact, anyone watching Moyers' program attentively would have been more than a little puzzled by Colson's criticism. Rousas J. Rushdoony, introduced by Moyers as the "godfather" of Christian Reconstruction, said again and again that he does not believe in salvation through political action. "The Constitution will not save this country," he said.

---

1. Bill Moyers, "God and Politics: On Earth As It Is In Heaven" (December 23, 1987), page 11 of transcript.

2. After the Moyers program, my former associate at American Vision, Peter Leithart, wrote to Colson, asking him to point out the passages in Reconstructionist literature that led Colson to his conclusion. Colson has never provided those references.

"The State is a bankrupt institution," he added. He admitted that Christian Reconstruction will not work unless "you have the vast majority of the people believing that this is the way things should be." (Democracy?) He told Moyers that he did not want America to be declared officially Christian, since "nothing official means anything unless it is personal with the people."[3]

Rushdoony didn't just stumble on this theme, either. For years, he has been warning about an overestimation of the power of politics. Rushdoony was warning about "messianic politics" and the "messianic state" before Colson ever became a Christian. In *The Politics of Guilt and Pity*, first published in 1970, Rushdoony described the implications of the anti-Christian idea that man is "over law." One of the consequences is that

> Man finds salvation through political programs, through legislation, so that *salvation is an enactment of the state.* . . . As a saving order, the state concerns itself with cradle-to-grave security, because, as the expression of man's divinity, it must play the role of god in man's life. It becomes man's savior.[4]

More recently, Rushdoony has noted that the "ancient, classical view of man . . . is a fertile ground for a radical statism and a radical anarchism." Because this view exalts man to the place of God, "[i]n its totalitarian form, it offers us a savior state as man's hope."[5] Notice that Rushdoony is arguing that a "messianic" view of politics is essentially anti-Christian and humanistic.

Gary North has emphasized the same point. In his book, *Political Polytheism*, North wrote:

> Every revolution needs slogans. Here is mine: *politics fourth*. First comes personal faith in Jesus Christ as Lord and Savior (not just Savior). Second comes Church renewal. There can be no successful

3. "God and Politics: On Earth As It Is In Heaven," page 4 of transcript.

4. Rousas J. Rushdoony, *Politics of Guilt and Pity* (Fairfax, VA: Thoburn Press, [1970] 1978), p. 145.

5. Rousas John Rushdoony, *Christianity and the State* (Vallecito, CA: Ross House Books, 1986), p. 17.

reformation of society without first beginning a reformation of the Church. Third comes family renewal. This involves pulling your children out of the public schools. Fourth comes local politics. At a minimum, this would involve public protests against abortion. From there we go to state and national politics.

Before any national political renewal can begin, we must first do what we can to make it clear to the politicians and the national government that a major religious transformation has taken place. Without the widespread movement of the Holy Spirit, this cannot happen.[6]

At the same time that leading Christian Reconstructionists caution against overestimation of politics, they also insist that political action is a legitimate life's calling for Christians. Scripture declares these truths clearly. Paul calls the civil magistrate a "servant" or "minister" of God (Romans 13:1-7). In the Old Testament, civil judges are called "gods" (*elohim*: judges, not Jehovah) because they stand in God's place (Psalm 82:1-4; cf. Exodus 21:6; 22:8, 28). Political leadership is, therefore, not only a legitimate calling, but a high calling.[7]

Christian Reconstructionists further insist that Jesus Christ is Lord of political leaders. Psalm 2 speaks of the exaltation of God's Son as King on Zion, and then applies this truth specifically to political leaders, judges, and kings (Psalm 2:7-12). Jesus Christ has been exalted above all rule and authority and power and dominion (Ephesians 1:20-23), and all authority in heaven and earth are His (Matthew 28:18-20). He is the King of kings and Lord of lords (1 Timothy 6:15). All political leaders are directly responsible to Jesus Christ in the discharge of their public office, as well as in their private lives.

Practically, this means that political leaders should seek the guidance of Scripture in framing their political positions and programs. Deuteronomy 17, which describes the duties of the future kings of Israel, emphasizes this point:

---

6. Gary North, *Political Polytheism: The Myth of Pluralism* (Tyler, Texas: Institute for Christian Economics, 1989), p. 559.

7. For a detailed analysis of Psalm 82:6 and related verses, see Gary DeMar and Peter Leithart, *The Reduction of Christianity: A Biblical Response to Dave Hunt* (Ft. Worth, TX: Dominion Press, 1987), pp. 76-83.

> Now it shall come about when he sits on the throne of his king-
> dom, he shall write for himself a copy of this law on a scroll in the
> presence of the Levitical priests. And it shall be with him, and he
> shall read it all the days of his life, that he may learn to fear the
> Lord his God, by carefully observing all the words of this law and
> these statutes, that his heart may not be lifted up above his country-
> men and that he may not turn aside from the commandment, to the
> right or the left; in order that he and his sons may continue long in
> his kingdom in the midst of Israel (vv. 18-20; cf. Joshua 1:8-9).

Note the reasons why God wants the king to have a copy of
the law. First, he is reminded that he is obligated to observe the
same law that his people observe. As a result, he does not become proud, arrogant, and oppressive, as if he were above the
law. Second, regular meditation on the Word of God prevents
the political leader from turning aside from God's commandments. Finally, the Lord promises a long and prosperous reign
to the faithful king. Though these words applied most directly
to the kings of Israel, they also apply to political rulers in all
ages, since the Word of God remains "useful for . . . every good
work" (2 Timothy 3:16-17).

Christian Reconstructionists think civil power should be
expanded to bring *negative sanctions against public immorality*,
beginning with a ban on all abortions. This infuriates the liberal
critics, who want few restraints on personal morality and great
restraints on personal wealth. They want the state to become an
agent bringing positive sanctions in history, which must be paid
for by taxation: *negative sanctions against productive people*. The
Reconstructionists have called for a massive reduction in the
power and activity of the state, including a massive reduction in
taxation. This infuriates the liberal critics, who see clearly that
this would de-fund their pet projects and drastically reduce
their power. Christian Reconstructionists believe that health
care, education, welfare, social security, and many other social
needs should be met by the church and family, not by the state.
It would be highly contradictory for Reconstructionists to want
salvation through politics while at the same time calling for a
"minimal state." No published critic of Christian Reconstruction
has even noticed this contradiction in the false accusation.

Question No. 9

ISN'T POSTMILLENNIALISM REALLY LIBERALISM?

In order to answer this question, we have to define the two terms: "postmillennialism" and "liberalism." First, what is postmillennialism? Postmillennialism is the belief that, before Christ returns, by the power of the Spirit, the kingdom of Jesus Christ will grow to enjoy a period of prosperity and growth throughout the world through the Church's faithfulness in fulfilling the Great Commission. In general, the nations of the world will be converted (cf. Genesis 12:3; Psalm 22:25-31; Isaiah 11:9; etc.). Reconstructionists go a step further to say that the converted nations will seek to order their common social and political life according to the Word of God in Scripture (cf. Isaiah 2:2-4; 65:17-25; etc.).

To put it more simply, postmillennialism is the affirmation that Christ "must reign *until He has put all His enemies under His feet*" (1 Corinthians 15:25). While men will always be sinners until Jesus returns, the Spirit will progressively turn the hearts of men away from unbelief and sin to righteousness and faith. Postmillennialism does not teach that a sinless utopia will be established before Christ returns, but simply insists that where sin abounded, grace much more abounded (Romans 5:20).

Second, what is "liberalism"? At the heart of theological liberalism are several important departures from orthodox Christianity. Liberalism denies that the Scriptures are true and accurate in every particular. The liberal may view the Scriptures with admiration, and even say such things as "the Scriptures are the source of all authority," but the liberal does not believe that the Scriptures are inerrant. Thus, liberals have historically attempted to explain (away) those portions of Scripture that they find troubling, and especially the miracles of Jesus. One liberal scholar "explained" Jesus' raising of Lazarus by saying that Lazarus was not dead, but buried prematurely. Jesus knew this, though no one else did. So, Jesus did not raise Lazarus; He just woke him up. (This is why liberalism is asleep!)

Liberalism not only tends to explain all the miracles of Scripture in a naturalistic and rationalistic manner, but also explains the growth of the kingdom in the same way. In liberal theology, the growth of the kingdom is not seen as the product of the Holy Spirit's supernatural renewal of men and women. Instead, the kingdom in liberal theology is seen as an ethical community that grows in history as the result of inherent evolutionary forces, and the inherent dignity and goodness of man. Thus, liberal optimism about the kingdom of God is opposite from the orthodox postmillennial position. The postmillennialist does not put his hope in man's inherent goodness, but in the power of the Spirit to transform sinners into saints.

Even the briefest glance at the historical background of postmillennialism shows that it is not at all identical with liberalism. Augustine (354-430), bishop of Hippo, was without question the most influential of the early fathers and was arguably the most influential thinker and writer in West European intellectual history. Augustine's eschatology is complex, but the note of optimism and progress is not absent. It appears that Augustine believed that progress in the knowledge of God would eventually lead to an earthly golden age. Conservative historian Robert Nisbet concludes that "there are grounds for belief that Augustine foresaw a progressive, fulfilling, and blissful period ahead, *on earth*, for humanity – prior to entry of the blessed into heaven."[1]

The Reformer John Calvin (1509-1564) likewise emphasized the victorious character of the kingdom of God. Commenting on 2 Thessalonians 2:8, Calvin writes,

---

1. Robert Nisbet, *History of the Idea of Progress* (New York: Basic Books, 1980), p. 67.

Paul, however, intimates that Christ will in the meantime, by the rays which he will emit *previously to his advent*, put to flight the darkness in which antichrist will reign, just as the sun, before he is seen by us, chases away the darkness of the night by the pouring forth of his rays.

This victory of the word, therefore, will show itself in this world. . . . He also furnished Christ with these very arms, that he may *rout his enemies*. This is a signal commendation of true and sound doctrine – that it is represented as sufficient for putting an end to all impiety, and as destined to be *invariably victorious, in opposition to all the machinations of Satan*.[2]

Calvin thus believed that the kingdom was already present, and that it was triumphantly advancing to a great climax.

This victorious outlook was embodied in the 1648 Westminster Larger Catechism. The answer to question 191 states:

In the second petition, (which is, *Thy kingdom come,*) acknowledging ourselves and all mankind to be by nature under the dominion of sin and Satan, we pray, that the kingdom of sin and Satan may be destroyed, the gospel propagated throughout the world, the Jews called, the fullness of the Gentiles brought in; the church furnished with all gospel-officers and ordinances, purged from corruption, countenanced and maintained by the civil magistrate: that the ordinances of Christ may be purely dispensed, and made effectual to the converting of those that are yet in their sins, and the confirming, comforting, and building up of those that are already converted: that Christ would rule in our hearts here, and hasten the time of his second coming, and our reigning with him for ever: and that he would be pleased so to exercise the kingdom of his power in all the world, as may best conduce to these ends.

Jonathan Edwards (1703-1758) expected an even fuller outpouring of the Spirit in the future, so that "the gospel shall be preached to every tongue, and kindred, and nation, and people, before the fall of Antichrist; so we may suppose, that it will be gloriously successful to bring in multitudes from every nation:

2. Quoted in Greg Bahnsen, "The *Prima Facie* Acceptability of Postmillennialism," *Journal of Christian Reconstruction* III, ed. Gary North (Winter 1976-1977), p. 70. Emphasis was added by Dr. Bahnsen.

and shall spread more and more with wonderful swiftness."[3] This great outpouring of the Spirit will be met with vicious opposition. Though Edwards admitted that "we know not particularly in what manner this opposition shall be made," one thing was certain: "Christ and his church shall in this battle obtain a complete and *entire victory* over their enemies."[4]

As a result, Satan's kingdom will be fully overthrown. In its place, Christ's kingdom will be "set up on the ruins of it, every where throughout the whole habitable globe."[5] These events will usher in a new era for the church. The church will no longer be under affliction, but will enjoy undiluted success. Edwards believed that "this is most properly the time of the kingdom of *heaven upon earth*." The Old Testament prophecies of the kingdom will be fulfilled in this era. It will be a time of great Spiritual knowledge, holiness, peace, love, and orderliness in the church. All of this would be followed by the great apostasy and the second coming of Christ.[6]

This view of the kingdom was adopted by many of the leading nineteenth-century theologians in the United States, especially those in Calvinistic seminaries. Princeton's Charles Hodge (1797-1878) wrote that "before the second coming of Christ there is to be a time of great and long continued prosperity." Hodge referred to one theory that claimed that this period would last 365,000 years, but he remained cautious: "During this period, be it longer or shorter, the Church is to enjoy a season of peace, purity, and blessedness as it has never yet experienced." Hodge claimed that "the prophets predict a glorious state of the Church prior to the second advent" because "they represent the Church as being thus prosperous and glorious on earth."[7]

The great Southern theologian Robert L. Dabney (1820-

---

3. Edwards, "History of Redemption," in *The Works of Jonathan Edwards*, 2 vols. (Edinburgh: Banner of Truth Trust, [1834] 1974), vol. 1, p. 606.

4. *Idem.*

5. *Ibid.*, pp. 607-8.

6. *Ibid.*, pp. 609-11.

7. Charles Hodge, *Systematic Theology*, 3 vols. (Grand Rapids, MI: Eerdmans, 1986 [1871-1873]), vol. 3, pp. 858-59.

1898) concurred with Hodge's views. Before the second coming, Dabney taught, the church would preach the gospel to all nations and would see "the general triumph of Christianity over all false religions, in all nations."[8] Benjamin Breckinridge Warfield (1851-1921), the great conservative theologian of Princeton, echoed the same themes of victory. Commenting on Revelation 19, he wrote,

> The section opens with a vision of the victory of the Word of God, the King of Kings and Lord of Lords over all His enemies. We see Him come forth from heaven girt for war, followed by the armies of heaven. . . What we have here, in effect, is a picture of the whole period between the first and second advents, seen from the point of view of heaven. It is the period of advancing victory of the Son of God over the world.[9]

Postmillennialist eschatology is certainly not the same as theological liberalism. Identifying postmillennialism with liberalism cuts both ways. Most cults are premillennial!

---

8. Robert L. Dabney, *Lectures in Systematic Theology* (Grand Rapids, MI: Zondervan, [1878] 1976), p. 838.

9. B. B. Warfield, "The Millennium and the Apocalypse," *Biblical Doctrines* (New York: Oxford University Press, 1929), pp. 647-648.

Question 10

WHAT ROLE DOES ISRAEL PLAY IN POSTMIL-LENNIALISM?

Since the publication of Hal Lindsey's malicious book, *The Road to Holocaust*, Reconstructionists have been branded with the label "Anti-Semitic." Lindsey's argument was that postmillennialism leaves no place in prophecy for the nation of Israel, and thus paves the way for Anti-Semitism and a possible Holocaust.[1] Of course, this argument implies that amillennialists and historical premillennialists are also Anti-Semitic.

Contrary to Lindsey's allegations, postmillennialism has always emphasized the important place that the ethnic Jews have in the future of the Church. Reconstructionist writer Gary North summarizes his own views by saying,

> [E]ven the Jews will be provoked to jealousy. Paul cited Deuteronomy 32:21 concerning the Jews: "But I say, Did not Israel know? First Moses saith, I will provoke you to jealousy by them that are no people, and by a foolish nation I will anger you" (Romans 10:19). The Gentiles have received the great blessing. "I say then, Have they [the Jews] stumbled that they should fall? God forbid; but rather through their fall salvation is come unto the Gentiles, for to provoke them to jealousy" (Romans 11:11). This becomes a means of *converting the remnant of Israel in the future*, and when they are converted, Paul says, just think of the *blessings* that God will pour out on the earth, given the fact that the fall of Israel was the source

---

1. Hal Lindsey, *The Road to Holocaust* (New York: Bantam Books, 1989). For an extended review of Lindsey's book, see Gary DeMar and Peter J. Leithart, *The Legacy of Hatred Continues: A Response to Hal Lindsey's The Road to Holocaust* (Tyler, TX: Institute for Christian Economics, 1989).

of great blessings for the Gentile nations. "Now if the fall of them be the riches of the world, and the diminishing of them the riches of the Gentiles, how much more their fullness?" (Romans 11:12). When the Jews received their promise, the age of blessings will come. When they submit to God's peace treaty, the growth of the kingdom will be spectacular. This is what Paul means by his phrase, "how much more." This leads to stage *ten*, the explosion of conversions and blessings. If God responds to covenantal faithfulness by means of blessings, just consider the implications of widespread conversions among the Jews. When the fullness of the Gentiles has come in, then Israel will be converted (Romans 11:25). The distinction between Jew and Gentile will then be finally erased in history, and the kingdom of God will be united as never before.[2]

As this quotation makes plain, North (as well as other Reconstructionists) rely on Paul's discussion in Romans 9-11 as the biblical basis for their view of the future of Israel. In sum, postmillennialism teaches that the Jews will someday be converted to Christ, and that this will spark a massive revival, which will produce abundant blessing for the entire world.

This understanding of the place of Israel in prophecy was not invented by Dr. North. In fact, it was a crucial feature in the development of the postmillennial position. As early as the sixteenth century, in the Reformation and immediate post-Reformation period, several theologians addressed the question of Israel's place in God's plans for the future. Theodore Beza, John Calvin's successor in Geneva, taught that the world would "be restored from death to life againe, at the time when the Jews should also come, and be called to the profession of the Gospel." Martin Bucer, the reformer of Strassbourg who had a direct influence on English Puritanism, wrote in a 1568 commentary on Romans that Paul prophesied a future conversion of the Jewish people. Peter Martyr Vermigli, who taught Hebrew in Strassbourg and later at Oxford, agreed.[3]

Historian Peter Toon describes the transmission of this inter-

---

2. Gary North, *Unconditional Surrender: God's Program for Victory* 3rd ed. (Tyler, TX: Institute for Christian Economics, [1981] 1988), pp. 340-41.

3. Quotations from J. A. DeJong, *As the Waters Cover the Sea: Millennial Expectations in the Rise of Anglo-America Missions, 1640-1810* (Kampen: J. H. Kok, 1970), p. 9.

pretation from the Continent to England, Scotland, and then to America:

> . . . the word 'Israel' in Romans 11:25ff., which had been understood by Calvin and Luther as referring to the Church of Jews and Gentiles, could be taken to mean 'Jews', that is non-Christian Jews whose religion was Judaism. Beza himself favoured this interpretation of Romans 11 and he was followed by the various editors of the influential *Geneva Bible*, which was translated in Geneva by the Marian exiles during the lifetime of Beza. In the 1557 and 1560 editions short notes explained that 'Israel' meant 'the nation of the Jews' but in later editions (e.g. 1599) the note on Romans 11 stated that the prophets of the Old Testament had predicted a future conversion of the nation of the Jews to Christ. Through this Bible and the writings of the Puritans (e.g. William Perkins, *Commentary on Galatians*, and various books by Hugh Broughton) the doctrine of the conversion of the Jewish people was widely diffused in England, Scotland, and New England.[4]

In England, the place of the Jews in prophecy was a prominent issue in the seventeenth century, and, significantly, this was true among postmillennial Calvinists. William Perkins, a leading Puritan teacher and writer, taught that there would be a future mass conversion of the Jews. Similarly, Richard Sibbes wrote that "The Jews are not yet come in under Christ's banner; but God, that hath persuaded Japhet to come into the tents of Shem, will persuade Shem to come into the tents of Japhet." Elnathan Parr's 1620 commentary on Romans espoused the view that there would be two "fullnesses" of the Gentiles: one prior to the conversion of the Jews and one following: "The end of this world shall not be till the Jews are called, and how long after that none yet can tell."[5]

Speaking before the House of Commons in 1649 during the Puritan Revolution, John Owen, a postmillennial theologian, spoke about "the bringing home of [God's] ancient people

---

4. Peter Toon, "The Latter-Day Glory," in *Puritans, the Millennium and the Future of Israel: Puritan Eschatology 1600-1660*, ed. Peter Toon (Cambridge: James Clarke, 1970), p. 24.

5. All quotations from DeJong, *As the Waters Cover the Sea*, pp. 27-28.

to be one fold with the fullness of the Gentiles . . . in answer to millions of prayers put up at the throne of grace, for this very glory, in all generations."[6]

Postmillennialist Jonathan Edwards outlined the history of the Christian Church in his 1774 *History of Redemption*. Edwards believed that the overthrow of Satan's kingdom involved several elements: the abolition of heresies and infidelity, the overthrow of the kingdom of the Antichrist (the Pope), the overthrow of the Muslim nations, and the overthrow of "Jewish infidelity":

> However obstinate [the Jews] have been now for above seven-teen hundred years in their rejection of Christ, and however rare have been the instances of individual conversions, ever since the destruction of Jerusalem . . . yet, when this day comes, the thick vail that blinds their eyes shall be removed, 2 Cor. iii.16. and divine grace shall melt and renew their hard hearts . . . And then shall the house of Israel be saved: the Jews in all their dispersions shall cast away their old infidelity, and shall have their hearts wonderfully changed, and abhor themselves for their past unbelief and obstinacy.

He concluded that "Nothing is more certainly foretold than this national conversion of the Jews in Romans 11."[7]

This view continued to be taught by postmillennialists throughout the nineteenth century. The great Princeton theologian Charles Hodge found in Romans 11 a prophecy that "the Gentiles, as a body, the mass of the Gentile world, will be converted before the restoration of the Jews, as a nation." After the fullness of the Gentiles come in, the Jewish people will be saved: "The Jews, as a people, are now rejected; as a people, they are to be restored. As their rejection, although national, did not include the rejection of every individual; so their resto-ration, although in like manner national, need not be assumed to include the salvation of every individual Jew." This will not be the end of history, however; rather, "much will remain to be accomplished after that event; and in the accomplishment of

6. Quoted in Iain Murray, *The Puritan Hope: Revival and the Interpretation of Prophecy* (London: The Banner of Truth Trust, 1971), p. 100.
7. Edwards, "History of Redemption," in *The Works of Jonathan Edwards*, vol. 1, p. 607.

what shall then remain to be done, the Jews are to have a prominent agency."[8]

This same view has been taught in the present century by some leading Reformed theologians. One of the high ironies of *The Road to Holocaust* is that Lindsey relies on a *postmillennialist*, the late John Murray of Westminster Theological Seminary, at crucial points in his exegesis of Romans 9-11![9] How Lindsey can then go on to warn about the potential "anti-Semitism" of postmillennialism is a leap of logic that we do not claim to fathom. In any case, Murray wrote this comment on Romans 11:26:

> If we keep in mind the theme of this chapter and the sustained emphasis on the restoration of Israel, there is no alternative than to conclude that the proposition, "all Israel shall be saved", is to be interpreted in terms of the fullness, the receiving, the ingrafting of Israel as a people, the restoration of Israel to gospel favour and blessing and the correlative turning of Israel from unbelief to faith and repentance. . . . the salvation of Israel must be conceived of on a scale that is commensurate with their trespass, their loss, their casting away, their breaking off, and their hardening, commensurate, of course, in the opposite direction.[10]

Many "Dominion Theologians" follow Murray's exegesis of this passage. I quoted Gary North's explanation of the conversion of the Jews above. Along similar lines, after citing Murray's exegesis of Romans 11, Ray R. Sutton, the pastor of Good Shepherd Episcopal Church in Tyler, Texas, and author of *That You May Prosper*, explains what he calls the "representative" or "covenantal" view of Israel, which holds that Israel "represents the *conversion* of the world to Christ." Sutton explains further:

> I hold to the [representative view of Israel's future], neither anti-semitic nor zionist. First, according to this position, Israel maintains

8. Charles Hodge, *A Commentary on Romans* (London: Banner of Truth Trust, [1864] 1972), p. 374. See also Hodge, *Systematic Theology*, vol. 3, pp. 804-13.

9. Lindsey, *Road to Holocaust*, pp. 176-77, 189.

10. John Murray, *The Epistle to the Romans*, 2 vols. in one (Grand Rapids, MI: Eerdmans, 1968), vol. 2, p. 98.

a special place in the plan of God. It is greatly loved by God. Because of its unique role in the conversion of the Gentiles, it is to be evangelized, not exterminated. It is to be called back to the God of Abraham, Isaac, Jacob, and Joseph, not excluded from a place in the world. It is to be cherished by the Church, the New Israel, not excoriated as a "Christ-killer"; remember, the *whole* world crucified Christ, for above His head were written in *all* the major languages of Jew and Gentile: "King of the Jews."

But second, the representative or covenantal view is not nationalistic. It does not believe there is magic in being a political unit, a nation. Just because Israel has become nationalized has little or nothing to do with its becoming "covenantalized"; in fact, being politicized has always stood in its way of accepting Christ as Savior and more importantly, *Lord.* The representative view can therefore advocate love for the Jew, while being able to reject his anti-Christian nation that persecutes Christians and butchers other people who need Christ just as much as they. It can work for the conversion of Israel without becoming the pawn of maniacal nationalism, a racial supremacy as ugly and potentially oppressive as its twentieth century arch enemy, Aryanism.[11]

The twentieth century has witnessed a great holocaust against the Jews. What millennial position dominated American culture during this time? It was dispensational premillennialism, not postmillennial Reconstructionism. Dispensationalists are quick to point out that postmillennialism fell out of favor with theologians after the first world war. Amillennialism was still prominent as was covenantal premillennialism. Certainly postmillennialism cannot be blamed for the holocaust since, according to Lindsey and company, there were very few men who were advocating the position after the first world war. Since dispensationalism did predominate during this period, what was its response to the persecution of the Jews under Hitler's regime?

Dwight Wilson, author of *Armageddon Now!*, convincingly writes that dispensational premillennialism advocated a "hands off" policy regarding Nazi persecutions of the Jews. Since, according to dispensational views regarding Bible prophecy, "the Gentile nations are permitted to afflict Israel in chastisement for

---

11. Ray R. Sutton, "Does Israel Have a Future?" *Covenant Renewal* (December 1988), p. 3.

her national sins,"[12] there is little or anything that should be done to oppose it. Wilson writes that "It is regrettable that this view allowed premillennialists to expect the phenomenon of anti-Semitism and tolerate it matter-of-factly."[13] Wilson is not a postmillennialist. The author describes himself as "a third-generation premillenarian who has spent his whole life in pre-millennialist churches, has attended a premillennialist Bible college, and has taught in such a college for fourteen years."[14] His views cannot be viewed as prejudiced against premillennialism.

Wilson described "premillenarian views" of anti-Semitism in the mid-thirties and thereafter as "ambivalent."[15] There was little moral outcry "among the premillenarians . . . against the persecution, since they had been expecting it."[16] He continues with startling candor:

> Another comment regarding the general European anti-Semitism depicted these developments as part of the on-going plan of God for the nation; they were "Foregleams of Israel's Tribulation." Premillennialists were anticipating the Great Tribulation, "the time of Jacob's trouble." Therefore, they predicted, "The next scene in Israel's history may be summed up in three words: purification through tribulation." It was clear that although this purification was part of the curse, God did not intend that Christians should partici-pate in it. Clear, also, was the implication that He did intend for the Germans to participate in it (in spite of the fact that it would bring them punishment) — *and that any moral outcry against Germany would have been in opposition to God's will. In such a fatalistic system, to oppose Hitler was to oppose God.*[17]

Other premillennial writers placed "part of the blame for anti-Semitism on the Jews: 'The Jew is the world's archtroubler. Most of the Revolutions of Continental Europe were fostered by

12. Dwight Wilson, *Armageddon Now!: The Premillenarian Response to Russia and Israel Since 1917* (Grand Rapids, MI: Baker Book House, 1977), p. 16.
13. *Idem.*
14. *Ibid.*, p. 13.
15. *Ibid.*, p. 94.
16. *Idem.*
17. *Idem.* Emphasis added.

Jews.' The Jews — especially the German Jews — were responsible for the great depression."[18]

Wilson maintains that it was the premillennial view of a predicted Jewish persecution prior to the Second Coming that led to a "hands off" policy when it came to speaking out against virulent anti-Semitism. "For the premillenarian, the massacre of Jewry expedited his blessed hope. Certainly he did not rejoice over the Nazi holocaust, he just fatalistically observed it as a 'sign of the times.' "[19] Wilson offers this summary:

> Pleas from Europe for assistance for Jewish refugees fell on deaf ears, and "Hands Off" meant no helping hand. So in spite of being theologically more pro-Jewish than any other Christian group, the premillenarians also were apathetic — because of a residual anti-Semitism, because persecution was prophetically expected, because it would encourage immigration to Palestine, because it seemed the beginning of the Great Tribulation, and because it was a wonderful sign of the imminent blessed hope.[20]

From a reading of Dwight Wilson's material, the argument has been turned on those dispensational premillennialists who have charged non-dispensationalists with being "unconsciously" anti-Semitic. The charge is preposterous, especially since postmillennialists see a great conversion of the Jews to Christ prophesied in the Bible prior to any such "Great Tribulation," while dispensationalism sees a great persecution yet to come where "two thirds of the children of Israel in the land will perish" during the "Great Tribulation."[21]

18. *Ibid.*, p. 95.
19. *Idem.*
20. *Ibid.*, pp. 96-97. See Wilson's comments on page 217.
21. John F. Walvoord, *Israel in Prophecy* (Grand Rapids, MI: Zondervan/Academie, [1962] 1988), p. 108.

Question No. 11

DO RECONSTRUCTIONISTS BELIEVE THAT REVOLUTION IS THE WAY TO ADVANCE GOD'S KINGDOM?

One of the major distortions of postmillennial and Reconstructionist teaching is that this position leads to revolutionary militancy. Some premillennial writers have attempted to paint postmillennialism in blood-red colors. Norman Geisler writes:

> Many evangelicals are calling for civil disobedience, even revolution, against a government. Francis Schaeffer, for example, insisted that Christians should disobey government when "any office commands that which is contrary to the word of God." He even urges a blood revolution, if necessary, against any government that makes such laws. He explains that "in a fallen world, force in some form will always be necessary."[1]

What makes this comment particularly interesting is the fact that Schaeffer was a *pre*millennialist, not a postmillennialist. Geisler admits that this is true, but then adds that "it appears that in actual practice at this point his views were postmillennial." This is certainly a strange and a very deceptive argument. Geisler cites Francis Schaeffer, a *pre*millennialist, to try to show that the *post*millennial position encourages revolution. And

---

1. Norman Geisler, "A Premillennial View of Law and Government," *The Best in Theology*, gen. ed. J. I. Packer (Carol Stream, IL: Christianity Today, 1986), p. 261-62. A revised version of this article appears as "A Dispensational Premillennial View of Law and Government" in J. Kerby Anderson, ed., *Living Ethically in the 90s* (Wheaton, IL: Victor Books, 1990), pp. 149-67.

Schaeffer is the *only* writer whom Geisler cites. Geisler does not cite a single postmillennial writer who advocates revolution, so it is sheer bias on his part to conclude that Schaeffer is operating as a postmillennialist.

Modern postmillennial Reconstructionists are not revolutionary because they have a more consistently biblical view of the future. Reconstructionists generally believe they have time, lots of time, to accomplish their ends. Moreover, they are not revolutionary because they believe that Christians achieve leadership by living righteously. Dominion is by ethical service and work, not by revolution. Thus, there is no theological reason for a postmillennialist to take up arms at the drop of a hat. Biblical postmillennialists can afford to wait for God to judge ungodly regimes, bide their time, and prepare to rebuild upon the ruins. Biblical postmillennialists are not pacifists, but neither are they revolutionaries.

Biblical postmillennialism provides the Christian with a *long-term* hope. Because of his long time-frame, the postmillennialist can exercise that chief element of true biblical faith: patience. Because he is confident that the Lord has given him time to accomplish the Lord's purposes, the postmillennialist need not take things into his own, sinful hands. The Lord will exalt us when He is ready, and when He knows that we are ready. Our calling is to wait patiently, praying and preparing ourselves for that responsibility, and working all the while to advance His kingdom. Historically, Christians who lack this long-term hope have taken things into their own hands, inevitably with disastrous consequences. Far from advocating militancy, biblical postmillennialism protects against a short-term revolutionary mentality.

Reconstructionists believe that Christians should follow the examples of biblical characters such as Joseph, Daniel, and Jesus Christ Himself. Joseph and Daniel both exercised enormous influence within the world's greatest empires. But they attained their positions by hard work, perseverance in persecution and suffering, and faithful obedience. Jesus Christ attained to His throne only by enduring the suffering of the cross. Christians are no different. We are not to attain positions of leadership by revolution or rebellion. Instead, we are to work at our callings, and wait on the Lord to place us in positions of influence, *in His time*.[2]

Gary North has called those who wish to advance the kingdom by revolution "romantic revolutionaries."[3] This is not a recent emphasis in North's writings. His first major book was *Marx's Religion of Revolution*, in which he insisted that "faithful men will remain orderly in all the aspects of their lives; they are not to create chaos in order to escape from law (Rom. 13; I Cor. 14:40). It is reserved for God alone to bring his total judgment to the world." In the biblical worldview, "it is God, and only God, who initiates the change."[4] North has pointed out repeatedly that the kingdom of God advances *ethically* as the people of God work out their salvation with fear and trembling. Revolutionaries are lawless. Their time frame is short. In fact, one of Dr. North's books, *Moses and Pharaoh*, is subtitled *Dominion Religion Versus Power Religion*. Power Religion, he writes,

> is a religious viewpoint which affirms that the most important goal for a man, group, or species, is the capture and maintenance of power. Power is seen as the chief attribute of God, or if the religion is officially atheistic, then the chief attribute of man. This perspective is a satanic perversion of God's command to man to exercise dominion over all the creation (Gen. 1:26-28). It is the attempt to exercise dominion apart from covenantal subordination to the true Creator God.
>
> What distinguishes biblical dominion religion from satanic power religion is *ethics*.[5]

---

2. See David Chilton, *The Days of Vengeance: An Exposition of the Book of Revelation* (Ft. Worth, TX: Dominion Press, 1987), pp. 511-12; James B. Jordan, "Rebellion, Tyranny, and Dominion in the Book of Genesis," in Gary North, ed., *Tactics of Christian Resistance*, Christianity and Civilization No. 3 (Tyler, TX: Geneva Ministries, 1983), pp. 38-80.

3. Gary North, "Editor's Introduction," *Christianity and Civilization*, Number 3 (Summer 1983), pp. xxxii-xxxvii.

4. North, *Marx's Religion of Revolution* (Nutley, NJ: The Craig Press, 1968), p. 99. This same quotation appears in the revised second edition (1989) on page 86.

5. (Tyler, TX: Institute for Christian Economics, 1985), p. 2. Dr. North distinguishes among "Power Religion," "Escapist Religion," and "Dominion Religion" (pp. 2-5). He makes it very clear that "Power Religion" is a militant religion that is unlawful and counterproductive.

Still, the Bible teaches that we are at war, and that we must prepare for it. The apostle Paul tells Christians to "put on the full armor of God" (Ephesians 6:11). At first, even Pilate considered Jesus' kingdom to be militaristic and political (John 18:28-40). In Acts, the Christians were described as a sect preaching "another king, Jesus" (Acts 17:7). These were the forerunners of The People for the American Way. They said of the first-century Christians, "These men who have upset the world have come here also; and Jason has welcomed them, and they all act contrary to the decrees of Caesar, saying that there is another king, Jesus" (vv. 6-7). There was another king, but those outside of Christ put a political and revolutionary slant on Christ's kingship.

PART III
WHY ARE CHRISTIAN RECONSTRUCTIONISTS
CONFRONTATIONAL?

Gary DeMar and Gary North

Question 12

ARE OUR CRITICS HONEST?

Gary DeMar

> *Thou therefore which teachest another, teachest thou not thyself? thou that preachest a man should not steal, dost thou steal? Thou that sayest a man should not commit adultery, dost thou commit adultery? thou that abhorrest idols, dost thou commit sacrilege? Thou that makest thy boast of the law, through breaking the law dishonourest thou God? (Romans 2:21-23).*

About a year before he was caught visiting a prostitute, Rev. Jimmy Swaggart went on national satellite television, weekend after weekend, attacking Dominion Theology. He said it is heretical. When Gary North journeyed to Baton Rouge to meet with Rev. Swaggart personally in the fall of 1986, to discuss the matter with him, Rev. Swaggart admitted that his information had come from Dave Hunt. He agreed to read at least some Christian Reconstruction literature before going on the attack again, and his attacks ceased. When he recognized that he did not have documented proof for his accusations, he stopped his public attacks. In this case, Jimmy Swaggart turned out to be more honest than Dave Hunt, who keeps misrepresenting us.

A few months before he left Lutheranism to join the Roman Catholic Church, Rev. Richard John Neuhaus described Christian Reconstruction as "an aberration of historic Christianity."[1]

---

1. Richard John Neuhaus, "Why Wait for the Kingdom?: The Theonomist Temptation," *First Things*, No. 3 (May 1990), p. 20.

What did Neuhaus find so aberrational? A hundred years ago, few people would have protested Reconstructionist distinctives. The theological climate has changed, however. (So, for that matter, has Neuhaus since he wrote his attack.)

Yet the attacks continue. Reconstructionism is called deviant, heretical, and so forth by its critics. Not merely wrong-headed, excessive, exaggerated, or even historically unprecedented, but heretical. This is strong language, far stronger than Reconstructionists use against their opponents. Yet it is the Reconstructionists who are called divisive and hostile. Why? More to the point, which doctrine of the Reconstructionists is heretical?

If the only position taken by the Reconstructionists that is unprecedented in church history is Van Til's assertion of the absolute authority of the Bible over all philosophy — biblical presuppositionalism — why do so few of the critics attack us at the one point where we are vulnerable to the accusation of new theology? Probably because more and more of them are coming to agree with us on this point: the myth of humanist neutrality.

Van Til was a Calvinist. He defended his position in terms of Calvinism. He said that Calvinism, with its doctrine of the absolute sovereignty of God, is the only Christian position that can systematically and consistently reject all compromises with humanism, for Calvinism alone grants no degree of autonomy to man, including intellectual autonomy. So, the critics have a problem: if they accept biblical presuppositionalism without accepting Calvinism, they have an obligation to show how this is intellectually legitimate. They have to refute Van Til. On the other hand, if they do not do this, yet they also remain convinced that neutrality is a myth, they have to ask themselves: In what way is Christian Reconstruction heretical?

Calvinism

Reconstructionists are Calvinists, i.e., defenders of the doctrine of predestination by God. This is certainly no aberration of historic Christianity. Many of the greatest ministers and theologians of the Christian church have been Calvinists. Many of the greatest ministers and theologians of our own day are Calvinists. Consider the words of Charles Haddon Spurgeon, the great nineteenth-century Baptist "Prince of Preachers":

> It is no novelty, then, that I am preaching; no new doctrine. I
> love to proclaim these strong old doctrines, which are called by the
> nickname Calvinism, but which are surely and verily the revealed
> truth of God as it is in Christ Jesus. By this truth I make a pilgrim-
> age into the past, and as I go, I see father after father, confessor
> after confessor, martyr after martyr, standing up to shake hands
> with me. Were I a Pelagian, or a believer in the doctrine of free-
> will, I should have to walk for centuries all alone. Here and there a
> heretic or no very honourable character might rise up and call me
> brother. But taking these things to be the standard of my faith, I see
> the land of the ancients peopled with my brethren — I behold multi-
> tudes who confess the same as I do, and acknowledge that this is the
> religion of God's own church.[2]

The doctrine now known to us as "Calvinism" was set forth
very plainly in the writings of Augustine (354-430).[3] It held
sway over the church for centuries until the church finally
plummeted into apostasy, specifically because of the theological
chain reaction set off by its rejection of Calvinism. Martin Luther (an Augustinian monk) and John Calvin revived the doctrine of the sovereignty of God and the particular biblical doctrine known as predestination. Luther with his *Bondage of the
Will* (1525),[4] and Calvin, with his *Institutes of the Christian Religion* (1536) and his nearly complete commentaries on the Bible,
gave the doctrine its fullest expression.

These men were not alone in their belief and application of
this life-transforming doctrine. As Rev. D. James Kennedy of
Coral Ridge Ministries (and the developer of Evangelism Explo-
sion) has said, this doctrine was held also by Melanchthon, by
Zwingli, by John Knox, and by Thomas Cranmer in England.
Without exception, all of the Reformers of the Protestant Refor-

---

2. Charles H. Spurgeon, *The New Park Street Pulpit: Containing Sermons Preached and
Revised by C. H. Spurgeon Minister of the Chapel During the Years 1855-1860*, 6 vols. (Grand
Rapids, MI: Zondervan, [1856-1861] 1963), Vol. 1, p. 313.

3. Benjamin B. Warfield, *Calvin and Augustine* (Philadelphia: Presbyterian & Reformed, [1905-9] 1956).

4. Martin Luther, *The Bondage of the Will*, trans. J. I. Packer and O. R. Johnston (Old
Tappan, NJ: Fleming H. Revell, [1525] 1957.

mation professed the doctrine of predestination by God. "All Protestant churches which came into being out of the Reformation hold to that doctrine in their creeds. The Presbyterians and the Reformed of Holland and Switzerland and Germany, Anglicans, the Huguenots, the Covenanters, the Puritans, the Pietists of Germany, the Pilgrims of America, were all firm believers in this great doctrine of predestination."[5]

It is no accident that it has been Calvinists who have developed a comprehensive social theory that places all men and institutions, including civil government, under the sovereign rule of God. Authority to rule is ministerial, derived from God and also limited by Him. The State's right to exist is not based on the "will of the people" but on the will of God (Romans 13:1-4). The Calvinist believes that

> the ultimate source of authority is not the state itself, as in Hegel and contemporary absolutist philosophers; nor in the people, as in modern democratic thought; nor in a classless society, as Marx taught; but in the will of the triune God. It is God who ordains the state, confers upon it its legitimate powers, and sets limits upon its actions. The state is not the source of law, nor of the concepts of right and wrong, or of justice and equity.[6]

Calvinistic social theory had its greatest impact on the Western world: A limited State and a free people bound by the sovereign rule of God. Arminianism now predominates in the church. This too has social and political implications. If man is sovereign in salvation, which Arminianism implies, since God cannot save until man exercises his will, then man is equally sovereign in the social and political spheres. To throw off Calvinism is to open the door to apostasy[7] and tyranny.[8] There is

---

5. D. James Kennedy, *Truths that Transform: Christian Doctrines for Your Life Today* (Old Tappan, NJ: Fleming H. Revell, 1974), p. 31.

6. C. Gregg Singer, *John Calvin: His Roots and Fruits* (Nutley, NJ: Presbyterian and Reformed, 1977), pp. 33-34.

7. The revivals of the early nineteenth century brought about a "Popular theology [that] had descended from Calvinism to Arminianism, and from there to universalism, and so on down the ladder of error to the pits of atheism." John B. Boles, *The Great Revival, 1787-1805: The Origins of the Southern Evangelical Mind* (Lexington, KY: The University Press of Kentucky, 1972), p. 100.

8. A. Mervyn Davies, *Foundation of American Freedom: Calvinism in the Development of*

no theological aberration in Christian Reconstruction's adherence to Calvinism.

Biblical Law

Reconstructionists believe that the whole Bible is the Christian's guide for every area of life: from personal holiness to civil righteousness. This includes God's law as it is found in all the Bible, not just "Old Testament Law" or the "Law of Moses."

> To orthodox Calvinism, the law of God is the permanent, unchanging expression of God's eternal and unchangeable holiness and justice.... God could not change this law, or set it aside, in His dealings with men, without denying Himself. When man sins, therefore, it is not God's nature to save him at the law's expense. Instead, He saves sinners by satisfying the law on their behalf.[9]

The Bible teaches that Jesus satisfied the requirements of the law in the sinner's place and only brought about a change in those laws that had specific reference to the redemptive work of Christ and those institutions and ceremonies that were specifically designed to keep Israel a separate people and nation (e.g., circumcision and food laws). The *law as a blueprint* for personal, familial, ecclesiastical, and civil righteousness was not abrogated by the work of Christ. This is the Calvinistic tradition that goes against Neuhaus's claim that the views of Reconstructionists are "an aberration of historic Christianity."

Few Christians would deny that the "moral law," as summarized in the Ten Commandments, is still binding upon the believer. But a question arises: How comprehensive is the moral law? "You shall not murder" (Exodus 20:13) is a moral law that has personal as well as social and civil applications. An individual (personal application) is forbidden to murder another person (social application), and the State has a duty to punish those who commit murder (civil application) (Romans 13:4). The

---

Democratic Thought and Action (Nashville, TN: Abingdon Press, 1955).

9. J. I. Packer, "The Redemption and Restoration of Man in the Thought of Richard Baxter," (1954), pp. 303-5. Quoted in Ernest F. Kevan, *The Grace of Law: A Study in Puritan Theology* (London: The Carey Kingsgate Press Limited, 1964). pp. 67-68.

same can be said about laws governing property, contracts, and criminal sexual practices like adultery, homosexuality, and bestiality. All of the laws governing these areas are moral laws having a tripartite application.

Since our task in this section is to deal with "historic Christianity," we will not survey what the Bible says about the abiding validity of God's law. This topic has been dealt with elsewhere in great detail.[10]

A steady confirmation of the abiding validity of God's law can be found with the earliest of the church fathers and continuing to our day. "Recognizing the value of the Law of God was no innovation by the Reformers. Irenaeus [c.175-c.195] had seen it; Augustine [354-430] knew it well; the medieval schoolmen, of whom Aquinas [1224-1274] was the best exponent, considered at length the application of the Law to the Christian."[11]

John Calvin's (1509-1564) exposition of the law and its application to society, including the civil magistrate, is set forth in comprehensive detail in his exposition of Deuteronomy 27 and 28, totalling two hundred sermons in all.

> After all, in reforming the city of Geneva, Calvin did not deliver two hundred lectures on common grace or natural law, but preached two hundred sermons on the book of Deuteronomy. He made full and direct applications from Deuteronomy into his modern situation, without apology. He viewed Biblical law as foundational and as the starting point for legal and socio-political reflection.[12]

The American Puritans, following in the tradition of Calvin, believed that it was possible to govern a modern commonwealth by the laws set forth in all of Scripture. For example, the "Puritans resolved to rule the [Massachusetts] Bay Colony with a strong hand but with a Christian heart."[13] This meant that the

---

10. See "Books for Further Reading and Study," below.

11. Geoffrey H. Greenhough, "The Reformers' Attitude to the Law of God," *The Westminster Theological Journal* 39:1 (Fall 1976), p. 81.

12. James B. Jordan, "Editor's Introduction," *The Covenant Enforced: Sermons on Deuteronomy 27 and 28* (Tyler, TX: Institute for Christian Economics, 1990), p. xxxiii.

13. Edwin Powers, *Crime and Punishment in Early Massachusetts, 1620-1692* (Boston,

Bible was used as the standard for personal, social, and civil justice, "but no Puritan believed that the entire Mosaic Code should be transposed bodily to the new Canaan."[14] While the Bible became the New Englanders' law book, much of English Common Law was rejected. "Burglary, robbery, larceny, and many other crimes against the person and property did not appear at all as death-penalty crimes in" the early Massachusetts Body of Liberties.[15] Why was the death penalty rejected for these crimes? The Bible did not mandate it.

These are not isolated historical cases advocating the binding nature of God's law. Martin Bucer, a contemporary of Calvin, in his *De Regno Christi*, wrote that "no one can describe an approach more equitable and wholesome to the commonwealth than that which God describes in his law." He further states that it is "the duty of all kings and princes who recognize that God has put them over his people that they follow most studiously his own method of punishing evildoers."[16] Similar sentiments can be found in the writings of Heinrich Bullinger (1504-1575), Bishop John Hooper (d. 1555), Hugh Latimer (1485-1555), Thomas Becon (1512-1567), John Knox (c. 1514-1572), Thomas Cartwright (1535-1603), William Perkins (1558-1602), Johannes Wollebius (1586-1629), George Gillespie (1613-1649), John Owen (1616-1683), John Cotton (1584-1652), Samuel Rutherford (1600-1661),[17] Thomas Shepard (1605-1649), John Eliot (1604-1690), Samuel Willard (1640-1707), Thomas Scott (1747-1821), E. C. Wines,[18] Ashbel Green,[19] J. B. Shearer,[20] and

MA: Beacon Press, 1966), p. 252.

14. *Ibid.*, p. 253. This, too, is the Reconstructionist position: "There are *cultural* discontinuities between biblical moral instruction and our modern society. This fact does not imply that the ethical teaching of Scripture is invalidated for us; it simply calls for hermeneutical sensitivity." Bahnsen, "The Reconstructionist Option," in Bahnsen and Gentry, *House Divided*, p. 32.

15. *Ibid.*, p. 254.

16. Martin Bucer, *De Regno Christi*, trans. Wilhelm Pauck and Paul Larkin, ed. Wilhelm Pauck, The Library of Christian Classics, vol. XIX *Melanchthon and Bucer* (Philadelphia, PA: The Westminster Press, 1969), p. 378.

17. Samuel Rutherford, *Lex, Rex, or the Law and the Prince* (Harrisonburg, VA: Sprinkle Publications, [1644] 1980).

18. E. C. Wines, "The Hebrew Theocracy," *The Biblical Repository* (October 1850), pp. 579-99.

19. Ashbel Green, *Obedience to the Laws of God the Sure and Indispensable Defence of*

many others.[21]

S. H. Kellogg wrote the following in the introduction to his exposition of Leviticus:

> It comes that the book is of use for today, as suggesting principles which should guide human legislators who would rule according to the mind of God. . . . For nothing can be more certain than this; that if God has indeed once stood to a commonwealth in the relation of King and political head, we shall be sure to discover in His theocratic law upon what principles, infinite righteousness, wisdom, and goodness would deal with these matters. We shall thus find in Leviticus that the law which it contains, from beginning to end, stands in contradiction to the modern democratic secularism, which would exclude religion from government and order all national affairs without reference to the being and government of God. . . .[22]

History is with the Reconstructionists as they advocate a return to God's law as the standard for righteous living, for the individual in self-government as well as elected officials in civil government. Our critics ignore most of this evidence. Why?

Postmillennialism

Reconstructionists believe in the advance of God's kingdom (i.e., *civilization*) and the progressive defeat of Satan's kingdom *prior* to Jesus' bodily return in glory. This view of eschatology has been called postmillennialism, because Jesus returns after (post) a great period of gospel prosperity and blessedness. Again, since Mr. Neuhaus has alleged that Christian Reconstruction is "an aberration of historic Christianity," we will only be considering the witness of history. There are numerous

---

Nations (Philadelphia, PA: John Ormrod, 1798).

20. J. B. Shearer, *Hebrew Institutions, Social and Civil* (Richmond, VA: Presbyterian Committee of Publications, 1910).

21. For a summary of the views of these men, see James B. Jordan, "Calvinism and 'The Judicial Law of Moses': An Historical Survey," *The Journal of Christian Reconstruction*, Symposium on Puritanism and Law, ed. Gary North V:2 (Winter 1978-79), pp. 17-48.

22. S. H. Kellogg, *The Book of Leviticus*, 3rd ed. (Minneapolis, MN: Klock & Klock, [1899] 1978), pp. 25-26.

biblical defenses of postmillennialism available to the reader.[23]

Millennial positions were not so clearly defined prior to and for an extended period after the Reformation of the sixteenth century as they are today. Christians did not describe themselves as pre-, a-, or post-millennialists. While a premillennialist is easy to spot because the system's characteristic is the one-thousand-year reign of Christ, bodily, on the *earth*, finding amillennialists and postmillennialists is a bit more difficult, since they teach a present reign of Christ who sits on His throne in heaven. Many amils and postmils can be spotted because of their opposition to "chiliasm,"[24] an ancient designation for premillennialism and its insistence on an earthly political kingdom (cf. John 6:15).

While it is true that premillennialism (or "chiliasm") has a long history, postmillennialism (or the idea that the gospel will have worldwide success before the return of Christ) has also had many adherents. In a homily on Matthew, John of Antioch, called Chrysostom (347-407), wrote:

> Let us show forth then a new kind of life. Let us make earth, heaven; let us hereby show the Greeks, of how great blessings they are deprived. For when they behold in us good conversation, they will look upon the very face of the kingdom of heaven.[25]

What effect will gospel proclamation have on the world? Did these early Christian writers expect the demise of culture (some did), to be overrun by pagan hordes? It was "Chrysostom's conviction that, when the outside world sees this Christian life burgeoning in a fashion that is gentle, unenvious, and socially responsible in every degree, the outer society will, itself, be

---

23. See "Books for Further Reading and Study," below.

24. "Chiliasm" is derived from the Greek *chiliad*, signifying a thousand. "Millennialism" is derived from the Latin *mille*, also signifying a thousand. Millennium is made up of two Latin words: *mille* (thousand) and *annum* (year). A millennium is a thousand years (Revelation 20:4).

25. Homily XLIII, 7 (Commentary on Matthew XII:38-39). Quoted in Ray C. Petry, *Christian Eschatology and Social Thought: A Historical Essay on the Social Implications of Some Neglected Aspects in Christian Eschatology to A.D. 150* (Nashville, TN: Abingdon Press, 1956), p. 100.

mightily impressed."[26] With such actions and attitudes, Chrysostom believed that it was possible to win "their native land!" This is the essence of the postmillennial vision.

> Thus they too will be reformed, and the word of godliness "will have free course," not less than in the apostles' time. For if they, being twelve, converted entire cities and countries; were we all to become teachers by our careful conduct, imagine how high our cause will be exalted.[27]

These same sentiments can be found throughout the entire history of the Christian church. The prospects for the advance of Christ's kingdom were paramount in the writings of many of the greatest thinkers of the church. Again we turn to the sixteenth-century protestant theologian John Calvin. J. A. De Jong in his doctoral dissertation on millennial expectations after 1640 writes of Calvin: "John Calvin's commentaries give some scholars cause for concluding that he anticipated the spread of the gospel and true religion to the ends of the earth."[28] John T. McNeill mentions "Calvin's conception of the victory and future universality of Christ's Kingdom throughout the human race, a topic frequently introduced in the Commentaries."[29]

> It is generally stated that postmillennialism came into prominence through the writings of the Anglican commentator Daniel Whitby (1638-1726), but prior to the publication of Whitby's widely read *Paraphrase and Commentary on the New Testament* in 1703, this outlook was being articulated by Puritan scholars such as Thomas Brightman, William Gouge, John Cotton, and John Owen. On October 24, 1651, Owen preached a sermon before the House of Commons on the theme of "The Kingdom of Christ" in which his postmillenarian outlook is quite evident. That God in his appointed time would "bring forth the Kingdom of the Lord Christ unto more glory and power than in former days, I presume you are persuad-

---

26. Petry, *Christian Eschatology and Social Thought*, p. 100.

27. *Idem.*

28. J. A. De Jong, *As the Waters Cover the Sea: Millennial Expectations in the Rise of Anglo-American Missions: 1640-1810* (Kampen, The Netherlands: J. H. Kok, 1970), p. 8.

29. *Calvin: Institutes of the Christian Religion,* ed. John T. McNeill, trans. Ford Lewis Battles, 2 vols. (Philadelphia, PA: Westminster Press, 1960), vol. 2, p. 904, n. 76.

ed," he stated to the assembly. He believed that the Scriptures foretold a time in history of "multitudes of converts, many persons, yea nations, Isa[iah] 60:7.8, 66:8, 49:18-22; Rev[elation] 7:9," and "professed subjection of the nations throughout the whole world unto the Lord Christ, Dan[iel] 2:44, 7:26, 27, Isa[iah] 60:6-9."[30]

Similar themes were addressed by Zwingli, Bucer, Peter Martyr, William Perkins, J. A. Alexander, A. A. Hodge, Charles Hodge, W. G. T. Shedd, Benjamin B. Warfield, Marcellus Kik, Roderick Campbell, John Murray (in his commentary on Romans, chapter 11), and Reconstructionist writers. Strains of postmillennialism can be found in the writings of the great English Baptist preacher of the nineteenth century, Charles Haddon Spurgeon,[31] and many others.[32] Charles Hodge, whose three-volume systematic theology is still used in seminaries today, considered postmillennialism the "common doctrine of the Church."[33] In 1859 the influential theological quarterly, the *American Theological Review*, could assert without fear of contradiction that postmillennialism was the 'commonly received doctrine' among American Protestants."[34] Our critics ignore most of this evidence. Why?

No One Likes Being Called a Heretic

In 1972 Dave Hunt wrote *Confessions of a Heretic*.[35] It is a moving story of how his long-term association with the anti-pentecostal Plymouth Brethren movement was finally broken with the charge of heresy and eventual excommunication because of his new-found pentecostal experiences. There are a number of parallels between what Dave Hunt experienced

30. Davis, *Postmillennialism Reconsidered*, p. 17.

31. Iain Murray, "C. H. Spurgeon's Views on Prophecy," in *The Puritan Hope: Revival and the Interpretation of Prophecy* (London: The Banner of Truth Trust, 1971), pp. 256-65.

32. Greg L. Bahnsen, "The *Prima Facie* Acceptability of Postmillennialism," *The Journal of Christian Reconstruction*, Symposium on the Millennium III:2 (Winter 1976-77), pp. 48-105. For an equally informative article, see James B. Jordan, "A Survey of Southern Presbyterian Millennial Views before 1930," *ibid.*, pp. 106-21.

33. Charles Hodge, *Systematic Theology*, 3 vols. (Grand Rapids, MI: Eerdmans, [1872-73] 1968), vol. 3, p. 861.

34. Davis, *Postmillennialism Reconsidered*, p. 19.

35. Dave Hunt, *Confessions of a Heretic* (Plainfield, NJ: Logos International, 1972).

among the Brethren and the way that he and others have been
treating Christian Reconstructionists. Just substitute *Reconstructionist* where you read *Pentecostal* or *gifts of the Spirit* in the following quotations.

> I grieved a long time that night in the dark of the living room –
> not for myself, but for my friends, and the frustration I felt at the
> misunderstanding that had come between us. No explanation I
> could make would satisfy them now that they had convinced them-
> selves that I was a Pentecostal.[36]

> I know something of the prejudice that surrounds this subject of
> the gifts of the Spirit, having denounced Pentecostals all my life
> purely on the basis of hearsay that I have only recently discovered
> was mostly false. I don't ask that you agree with me, nor do I see
> that [another Christian] should demand that I agree with him on
> every point of doctrine or be put out of the assembly. This is not the
> basis for our fellowship in Christ.[37]

In addition, there are numerous places in *Confessions of a
Heretic* where Dave Hunt sounds like – dare I say it? – a Reconstructionist! He decried the modern conception of "the separation of church and state." He believed that Jesus should reign
in every area of life, including the political realm.

> Thus the way had been paved for Satan's *coup d'etat* – "the sepa-
> ration of church and state." This seemingly reasonable arrangement
> between political and religious institutions had effectively barred
> Christ from the very places that need him most, where he should
> and must reign. Christianity had become a game played off to the
> side a few hours each week, in or on certain designated tax-exempt
> properties remote from real or ordinary life, unrelated to every-
> thing vital in the affairs of men.
> That which had been intended by Christ to pervade every pulse-
> beat of life is now sealed off in a tiny sector of society that we know
> as organized religion. Institutionalized Christianity is allowed to put
> in a brief appearance outside these narrow confines on certain
> specified occasions – an "invocation" here and a "benediction" there

36. *Ibid.*, p. 139.
37. *Ibid.*, p. 169.

— but must be careful even at such times not to overstep its limited license. There must be no significant intrusion of "religion" into real life — affairs of state, education, social action, pleasure.[38]

Dave Hunt should recall some of the experiences he encountered in his dealings with the Plymouth Brethren movement so he can understand how others feel when they too are unjustly treated. In addition, he might want to explain why his earlier works sound suspiciously like present-day Reconstructionist writings.

Conclusion

There is a tendency among heresy hunters to look for the most controversial doctrines of a theological system and then to evaluate the entire system solely in terms of the controversial doctrines. If you are a die-hard dispensationalist, then postmillennialism is going to look aberrational to you. As has been shown, however, many fine Christians have held to a postmillennial eschatology. The same can be said for the Reconstructionist's adherence to Calvin's doctrine of salvation and his view of the law. Of course, this does not make the positions orthodox, but it ought to make people think twice about condemning a group of believers because they hold an opposing doctrinal position that has biblical and historical support. The three doctrines listed above — Calvinistic soteriology, biblical ethics, and postmillennial eschatology — are set forth in masterful detail in the Westminster Confession of Faith and Catechisms, documents that have been subscribed to by millions of Christians worldwide for nearly 350 years. Until at least these documents are wrestled with, would-be heresy hunters would do well to choose another line of work. Until they do, however, we Reconstructionists are compelled to defend ourselves. The question then is: How? This is discussed in Chapter 13 by Gary North.

---

38. *Ibid.*, p. 191.

Question 13

WHAT IS THE PROPER RESPONSE?

Gary North

One witness shall not rise up against a man for any iniquity, or for any sin, in any sin that he sinneth: at the mouth of two witnesses, or at the mouth of three witnesses, shall the matter be established. If a false witness rise up against any man to testify against him that which is wrong; Then both the men, between whom the controversy is, shall stand before the LORD, before the priests and the judges, which shall be in those days; And the judges shall make diligent inquisition: and, behold, if the witness be a false witness, and hath testified falsely against his brother; Then shall ye do unto him, as he had thought to have done unto his brother: so shalt thou put the evil away from among you. And those which remain shall hear, and fear, and shall henceforth commit no more any such evil among you (Deuteronomy 19:15-20).

Our critics have repeatedly misrepresented us. This includes Christian critics. They claim that we are heretical. Why? Mainly because we proclaim biblical law. We say that biblical law is Christianity's tool of dominion.[1] We believe in social progress.[2] We therefore believe in the need for social change and the legitimacy of Christian social action.

Christians today think just as humanists do regarding social change. When they hear the phrase "social change," they automatically think to themselves "politically directed change." This

---

1. Gary North, *Tools of Dominion: The Case Laws of Exodus* (Tyler, Texas: Institute for Christian Economics, 1990).

2. Gary North, *Dominion and Common Grace: The Biblical Basis of Progress* (Tyler, Texas: Institute for Christian Economics, 1987).

is humanism's view of social change, not the Bible's. This reveals the extent to which modern pietism has been influenced by contemporary humanism's worldview. When pietists hear the words "Christian Reconstruction," they, like the humanists, think of a theology based on the ideal of political action through legislative reform — a narrow ideal, indeed. This would mean the rule of biblical law. They oppose Christian Reconstruction for this reason. There has developed a kind of unstated operational alliance between them. They are united against biblical law.[3]

There are times when I think that Christian Reconstructionists are today the only people who think that political action is *not* primary. But no matter how many times we say this in print, our critics refuse to listen. They interpret our words in their own way. They systematically refuse to understand what we have in mind, meaning what we have repeatedly written. (One reason for their confusion is that they refuse to read what we write.)

This book is a short, concise, and representative example of what Christian Reconstructionism is, and also what it isn't. It is short enough and cheap enough to give even the laziest critic an accurate survey of Christian Reconstructionism. There will be no further excuse for misrepresenting our position.

Will this end the misrepresentation? Not a chance! Misrepresentation sells almost as well as sensationalism does. Therefore, this book is not merely a positive statement of our position. It is also a rebuttal. We are tired of the lies and misrepresentations. We intend to leave the liars without excuse.

This presents us with a dilemma. Should we respond at all? Or should we remain passively quiet, as if we had not been attacked, and not merely attacked, but misrepresented and in some cases even slandered? Should we give our followers the impression by our silence that we are *incapable* of answering, thereby giving credence to our attackers' accusations? Or should we present our case forcefully, which of necessity means refuting our opponents' cases forcefully? If we do, our opponents

---

3. See Chapter 9, above.

will wrap themselves in the swaddling clothes of humility and call us confrontational, uncharitable, and unchristian. They place humility at the top of the list of desirable Christian attributes in modern political pluralism's naked public square — far, far above the Ninth Commandment, which they ignore with impunity when discussing Christian Reconstruction.

Fools Rush In

Because I am heavily involved in promoting a very controversial variety of Christianity, I receive my share of criticism, mostly from other Christians. Non-Christians for the most part pay no attention to us: one non-profit Public Broadcasting System TV documentary by Lyndon B. Johnson's former press agent, one *Wall Street Journal* editorial page essay by a theologically liberal sociologist, and that is about it. Nothing of any consequence happened after either event, so I assume that no one is paying much attention to us in humanism-land.

Not so in Christian circles. Christian leaders recognize the obvious: if we are correct in our views, then they are incorrect. Not only incorrect: they are hindering the expansion of the kingdom of God by their narrow definitions of what constitutes evangelism, Christian social service, and personal responsibility in such areas as education, abortion, and public policy. They have so narrowed the range of legitimate Christian concern that they have become operational allies of secular humanists. In the name of God, they have rented out about 98% of His world to Satan's earthly representatives, using a lease contract that reads: "Irrevocable until the Second Coming of Christ."

They do not see the obvious: *kingdom* means *civilization*. God's kingdom is a cosmic civilization linking heaven and earth. He is the King of both realms. But their view of kingship is flawed. They believe that God is indeed king of heaven, but on earth He is a king only of the regenerate heart, the Christian family, and the local congregation. In their view, God is king in name only over everything else. To them, "civilization" means the devil's realm, and they make it clear that Christians should not set foot in it. The focus of their concern has been the personal vices of liquor and tobacco. In the doggerel that used to be applied to the fundamentalists (and still should be), "I don't drink, and I don't chew, and I don't go with the boys who do!" Demon rum is still their primary enemy, not demon public education.

The more books I write, the more letters I receive from critics who call themselves Christians. These letters are for the most part rational and coherent. This is probably because Christian Reconstruction is still a comparatively small intellectual movement with only a few thousand regular readers per organization. (The publicly announced estimate of some 20 million Christian Reconstructionists was made by an overly optimistic gentleman whose non-profit foundation, I can assure you, is not being sent a dollar a year by each of these supposed 20 million disciples.) The percentage of certifiable crazies in any population is limited, so I get only moderate amounts of mail from them. Those people who write to me are often donors who just want clarification. I usually answer donors' questions, even silly ones. Sometimes, I am downright civil.

A few of these letters are sent by people who, if they are not fools, certainly do a passable imitation. If I were to answer every critical letter, it would only encourage the crazies. They would just write more letters, demanding more responses. In the name of Christian humility, they always demand my immediate detailed response. Any leader in any field who gets involved in writing detailed letters to the crazies on his mailing list (let alone outsiders) places a low value on his time. His written replies will only encourage the nuttier of the letter-writers. It makes them feel important. They are not important. They are loonies. (The ones who enrage me most are the racists, who implicitly place genetics above the covenant as an explanation for social change. They are a fading influence today, but they still exist in right-wing circles. I am not charitable with these people. They belong on someone else's mailing list. The sooner they are off of mine, the better.)

Question: Should the President of the United States or the prime minister of some nation answer every letter from every critic? No? Then neither should any other leader. You have to pick and choose which letters get answered. If you don't do this, it interferes with your productive work. What is true for political leaders is true for theological innovators, too.

The "Experts" Among Us

But it is not the letter-writers who are our main problem. It is the "experts" who go into print with their criticisms. The Christian newsletter field is open to anyone, including theological basket cases. Sometimes I think, *especially* theological basket cases.

What I have noticed over the last three years (when the critics finally discovered us, about fifteen years too late) is that the more outraged the critic, and the more inflamed his rhetoric, the less intellectually competent he is, and the less informed about the worldview that he is criticizing. Men put their names on typeset nonsense in the hope that their efforts will pass for responsible criticism of Christian Reconstruction. Unfortunately, in their theologically and educationally limited Christian circles, it very often does pass for responsible criticism. The Christian reading public on the whole still moves its collective lips when it reads. Jim Bakker didn't get where he is today by appealing to sophisticated people. Neither did Hal Lindsey.

These critics do not understand or respect the enormous moral and intellectual burden associated with the printed page. When I write, I do so in constant fear of including an erroneous footnote reference or date, let alone some obvious misrepresentation of another person's intellectual position. But our critics are so sure that they are doing God's work that such things as getting their opponents' positions straight are regarded as minor details not worth bothering about. The Ninth Commandment means little to them. Polemics does. They would rather impress their poorly informed readers than present serious theoretical or practical objections to our position.

Question: How should we Reconstructionists answer them? Should we answer them at all? If we refuse to answer them, what are the likely consequences? Will a challenge from us be viewed as unchristian? Will silence be interpreted as a sign of weakness, both by our opponents and our followers?

Answering Fools

Answer not a fool according to his folly, lest thou also be like unto him (Proverbs 26:4).

Answer a fool according to his folly, lest he be wise in his own conceit (Proverbs 26:5).

Well, which is it? Answer the fool or remain silent? Or is there a third alternative?

These are probably the two most visibly contradictory verses in the Bible, yet Proverbs lists them one after the other without explanation. It can hardly be because the author somehow failed to notice that they are visibly contradictory. There has to be another explanation.

First, I do not think they are antithetical in the way that the familiar English proverbs, "Out of sight, out of mind" and "absence makes the heart grow fonder," are antithetical. I think they deal with two different situations. The trouble is, we do not know for certain what these situations are. We have to do our best to figure out the intention of the author by a careful investigation of his language, in order to discover what the fundamental differentiating factor is.

Second, the two proverbs have a single underlying message: *in this life we must deal with fools.* We are required to recognize them as fools. Developing the ability to evaluate people biblically is fundamental to wisdom: distinguishing the fools from other kinds of critics.

In one of the most important postmillennial passages in Scripture, Isaiah 32, we are given this prophecy regarding the coming millennial era of blessings: "The vile person shall be no more called liberal, nor the churl said to be bountiful" (Isa. 32:5). In our day, as in Isaiah's day, vile people are called liberal. I offer as a classic recent example the defensive responses of the highly paid functionaries of America's National Endowment of the Arts. Critics had identified as reprehensible such taxpayer-financed "works of art" as the "piss Christ": a photograph of a crucifix in a glass case filled with urine. (Who says the U.S. government cannot lawfully use tax money — $15,000 — to promote religious symbols? The symbols just have to be submerged in urine first.) When U.S. Senator Jesse Helms protested this use of taxpayers' money, he was liberally attacked in the liberal press as a censor and potential book-burner. Who is the liberal? Who is the churl? God tells us to make such distinctions.

Avoiding Folly

The differentiating factor in the two proverbs is the spiritual condition of the responder. "Answer not a fool according to his folly, lest thou also be like unto him" (Proverbs 26:4). Any Christian who has a tendency toward foolishness — shooting from the lip, for example — should keep his mouth tightly shut (Proverbs 17:28). If the churl is sarcastic, the targeted victim should not be sarcastic. This strategy, by the way, is a very good debate technique. It may be that the most important public debate of modern times was lost because an anti-Christian honored this rule, and his Christian opponent didn't.

The story comes down to us of a crucial 20-minute debate at Oxford University in 1860 between Bishop Samuel Wilberforce and Thomas Huxley. The subject was Darwinian evolution, a theory first presented to the public in 1858 with zero effect,[4] and presented again the following year in *The Origin of Species* with revolutionary effect. (The book and its sequel offered the most important intellectual defense of racism ever written; they laid the theoretical foundations of modern racist theory.)[5] Huxley was taking Darwin's place at the podium, as he did for the remainder of Darwin's life. Darwin never appeared in public debate; this legendary hypochondriac avoided all such distasteful confrontations.[6] But Huxley became a mighty representa-

---

4. In a co-authored scholarly essay (with Alfred R. Wallace).

5. Its subtitle is *The Preservation of Favored Races in the Struggle for Life*. We learn in his *Descent of Man* (1871) of the "mongrel population of Negroes and Portuguese" (Modern Library edition, p. 535) and of the fact that Negroes make excellent musicians in civilized societies, "although in their native countries they rarely practice anything that we should consider music" (pp. 878-79). All that is missing is a discussion of their natural rhythm.

6. Perhaps he was sicker than we think. This, at least, is the theory of John P. Koster in his book, *The Atheist Syndrome* (Brentwood, Tennessee: Wolgemuth & Hyatt, 1989), ch. 3.

tive.[7] He became known as Darwin's Bulldog.

Wilberforce, Bishop of Oxford, son of the great Christian social activist William Wilberforce, was not a scientist, yet he agreed on a few days' notice to debate the man who would develop and promote the Darwinian position tirelessly over the next generation. Presenting his 10-minute negative case first, the Bishop referred to Darwin's theory of mankind's simian ancestors, and then he made a seemingly clever remark to Huxley, asking him whether it was through his grandmother or his grandfather that he traced his simian ancestry. Huxley is said to have turned to a colleague and said, "The Lord hath delivered him into mine hands." Huxley took the podium and declared that he would not be ashamed to have a monkey for his ancestor, but he would be "ashamed to be connected with a man who used great gifts to obscure the truth."

This story comes to us from *The Macmillan Magazine*, published almost 40 years after the event, in an article called "A Grandmother's Tales." It was hardly a primary source document. We need not accept it as a faithful account of what happened. Nevertheless, it has come down to us as a true account of what took place. Listen to a modern historian's summary of what happened, and bear in mind that this account is accepted as fact by most historians:

> The sensation was immense. A hostile audience accorded him nearly as much applause as the Bishop had received. One lady, employing an idiom now lost, expressed her sense of intellectual crisis by fainting. The Bishop had suffered a sudden and involuntary martyrdom, perishing in the diverted avalanches of his own blunt ridicule. Huxley had committed forensic murder with a wonderful artistic simplicity, grinding orthodoxy between the facts and the supreme Victorian value of truth-telling.[8]

---

7. Huxley had become a Darwinist after having been sent a copy of *Origin* to review in the London *Times*. He was the second reviewer to be asked to review it. The first reviewer had sent it back, claiming that he did not have sufficient knowledge of the field. What if the first reviewer had reviewed it? Would Huxley and his famous descendants have made a difference in history?

8. William Irvine, *Apes, Angels, and Victorians: The Story of Darwin, Huxley, and Evolution* (New York: McGraw-Hill, 1955), p. 7.

Huxley did not answer Wilberforce according to the Bishop's folly. He did answer him, however. Whatever else he actually said in those ten minutes is long forgotten. It was probably forgotten by the next day. What was remembered was his effective countering of the Bishop's failure to grasp the vulnerability of an overly clever sarcastic remark. Sometimes it is better to play the wounded lamb than to play the wounded water buffalo, let alone the clever comic.

Do not answer a fool according to his folly. Except, of course, when you should.

Knocking the Stuffings Out of a Stuffed Shirt

"Answer a fool according to his folly, lest he be wise in his own conceit" (Proverbs 26:5). There are times when a direct response is just what the doctor ordered. You can legitimately use ridicule in order to identify the ridiculous. This is Solomon's implicit advice, and it was Augustine's explicit advice.[9] Nevertheless, you have to know how and when to exercise this skill. You must also calculate the risk. Bishop Wilberforce apparently neglected to do either.

What I have learned over the years is that we Christian Reconstructionists are constantly confronting people with minimal intellectual abilities and minimal professional training, as well as (very occasionally) people with considerable intellectual abilities who have decided to rush into print without first doing their homework. They are not the type of fool identified in the Bible: people who have said in their hearts that there is no God (Psalm 14:1). Darwin was a fool. Huxley was a fool. Marx was a fool. Freud was a fool. Our published critics, in contrast, are for the most part just not very bright. And when they are bright, they have been lazy. They let their less intellectually gifted peers do their initial homework for them; then they cite as authoritative these half-baked published reports.[10] It is wiser to

---

9. *City of God*, XVIII:49.

10. An example of this is provided by Dr. Peter Masters, who occupies Charles Spurgeon's pulpit. Dr. Masters promotes the book by House and Ice, *Dominion Theology: Blessing or Curse?*, as if Bahnsen and Gentry had not demolished it in *House Divided*. See

do your own homework; that way, you avoid sticking your finger (or worse) into a Reconstructionist buzz saw.

There is another aspect of the critics that must be confronted. Some of them really are intellectually corrupt. They lie. They cheat. They steal (other people's footnotes). Hal Lindsey, who multiplies ex-wives the way Reconstructionists multiply books, is one such critic. They have adopted this rule: "Thou shalt not bear false witness, except against other Christians."

Dealing With Lightweights

Actually, these people are easy to handle. In the summer of 1989, Lindsey's book, *The Road to Holocaust,* appeared. The book accuses Reconstructionists and all other non-dispensationalists of anti-Semitism. If you are not a premillennial dispensationalist, Lindsey writes, you are a latent anti-semite. To say that this thesis is absurd is not doing it justice. It really is one of the stupidest Christian books ever published, in a field in which there is heavy competition. The book did not achieve much success, although a paperback version is now available, one which Lindsey refused to revise, even when he knew that he had spelled people's names incorrectly and had made other equally obvious misstatements of fact.

How did we deal with him? First, his publisher (Bantam) erred in releasing the book a month early, in June of 1989, instead of July, as Bantam had previously announced in trade publication advertising that it would. This was a major mistake. The Christian Bookseller Association's summer convention was scheduled for July. So, with his book in our hands in June, we wrote a 75-page book in response, had it typeset, printed, and delivered to the CBA convention on the day it opened.[11] We had previously rented a book table there. We then handed out hundreds of copies of the book free of charge. We de-fused Lindsey's book before it hit most Christian book stores.

---

the two-page promotion of the book in Masters' critical essay, "World Dominion: The High Ambition of Reconstruction," *Sword & Trowel* (May 24, 1990), pp. 19-20.

11. Gary DeMar and Peter J. Leithart, *The Legacy of Hatred Continues* (Tyler, Texas: Institute for Christian Economics, 1989).

Was Lindsey upset? I think so. He indicated as much at the convention, as did his outraged secretary. He had not understood our mastery of the wonders of microcomputer technology. More to the point, he had never taken on anyone in print with academic training in his whole career. He simply cannot "duke it out" intellectually with the big boys, which is why he refuses to debate any Christian Reconstructionist in public. He got his head handed to him, but only a few Reconstructionists know of *The Legacy of Hatred Continues*. He prefers to keep his wounds relatively private. (He may also suspect that the very first question I would ask him in any public debate is this: "On what legal basis did each of your wives gain her divorce?")[12] Unlike Dave Hunt, who really is a glutton for punishment, Hal Lindsey knows that he was beaten, and beaten soundly. He has not written a reply. He has not revised his book. If he does reply in print, we will respond again, but in far greater detail. He knows this. So far, he has confined his comments to local radio talk shows, where we have difficulty calling in, although on one occasion, Gary DeMar did get through. Was Lindsey surprised! The show was being broadcast locally in Texas, and DeMar was in Atlanta. (A local listener had tipped off DeMar.)

Here is my strategy at ICE. Every critic who writes a book-length criticism of Christian Reconstruction gets a book-length reply within six months, if his book was not self-published. This is guaranteed. Our reply may be released within three months. In Hal Lindsey's case, it took only 30 days. If the critic replies to us in another book, he will get another book-length response. In the case of Westminster Theological Seminary's remarkably mediocre and unfocused book, which took the sixteen authors about five years to get into print, we produced three

---

12. Some readers may wonder why I keep returning to this marital fact of Hal Lindsey's life. I do so because he holds the public office of minister of the gospel. The Bible is very clear about the requirements of this office: a man is not to serve as an elder unless he is the husband of one wife (I Tim. 3:2). This does *not* mean "one wife at a time." Unless he brought biblical grounds of divorce against his ex-wives, and then proved these charges in a church court, Lindsey is an adulterer, according to Jesus (Matt. 5:31-32). But adultery has become a way of life in modern Christian circles, so my accusation is shrugged off as bad etiquette on my part. It is in such a moral environment that a man such as Lindsey can become a national spiritual leader.

volumes of replies within a few months.[13] Microchip technology and a comprehensive paradigm make this possible. I had one chapter written and typeset in one day and the book to the printer's within three weeks: only two weeks after the Westminster book was officially released to the book-buying public.[14]

Remember the tar baby in the Uncle Remus story?[15] That is my working model. Punch me once, and you won't get out. This strategy works. It is costly, but it works. When the critic wearies of the exchange and fails to reply to our latest book-length reply, we then tell the world: "See, he couldn't answer us. He clearly has no intellectually defensible position." Tactic or not, it really is true: the critics cannot defend their position. It just takes some of them a long time to figure this out. There are some amazingly slow learners out there.

Just how seriously should we take critics who begin their articles, as both Richard John Neuhaus and Errol Hulse began theirs, with the frank admission that we Reconstructionists have written too much for any critic to be expected to read?[16] Then they attacked us anyway!

As the Critics Multiply

Consider Richard John Neuhaus. He is liberal theologically, but he has the reputation of being somewhat conservative culturally. He is also, by neo-evangelical standards, a scholar. (At the time he wrote his critical essay, he was still in the neo-evangelical camp. A few months later, he joined the Roman Catholic Church.) Previously, he had been unceremoniously booted out of his former employer's New York offices.[17] In *First Things'*

---

13. William S. Barker and W. Robert Godfrey (eds.), *Theonomy: A Reformed Critique* (Grand Rapids, Michigan: Zondervan Academie, 1990). The replies are: Gary North, *Westminster's Confession*, Greg Bahnsen, *No Other Standard*, and North (ed.) *Theonomy: An Informed Critique.*

14. North, *Millennialism and Social Theory* (Tyler, Texas: Institute for Christian Economics, 1990), ch. 9: "The Sociology of Suffering."

15. He became the glue bunny — non-racial — in a recent Disney book version.

16. Richard John Neuhaus, "Why Wait for the Kingdom?: The Theonomist Temptation," *First Things* 3 (May 1990), p. 14; Errol Hulse, "Reconstructionism, Restorationism or Puritanism," *Reformation Today*, No. 116 (July-Aug. 1990), p. 25.

17. The Rockford Foundation.

third issue, he attacked Christian Reconstructionism. His attack was not a book; it was merely a short essay in a new, unknown journal, written by a man in theological transition. It had very little impact even before he switched churches.

Here is our problem. We freely acknowledge that Rev. Neuhaus is a literate man. He is vaguely conservative socially. He has his own small-circulation magazine. What is the proper response? Write a whole book? But hardly anyone in the evangelical Christian world has ever heard of him. Wouldn't a whole book be overkill?

Should we answer him line by line? Where? In a newsletter? This would be boring to most of our readers. Also, he is not exactly skating on thick theological ice. He calls us heretics, yet he himself does not believe that Jews need to accept Christ as Savior in order to be saved. Calling us heretics demonstrates, to put it bluntly, considerable *chutzpa* on his part.

A few of the more literate of our followers nevertheless worry about what Rev. Neuhaus has said. I received exactly one letter that asked, basically: "What do you say in response to Dr. Neuhaus?" Mainly I say this: I wrote a 700-page book refuting Neuhaus' civic theology of political pluralism, *Political Polytheism*. I specifically identified his position as intellectually and theologically indefensible, and showed why it is.[18] Did he respond to me in his 1990 article? Hardly; he did not refer once to the book. Just how seriously should I take Mr. Neuhaus? Not very.

Besides, how many Neuhauses are there in the world? How many Anson Shupes?[19] How many times must we answer the same unsubstantiated accusations, the same misrepresentations, and even the same misspellings, repeated endlessly? What profit is there in replying to people who freely admit — as Neuhaus admitted — that we Reconstructionists write too many books for them to read. They still go into print with their unsupported accusations.

Some of our followers have a bad case of "What have I gotten

---

18. North, *Political Polytheism*, ch. 2.

19. Anson Shupe, "Prophets of a Biblical America," *Wall Street Journal* (April 12, 1989).

myself into?" They are in tight little groups of antinomian pietists, and they have identified themselves as Reconstructionists.
Now the little group's spokesman has publicly called us heretical, or worse. What to do? They feel they must respond, but
they don't feel competent to do it. So, they expect one of us to
respond to the little group's critic. They see this as our duty.
They do not recognize that we are increasingly coming under
fire from late-responding leaders of lots of little groups. We
dare not waste time responding to every newsletter attack, yet
each member of each little fringe group expects us to respond.

Residents of Dispensational Ghettos

Those who have still not made the break from dispensationalist churches (mainly charismatics who have become postmillennial) may even worry about what Dave Hunt has said recently, even though Mr. Hunt is arguably the world's second-
worst debater,[20] even though he has steadfastly refused to reply to two volumes of detailed material aimed directly at
him,[21] even though he is an accountant rather than a theologian, even though the man is too lazy to provide indexes for his
books. I had one person write to me telling me that I just had
to write a reply to Hunt's *Whatever Happened to Heaven?*, as if
Gary DeMar's two volumes had not already publicly disembow-
eled Hunt. Why should I? It is not written only about Reconstruction. He refuses to respond to DeMar, just as Ronald Sider's second edition of *Rich Christians in an Age of Hunger* failed
to reply to David Chilton's *Productive Christians in an Age of
Guilt-Manipulators*. It should be clear to anyone who has read
both sides who won each of these debates. It was not our critics.
If they refuse to respond to our arguments, why is it our responsibility to repeat them again?

Ron Sider has had the wisdom to stop writing about world

---

20. After Tommy Ice. For proof, order a copy of the 1988 debate: Gary DeMar and
Gary North vs. Dave Hunt and Tommy Ice. Two audiotapes: $10; videotape: $30. Institute for Christian Economics, P. O. Box 8000, Tyler, TX 75711.

21. Gary DeMar and Peter J. Leithart, *The Reduction of Christianity: A Biblical Response
to Dave Hunt* (Ft. Worth, Texas: Dominion Pres, 1988); DeMar, *The Debate over Christian
Reconstruction* (Ft. Worth, Texas: Dominion Press, 1988).

hunger and the need for a "graduated tithe." He writes today mainly about the evils of abortion and homosexuality, which is why he has become a pariah among his former *Sojourner* colleagues. But Dave Hunt refuses to go away quietly. He writes his book-length dispensational tracts as if he had somewhere answered DeMar's point-by-point refutation. "Gary who?", he asks. He pretends that he was not repeatedly and in full public view taken apart theologically. He can get away with this only because his followers do not read serious books. Now he needs to answer the Passantinos' book, *Witch Hunt* (I suggested the title), which went through three printings in four months. I will not hold my breath waiting for his reply.

Dave Hunt's problem is that he is intellectually incompetent in matters of theology, a fact he freely attests to by his constant refrain during public debates when he is losing the argument: "I'm not a theologian, but. . . ." He surely isn't, no "buts" about it. He systematically refuses to respond, line by line, to our previous published criticisms of his "facts," his logic, and his outright lies.[22] What is our appropriate response? We have written two full-length books against him. He has yet to respond. What now?

I'll tell you what. We will go on down the road, presenting a comprehensive positive alternative to Hunt's ever-predicted, never-fulfilled rapture. The best defense is a good offense. Dave Hunt can't beat something with nothing. The best answer to bad negative theology is good positive theology. The best answer to historical despair is the gospel of Jesus Christ.

This Book Is Our Answer

In my section of this book, I stated the Christian Reconstructionist position on the kingdom of God in history, which is the major target of the critics. DeMar in his section answered eleven

---

22. I refer here to his retrospective misdating, in his newsletter, of the dates and circumstances of our request that he read *The Reduction of Christianity* and offer any rebuttals, a courtesy that he did not show his targets in *The Seduction of Christianity*. It was a courtesy that Ice and House also refused us, and which Hal Lindsey refused us, even when we asked to see their respective manuscripts. Who, I ask, are the "mean, vindictive, uncharitable" authors, and who are the victims?

of the most frequently asked questions about Christian Reconstruction. We have kept the book simple — so simple that even
a *Christianity Today* editor will be able to follow it.

It is our hope that readers will take these answers seriously.
It is also our hope that our future critics will think carefully
about these answers before going into print to tell people what
we believe. We exercise faith that they will do this. You know
what faith is: ". . . the substance of things hoped for, the evidence of things not seen" (Hebrews 11:1). After all, we are
postmillennialists. Optimism in the face of contrary recent evidence is basic to our eschatological perspective.

To all of our dedicated but nervous readers, we implore you
to make sure that before you get the heebie-jeebies the next
time you read some criticism of our movement in the pages of
yet another obscure little Christian newsletter or magazine,
written by someone who has yet to write his first book, you get
out your dog-eared copy of this book and see if the critic has
read it. See if he is responding to what we have written here.
See if he even knows what questions to ask.

Our critics so far have been utterly incompetent. How do I
know this? Because I know the "soft underbelly" of the Christian Reconstruction position. Every insider knows where the
weak chinks are in his movement's armor. The best test of a
critic's mastery of his opponent's system is his ability to go
straight for his opponent's weakest spots. He will not be side-
tracked. If he can do this, he will draw blood. He will create
consternation and confusion within his opponent's camp. This
has not happened so far, yet Rushdoony's *Institutes of Biblical
Law* was published in 1973, and Bahnsen's *Theonomy in Christian
Ethics* appeared in 1977. If the critics had answers, we would
have heard by now.

Our critics have been remarkably easy to refute, usually by
citing verbatim what we have already published that they never
read or at least forgot. It is safe to say that they have not known
what they were doing. Critics who expose themselves publicly to
refutations as thorough and as specific as DeMar and Leithart's
The Reduction of Christianity or Bahnsen and Gentry's *House
Divided* need not be taken seriously.

Why Are We So Confident?

Because we have already won the intellectual battle. Our critics waited too long to respond. When a movement has been given time to get over a hundred books and scholarly journals into print, it is too late for its critics to *begin* responding. The critics now have too much to read, and they refuse to do the necessary work. When the new movement has already made converts in the major rival organizations, in some cases the next generation of leaders, it is way too late. When the critics keep repeating as the gospel truth both facts and opinions that have been refuted, line by line, in previous Reconstructionist responses, usually in book-long responses, the critics are admitting in public two things: (1) they have no answers to our position and (2) they have not bothered to read our detailed replies. This is the case today. When the critics think they can defeat the new movement by attacking the leaders' styles or personalities rather than their ideas, it is way, way too late. The main theological battle is already over. We are now in the "mopping-up" phase.

There is something else. Our ideas are now in wide circulation. They no longer depend on the skills or integrity of any one person. We Christian Reconstructionists practice what we preach. We are a decentralized movement. We cannot be taken out by a successful attack on any one of our institutional strongholds or any one of our spokesmen. Our authors may come and go (and have), but our basic worldview is now complete. We have laid down the foundations of a paradigm shift.

Our critics are so deeply committed to the prevailing Establishment — political and religious pluralism — that when the humanist order self-destructs, it will take down the critics. They have all built their institutions on the sand of humanist social theory and humanist social order.[23] What today appears to be their great advantage — their acceptance of and by the prevailing social order — will become a distinct liability in and after a major crisis. That crisis is coming, long before Jesus does.

---

23. North, *Millennialism and Social Theory.*

Running for Cover

When Wayne House refused to debate Greg Bahnsen in public, having bragged previously that none of us would meet him in a formal debate, and after he left the prestige of Dallas Theological Seminary for the obscurity of Western Baptist College, it was obvious who had won the theological debate. Neither House nor Ice is ready today to defend himself in formal debate from the devastating responses in *House Divided*. They are both back-peddling (e.g., in their traditional dispensational assertion, known by every church historian to be false, that postmillennialism was invented by Unitarian Daniel Whitby in the early 1700's, despite the obvious postmillennialism of Puritanism in the 1600's). Dispensational theology is in sad shape. Worse: it is in terminal shape.

John Walvoord's remarkably embarrassing attempt to respond to *House Divided*[24] only adds to our conviction that dispensationalism is an intellectually dead system whose own supporters refuse to defend its details in public. They are now redesigning the whole system. When the leading theologian of the movement (Walvoord) says in print that an entire book is needed to reply to *House Divided*, which is itself a response to the one attempted defense of dispensational theology in a generation,[25] and then says he does not intend to write such a book, you know the dispensational movement is in its final stages. The movement has yet to respond to O. T. Allis' 1945 book, *Prophecy and the Church*. Wait until John Gerstner's gigantic critique becomes available! Dispensationalism is now intellectually terminal. Rigor mortis has visibly set in. It is only a matter of time before it becomes institutionally terminal. When faith in Marxism faded in the Soviet Union, the system was doomed. So shall dispensationalism fade. Ideas do have consequences. A headless movement cannot survive long.

---

24. *Bibliotheca Sacra* (July-Sept. 1990). For my response, see "First, the Head Goes Soft," *Dispensationalism in Transition*, III (Aug. 1990).

25. H. Wayne House and Thomas D. Ice, *Dominion Theology: Blessing or Curse?* (Portland, Oregon: Multnomah Press, 1988).

Unserious Spokesmen

A serious author takes care to get things correct. I do not want to make mistakes in my writing. A critic may point out a serious error, or even a messed-up footnote. I always revise my books when they are reprinted. I am serious. Our critics seldom are. When Hal Lindsey repeatedly attacks books written by a "John Rousas Rushdoony," when the man's name is Rousas John Rushdoony, he shows that he is not serious. When he allows a paperback version of *The Road to Holocaust* to appear a year later without any corrections, despite our detailed response, he shows that he is dishonest. We knew that from the beginning. Yet this man is the spokesman for an entire theological movement, rivaled only by Dave Hunt. Dispensationalism is no longer a serious theological movement.

I can appreciate a diatribe that draws blood, having written my share of them. I am a scholar by training, and I respect good scholarship even among my ideological foes. There is so little competent writing out there that I am always happy to read something accurate, even if it is critical of me. But what is obvious to all of us in the leadership of this little movement is that the most competent of the theologians and scholars who do not share our perspective are either content to remain silent or have themselves quietly adopted considerable portions of our position. In some cases, they have become Reconstructionist "moles."

I remember in the mid-1970's when a few pastors in the Presbyterian Church of America approached F. N. Lee, the denomination's most articulate and scholarly theologian, asking him to refute Rushdoony's *Institutes of Biblical Law*. Lee was already a postmillennial theonomist by that time. (Rushdoony had persuaded Craig Press to publish Lee's *Communist Eschatology*.) This sort of thing has happened more than once. The critics call in their big guns, and the big guns then proceed to blow a hole in the critics' defenses. It must be very discouraging to them. If it isn't, it should be.

Here is the plight of our institutional opponents: *we keep picking off the best and the brightest of their disciples.* The best and the brightest people want to make a difference in history, and they are attracted to a theological position that teaches that Christianity can and will transform world civilization. They are not instinctively attracted to eschatological positions that proclaim progressive Christian impotence as a way of life.[26] When they see a theological alternative, they adopt it.

Conclusion

It boils down to this: *our critics can't beat something with nothing*. We have offered, and continue to update, a consistent, comprehensive, Bible-based alternative to a collapsing humanist order. What do our critics offer as their workable alternative? If it is just another round of "Come quickly, Lord Jesus," then they are not offering much. That prayer is legitimate only when the one who prays it is willing to add this justification for his prayer: "Because your church has completed her assigned task faithfully (Matthew 28:18-20), and your kingdom has become manifest to many formerly lost souls." This is surely not a prayer that is appropriate today. (It was appropriate for John because he was praying for the *covenantal coming* of Jesus Christ, manifested by destruction of the Old Covenant order. His prayer was answered within a few months: the destruction of Jerusalem.)[27]

One last note: for those who still think my style is intemperate and unnecessarily personal, please read Mark Edwards' two scholarly books on Luther's polemics. Get a feel for what a master polemicist and pamphleteer did, and why he successfully launched the Protestant Reformation. Then re-read Calvin's *Institutes*. When it comes to invective, I am a piker.[28]

---

26. North, *Millennialism and Social Theory*.

27. David Chilton, *The Days of Vengeance: An Exposition of the Book of Revelation* (Ft. Worth, Texas: Dominion Press, 1987); Kenneth L. Gentry, Jr., *Before Jerusalem Fell: Dating the Book of Revelation* (Tyler, Texas: Institute for Christian Economics, 1989).

28. Mark U. Edwards, Jr., *Luther and the False Brethren* (Stanford, California: Stanford University Press, 1975); *Luther's Last Battles: Politics and Polemics, 1531-46* (Ithaca, New York: Cornell University Press, 1983).

CONCLUSION

Gary DeMar

CONCLUSION

One of the recurring criticisms of Christian Reconstruction-ism is that it will not work. In fact, we're told that it has been tried, and it didn't work. This is a strange objection since Reconstructionists are often accused of developing a new system. How can we be accused of developing a new theology and at the same time be told that what we espouse was tried in the past but ended in utter failure? If it was tried and failed, then what we are advocating has been advocated before. As has been demonstrated, Christian Reconstructionist distinctives have been around for quite some time and have always been within the circle of orthodoxy, closer to the center than much of what today passes as orthodoxy. The newness of the position is in its forthrightness and consistency, not in its doctrinal formulations.

But was it a failure? Certainly it was if you compare its past results with utopian dreams of a sinless world. But it was a resounding success if you compare it to today's decadent culture. It is because of the abandonment of Christian Reconstructionist distinctives that our nation is sinking in the moral abyss. Other competing religious systems, with comprehensive worldviews that affect this world, are replacing a once vibrant Christianity.

A Gospel for Adults

Consider that the average age of a convert to Christianity is sixteen, while the average age of a convert to Islam is thirty-one! Why the difference? One of the main reasons for the differences is the application of the two religions to the present circumstances of individual believers in a world of disorder. The older a person gets, the more responsibilities he or she has. For centuries the church addressed the areas of law, education, and politics, to name only a few. The Bible was very much a "this-worldly religion." Sadly, this no longer seems to be the case. Islam, as a rival faith, has supplanted Christianity in the vital area of a this-world application of God's Word. Secularism, previously Christianity's greatest nemesis, has been doing it for centuries in the name of "enlightenment." Islam with its emphasis on imminence and practicality is growing in influence.

> Islam is practical. It is considered a this-worldly religion in contrast to Christianity, which is perceived as abstract in the extreme. Muhammad left his followers a political, social, moral, and economic program founded on religious precepts. Jesus, however, is said to have advocated no such program; it is claimed that the New Testament is so preoccupied with his imminent return that it is impractical for modern life.[1]

Christians have forsaken God's Bible-revealed law as the universal standard for righteousness in the areas of economics, education, politics, and the judicial system. Instead, they have adopted escapism (Jesus could return at any moment) and a form of ethical pluralism (the Bible is only one law among many from which to choose). Ethical pluralism means that *all moral views are valid except any moral view that does not believe that all moral views are valid*. So, Christianity as the Bible conceives of it is not an acceptable ethical standard on how the world should work. The absolutist position that the Reconstructionists take is anathema to the modern mind, and its rejection of ethical pluralism makes it the scourge of the Christian community.

With pluralism you get an "anything goes" ethic. Since most Americans (and most Christians) believe that ethical pluralism is legitimate, they often remain silent in the midst of the storm of moral anarchy that is battering our nation. They have been propagandized into believing that this is the American way. Bob Greene, a syndicated columnist with the *Chicago Tribune*, was shocked when he realized that millions of parents sat and

---

1. Larry Postan, "The Adult Gospel," *Christianity Today* (August 20, 1990), p. 24.

watched a Madonna concert originating from France and tele-cast on HBO.

> What is amazing is not what came across the screen. We live in an anything-goes age, and to say the concert was shocking would be incorrect, because society today is basically unshockable. No, the show's content, although witless and purposely vulgar, was not the surprising thing. The surprising thing was that an insignificant number of those parents called HBO to object to what was shown. Apparently the parents of America have totally given up on hoping that they can control the entertainment environment their children are exposed to.[2]

But it's far worse than parents allowing their children to watch a Madonna concert on HBO. "It's about a country that has been so beaten down by a lessening of standards for what is accept-able in public and what isn't that something like the Madonna concert can be telecast to millions of families, and it doesn't even cause a ripple of controversy or complaint."[3] The citizenry has been propagandized into believing that morals are solely a personal matter. What used to be consider gross evils are now accepted as legitimate alternative lifestyles that ought to be sanctioned by law.

> The legalization of abortion.
> The decriminalization of homosexuality.
> Self-professed homosexuals running for political office and winning.
> Churches ordaining homosexuals.
> The abolition of the Christian religion from public schools and nearly every vestige of American life.
> Pornographic displays of so-called "homoerotic art" paid for by tax dollars.
> The rewriting of textbooks to teach that capitalism and communism are legitimate economic options for nations.

In addition, there is so much anti-Christian bigotry and de-

---

2. Bob Greene, "Madonna Concert Shows What We've Become," *Marietta Daily Journal* (August 15, 1990), p. 7A.
3. *Idem.*

bauchery in our nation that it would be impossible to come up with a comprehensive list. But consider how far we have fallen as a nation when the ACLU sues a North Carolina judge because he starts each court session with prayer, a brief plea to God for justice.[4] These are the offending words:

> O Lord, our God, our Father in Heaven, we pray this morning that you will place your divine guiding hand on this courtroom and that with your mighty outstretched arm you will protect the innocent, give justice to those who have been harmed, and mercy to us all. Let truth be heard and wisdom be reflected in the light of your presence here with us today. Amen.

If there is no God there is no law. How can a judge render a just decision if there is no fixed standard of justice? Since the courts have consistently voted to uphold Darwinian evolutionism, how can there ever be an ethical absolute?

Florida no longer requires Notaries to affirm "so help me God" on their written oath of office. Presidents since George Washington have taken their oath of office with a hand on an open Bible. They end their oath with "so help me God." The Rev. Gerard LaCerra, chancellor of the Archdiocese of Miami, understands the implications of such an action: "What are we supposed to base our commitments on if something like this is removed? The State?"[5]

A third-grader's valentines were censored because they contained references to Jesus Christ. School officials changed their minds after learning they could be sued over the matter. Charles Colson recounts a message he heard at a meeting of 100 evangelical leaders and political activists who assembled to respond to the rising tides of anti-Christian bigotry.

> A friend I greatly respect was speaking, citing one example after another. They were bizarre stories: like the high-school students

---

4. For a critique of the ACLU written by a Christian Reconstructionist, see George Grant, *Trial and Error: The American Civil Liberties Union and Its Impact on Your Family* (Brentwood, TN: Wolgemuth & Hyatt, 1989).

5. " 'God' removed from notaries' oath," *The Kansas City Star* (February 18, 1990), p. 2A.

informed that they could not wear their fellowship of Christian Athletes T-shirts to school (though satanic T-shirts were okay); or the court decision forcing Zion, Illinois, to change its 88-year-old city seal because it included religious symbols. Or the fact that *The Last Temptation of Christ* was shown in an Albuquerque high school, while the Genesis Project's *Jesus* film, whose script is all Scripture, would not be allowed near school grounds.[6]

The failure is Christians' refusal to believe that the public arena is a place of ministry and that God's law has application there. Christians have failed to be advocates of righteousness in areas beyond personal and familial piety. There has been a steady erosion among evangelicals and fundamentalists over the adoption of a comprehensive biblical worldview.

Our nation was founded on the belief that religious man undergirds a society. "In the last resort, our civilization is what we think and believe. The externals matter, but they cannot stand if the inner convictions which originally produced them have vanished."[7]

Government is only as good as the people who create it. Family, church, and civil governments reflect self-government, whether good or bad. At the civil level, a nation gets what it votes for. Civil government, no matter how righteously conceived, cannot make people better. Leadership, like water, rises to its own level, the righteousness of the people. The maintenance of good government is dependent on good people.

A nation will exhibit either self-government or the State will implement tyranny. On May 28th, 1849, Robert C. Winthrop (1809-1894), descendant of Governor John Winthrop, first governor of Massachusetts Bay Colony, addressed the Annual Meeting of the Massachusetts Bible Society in Boston showing that there is no third way.

All societies of men must be governed in some way or other. The less they may have of stringent State Government, the more they must have of individual self-government. The less they rely on

---

6. Charles Colson, "From a Moral Majority to a Persecuted Minority," *Christianity Today* (May 14, 1990), p. 80.
7. Paul Johnson, *The Enemies of Society* (New York: Atheneum, 1977), p. 117.

public law or physical force, the more they must rely on private moral restraint. Men, in a word, must necessarily be controlled, either by a power within them, or by a power without them; either by the word of God, or by the strong arm of man; either by the Bible, or by the bayonet. It may do for other countries and other governments to talk about the State supporting religion. Here, under our own free institutions, it is Religion which must support the State.[8]

"Choose for yourselves today whom you will serve. . ." (Joshua 24:15).

---

8. Cited in Verna M. Hall, ed., *The Christian History of the American Revolution* (San Francisco, CA: Foundation for American Christian Eduction, 1976), p. 20.

BOOKS FOR FURTHER READING AND STUDY

BOOKS FOR FURTHER READING AND STUDY

No book as brief as this one can do justice to the full range of issues raised by the Christian Reconstruction perspective. Critics of the Reconstruction movement have had a tendency to dismiss its main features as if it were somehow deviant theologically. Yet the critics are not always aware of the large body of scholarly literature, not only within Christian Reconstructionism, but also belonging to the Reconstructionists' theological predecessors.

There has been a distinct tendency for those holding dispensational and amillennial views to dismiss postmillennialism as a dead system. For decades, each has spent most of its time and energy attacking the other. The arrival of theonomic postmillennialism (Rushdoony, Bahnsen, and Lee) and later of five-point covenantal postmillennialism (Sutton and North) caught both rival groups by surprise.

Because there is an extensive body of literature on Calvinism and predestination, we have not included that list here. A basic work is Loraine Boettner's *The Reformed Doctrine of Predestination* (1933). Martin Luther's classic, *The Bondage of the Will* (1525), is still worth reading, especially by Lutherans.

The easiest introduction to the basic theological issues of Christian Reconstruction is Gary North's *Unconditional Surrender: God's Program for Victory*, first published in 1981, with a revised edition in 1988 (Institute for Christian Economics).

Theonomic Studies in Biblical Law

Bahnsen, Greg L. *By This Standard: The Authority of God's Law Today*. Tyler, TX: Institute for Christian Economics, 1985. An introduction to the issues of biblical law in society.

Bahnsen, Greg L. *Theonomy and Its Critics*. Tyler, TX: Institute for Christian Economics, 1991. A detailed response to the major criticisms of theonomy, focusing on *Theonomy: A Reformed Critique*, a collection of essays written by the faculty of Westminster Theological Seminary (Zondervan/Academie, 1990).

Bahnsen, Greg L. *Theonomy in Christian Ethics*. Nutley, New Jersey: Presbyterian and Reformed, (1977) 1984. A detailed apologetic of the idea of continuity in biblical law.

DeMar, Gary. *God and Government*, 3 vols. Brentwood, Tennessee: Wolgemuth & Hyatt, 1990. An introduction to the fundamentals of biblical government, emphasizing self-government.

Jordan, James. *The Law of the Covenant: An Exposition of Exodus 21-23*. Tyler, TX: Institute for Christian Economics, 1984. A clear introduction to the issues of the case laws of the Old Testament.

North, Gary. *The Dominion Covenant: Genesis*. Tyler, TX: Institute for Christian Economics, (1982) 1987. A study of the economic laws of the Book of Genesis.

North, Gary. *Moses and Pharaoh: Dominion Religion vs. Power Religion*. Tyler, TX: Institute for Christian Economics, 1985. A study of the economic issues governing the Exodus.

North, Gary. *Political Polytheism: The Myth of Pluralism*. Tyler,

TX: Institute for Christian Economics, 1989. A 700-page critique of the myth of neutrality: in ethics, social criticism, U.S. history, and the U.S. Constitution.

North, Gary. *The Sinai Strategy: Economics and the Ten Commandments*. Tyler, TX: Institute for Christian Economics, 1986. A study of the five-point covenantal structure (1-5, 6-10) of the Ten Commandments. Includes a detailed study of why the Old Covenant's capital sanction no longer aplies to sabbath-breaking.

North, Gary. *Tools of Dominion: The Case Laws of Exodus*. Tyler, TX: Institute for Christian Economics, 1990. A 1,300-page examination of the economics of Exodus 21-23.

Rushdoony, Rousas John. *The Institutes of Biblical Law*. Nutley, New Jersey: Presbyterian and Reformed, 1973. The foundational work of the Christian Reconstruction movement. It subsumes all of biblical law under the Ten Commandments. It includes three appendixes by Gary North.

Sutton, Ray R. *That You May Prosper: Dominion By Covenant*. Tyler, TX: Institute for Christian Economics, 1987. A detailed study of the five points of the biblical covenant model, applying them to church, State, and family.

General Works on Eschatology

Clouse, Robert G., ed. *The Meaning of the Millennium: Four Views*. Downers Grove, IL: InterVarsity Press, 1977. Advocates of the four major views of the millennium present each case.

Erickson, Millard J. *Contemporary Options in Eschatology: A Study of the Millennium*. Grand Rapids, MI: Baker, 1977. Examines modern views of eschatology: millennium, and tribulation.

Works Defending Postmillennialism or Preterism

Adams, Jay. *The Time Is At Hand*. Phillipsburg, NJ: Presbyterian and Reformed, 1966. Amillennial, preterist interpretation of Revelation.

Alexander, J. A. *The Prophecies of Isaiah, A Commentary on Matthew* (complete through chapter 16), *A Commentary on Mark*, and *A Commentary on Acts*. Various Publishers. Nineteenth-century Princeton Old Testament scholar.

Boettner, Loraine. *The Millennium*. Revised edition. Phillipsburg, NJ: Presbyterian and Reformed, (1957) 1984. Classic study of millennial views, and defense of postmillennialism.

Brown, John. *The Discourses and Sayings of Our Lord* and commentaries on *Romans, Hebrews*, and *1 Peter*. Various Publishers. Nineteenth-century Scottish Calvinist.

Campbell, Roderick. *Israel and the New Covenant*. Tyler, TX: Geneva Divinity School Press, (1954) 1981. Neglected study of principles for interpretation of prophecy; examines themes in New Testament biblical theology.

Chilton, David. *The Days of Vengeance: An Exposition of the Book of Revelation*. Ft. Worth, TX: Dominion Press. Massive postmillennial commentary on Revelation.

Chilton, David. *The Great Tribulation*. Ft. Worth, TX: Dominion Press, 1987. Popular exegetical introduction to postmillennial interpretation.

Chilton, David. *Paradise Restored: A Biblical Theology of Dominion*. Ft. Worth, TX: Dominion Press, 1985. Study of prophetic symbolism, the coming of the Kingdom, and the book of Revelation.

Clark, David S. *The Message from Patmos: A Postmillennial Commentary on the Book of Revelation*. Grand Rapids, MI: Baker, 1989. Brief preterist and postmillennial commentary.

Davis, John Jefferson. *Christ's Victorious Kingdom: Postmillennialism Reconsidered*. Grand Rapids, MI: Baker, 1986. Biblical and historical defense of postmillennialism.

DeMar, Gary and Peter Leithart. *The Reduction of Christianity: A Biblical Response to Dave Hunt*. Ft. Worth, TX: Dominion Press, 1988. Critique of Dave Hunt, and historical and biblical defense of postmillennialism.

Edwards, Jonathan. *The Works of Jonathan Edwards*. 2 volumes. Edinburgh: The Banner of Truth Trust, (1834) 1974. Volume 2 includes Edwards' "History of Redemption."

Gentry, Kenneth L. *The Beast of Revelation*. Tyler, TX: Institute for Christian Economics, 1989. Preterist study of the identity of the beast in Revelation.

Gentry, Kenneth L. *Before Jerusalem Fell*. Tyler, TX: Institute for Christian Economics, 1989. Exhaustively researched study on the dating of Revelation.

Henry, Matthew. *Matthew Henry's Commentary*. 6 volumes. New York: Fleming H. Revell, (1714). Popular commentary on the whole Bible.

Hodge, A. A. *Outlines of Theology*. Enlarged edition. London: The Banner of Truth Trust, (1879) 1972. Nineteenth-century introduction to systematic theology in question-and-answer form.

Hodge, Charles. *Systematic Theology*. 3 volumes. Grand Rapids, MI: Eerdmans, (1871-73) 1986. Old standard Reformed text; volume 3 includes extensive discussion of eschatology.

Kik, J. Marcellus. *An Eschatology of Victory*. N.p.: Presbyterian and Reformed, 1975. Exegetical studies of Matthew 24 and Revelation 20.

Murray, Iain. *The Puritan Hope: Revival and the Interpretation of Prophecy*. (Edinburgh: Banner of Truth, 1971). Historical study of postmillennialism in England and Scotland.

North, Gary, ed. *The Journal of Christian Reconstruction*, Symposium on the Millennium (Winter 1976-77). Historical and theological essays on postmillennialism.

North, Gary. *Millennialism and Social Theory*. Tyler, TX: Institute for Christian Economics, 1990. A study of the failure of premillennialism and amillennialism to deal with social theory.

Owen, John. *Works*, ed. William H. Goold. 16 volumes. Edinburgh: The Banner of Truth Trust, 1965. Seventeenth-century preacher and theologian; volume 8 includes several sermons on the Kingdom of God, and volume 9 contains a preterist sermon on 2 Peter 3.

Rushdoony, Rousas John. *God's Plan for Victory: The Meaning of Postmillennialism*. Fairfax, VA: Thoburn Press, 1977. Theological study of the implications of postmillennialism for economics, law, and reconstruction.

Rushdoony, Rousas John. *Thy Kingdom Come: Studies in Daniel and Revelation*. Phillipsburg, NJ: Presbyterian and Reformed, 1970. Exegetical studies in Daniel and Revelation, full of insightful comments on history and society.

Shedd, W. G. T. *Dogmatic Theology*. 3 volumes. Nashville, TN: Thomas Nelson, (1888) 1980. Nineteenth-century Reformed systematics text.

Strong, A. H. *Systematic Theology*. Baptist postmillennialist of late nineteenth and early twentieth centuries.

Sutton, Ray R. "Covenantal Postmillennialism," *Covenant Renewal* (February 1989). Discusses the difference between traditional Presbyterian postmillennialism and covenantal postmillennialism.

Terry, Milton S. *Biblical Apocalyptics: A Study of the Most Notable Revelations of God and of Christ*. Grand Rapids, MI: Baker, (1898) 1988. Nineteenth-century exegetical studies of prophetic passages in Old and New Testaments; includes a complete commentary on Revelation.

Postmillennialism and the Jews

De Jong, J. A. *As the Waters Cover the Sea: Millennial Expectations in the Rise of Anglo-American Missions 1640-1810*. Kampen: J. H. Kok, 1970. General history of millennial views; throughout mentions the importance of prophecies concerning the Jews.

DeMar, Gary and Peter Leithart. *The Legacy of Hatred Continues: A Response to Hal Lindsey's The Road to Holocaust* (Tyler, TX: Institute for Christian Economics, 1989. A brief but thorough refutation to Hal Lindsey's claim that all nondispensational eschatologies are anti-Semitic.

Fairbairn, Patrick. *The Prophetic Prospects of the Jews, or, Fairbairn vs. Fairbairn*. Grand Rapids, MI: Eerdmans, 1930. Nineteenth-century scholar Fairbairn changed his mind about the conversion of the Jews; this volume reproduces his early arguments for the historic postmillennial position, and his later arguments against it.

Schlissel, Steve and David Brown. *Hal Lindsey and the Restoration of the Jews*. Edmonton, Alberta, Canada: Still Waters Revival Books, 1990. A Jewish-born Reconstructionist pastor responds to Hal Lindsey's claim that Christian Reconstruction is anti-Semitic. Schlissel's work is combined with David Brown's work that demonstrates that *postmillennialism* is the "system of prophetic interpretation that historically furnished the Biblical basis for the most glorious future imaginable for the Jews!"

Sutton, Ray R. "A Postmillennial Jew (The Covenantal Structure of Romans 11)," *Covenant Renewal* (June 1989). Sutton has a conversation with a postmillennial Messianic Jew.

Sutton, Ray R. "Does Israel Have a Future?" *Covenant Renewal* (December 1988). Examines several different views of Israel's future, and argues for the covenantal view.

Toon, Peter, ed. *Puritans, the Millennium and the Future of Israel: Puritan Eschatology 1600-1660*. Cambridge: James Clarke, 1970. Detailed historical study of millennial views with special attention to the place of Israel in prophecy.

Works Critical of Dispensationalism

Allis, Oswald T. *Prophecy and the Church*. Phillipsburg, NJ: Presbyterian and Reformed, 1945. Classic comprehensive critique of dispensationalism.

Bacchiocchi, Samuele. *Hal Lindsey's Prophetic Jigsaw Puzzle: Five Predictions That Failed!* Berrien Springs, MI: Biblical Perspectives, 1987. Examines Lindsey's failed prophecies, yet argues for an imminent Second Coming.

Bahnsen, Greg L. and Kenneth L. Gentry. *House Divided: The Break-Up of Dispensational Theology*. Ft. Worth, TX: Dominion Press, 1989. Response to H. Wayne House and Thomas Ice, *Dominion Theology: Blessing or Curse?* Includes a comprehensive discussion of eschatological issues.

Bass, Clarence B. *Backgrounds to Dispensationalism: Its Historical Genesis and Ecclesiastical Implications*. Grand Rapids, MI: Baker, 1960. Massively researched history of dispensationalism, with focus on J. N. Darby.

Boersma, T. *Is the Bible a Jigsaw Puzzle: An Evaluation of Hal Lindsey's Writings*. Ontario, Canada: Paideia Press, 1978. An examination of Lindsey's interpretive method, and exegesis of important prophetic passages.

Bray, John L. *Israel in Bible Prophecy*. Lakeland, FL: John L. Bray Ministry, 1983. An amillennial historical and biblical discussion of the Jews in the New Covenant.

Brown, David. *Christ's Second Coming: Will It Be Premillennial?*

Edmonton, Alberta, Canada: Still Water Revival Books, (1876) 1990. Detailed exegetical study of the Second Coming and the Millennium by a former premillennialist.

Cox, William E. *An Examination of Dispensationalism*. Philadelphia, PA: Presbyterian and Reformed, 1963. Critical look at major tenets of dispensationalism by former dispensationalist.

Cox, William E. *Why I Left Scofieldism*. Phillipsburg, NJ: Presbyterian and Reformed, n.d. Critical examination of major flaws of dispensationalism.

Crenshaw, Curtis I. and Grover E. Gunn, III. *Dispensationalism Today, Yesterday, and Tomorrow*. Memphis, TN: Footstool Publications, (1985) 1989. Two Dallas Seminary graduates take a critical and comprehensive look at dispensationalism.

DeMar, Gary. *The Debate Over Christian Reconstruction*. Ft. Worth, TX: 1988. Response to Dave Hunt and Thomas Ice. Includes a brief commentary on Matthew 24.

Feinberg, John A. *Continuity and Discontinuity: Perspectives on the Relationship Between the Old and New Testaments*. Westchester, IL: Crossway, 1988. Theologians of various persuasions discuss relationship of Old and New Covenants; evidence of important modifications in dispensationalism.

Gerstner, John H. *A Primer on Dispensationalism*. Phillipsburg, NJ: Presbyterian and Reformed, 1982. Brief critique of dispensationalism's "division" of the Bible. Expect a major work on dispensationalism in the near future.

Halsell, Grace. *Prophecy and Politics: Militant Evangelists on the*

Road to Nuclear War. Westport, CN: Lawrence Hill, 1986. Journalist enters the world of dispensationalist Zionism, and warns of political dangers of dispensationalist prophetic teachings.

Hendriksen, William. *Israel and the Bible*. Grand Rapids, MI: Baker, 1968. Amillennial discussion of the place of the Jews in the New Covenant.

Jordan, James B. *The Sociology of the Church*. Tyler, TX: Geneva Ministries, 1986. Chapter entitled, "Christian Zionism and Messianic Judaism," contrasts the dispensational Zionism of Jerry Falwell, et. al. with classic early dispensationalism.

MacPherson, Dave. *The Incredible Cover-Up*. Medford, OR: Omega Publications, 1975. Revisionist study of the origins of the pre-trib rapture doctrine.

Mauro, Philip. *The Seventy Weeks and the Great Tribulation*. Swengel, PA: Reiner Publishers, n.d. Former dispensationalist re-examines prophecies in Daniel and the Olivet Discourse.

Miladin, George C. *Is This Really the End?: A Reformed Analysis of The Late Great Planet Earth*. Cherry Hill, NJ: Mack Publishing, 1972. Brief response to Hal Lindsey's prophetic works; concludes with a defense of postmillennial optimism.

Provan, Charles D. *The Church Is Israel Now: The Transfer of Conditional Privilege*. Vallecito, CA: Ross House Books, 1987. collection of Scripture texts with brief comments.

Vanderwaal, C. *Hal Lindsey and Biblical Prophecy*. Ontario, Canada: Paideia Press, 1978. Lively critique of dispensationalism and Hal Lindsey by a Reformed scholar and pastor.

Weber, Timothy P. *Living in the Shadow of the Second Coming: American Premillennialism 1875-1982*. Grand Rapids, MI: Zondervan/Academie, 1983. Touches on American dispensationalism in a larger historical and social context.

Wilson, Dwight. *Armageddon Now!: The Premillenarian Response to Russia and Israel Since 1917*. Tyler, TX: Institute for Christian Economics, (1977) 1991. Premillennialist studies history of failed prophecy, and warns against newspaper exegesis.

Woodrow, Ralph. *Great Prophecies of the Bible*. Riverside, CA: Ralph Woodrow Evangelistic Association, 1971. Exegetical study of Matthew 24, the Seventy Weeks of Daniel, the doctrine of the Anti-Christ.

Woodrow, Ralph. *His Truth Is Marching On: Advanced Studies on Prophecy in the Light of History*. Riverside, CA: Ralph Woodrow Evangelistic Association, 1977. Exegetical study of important prophetic passages in Old and New Testaments.

Zens, John. *Dispensationalism: A Reformed Inquiry into Its Leading Figures and Features*. Nashville, TN: Baptist Reformation Review, 1973. Brief historical and exegetical discussion by a (then) Reformed Baptist.

SCRIPTURE INDEX

OLD TESTAMENT

Genesis

1:26-28	30, 142
1:28	56
2:18-24	114
3:17-19	30
4:19-23	114
6:5	116
8:21	116
9:6-7	16
12:3	127
13:9	16
18:19	16
26:5	16
26:34	114
28:9	114
29:15	114
36:2	114

Exodus

5:20-21	70
18	68, 74
20:10	85n
20:12	86
20:13	15, 17, 86
20:14	17
20:16	1
20:17	17
21-23	16
21:6	125
21:17	86
21:22-25	82
22	17
22:1-9	82
22:8	125
22:21	122
22:28	125
22:36	16
23:9	122

Leviticus

18:3-4	118
18:18	114
18:24-28	119
19:18	107
20:9	107

Deuteronomy

4:5-8	37
5:16-20	105
6:13	105
6:16	105
8:3	105
15:1-5	17
19:13-20	160
19:15	86
19:19	1
25:4	86

Joshua

1:8-9	126
2:11	33
24:15	188

I Samuel

1:1-2	114

II Samuel

16:5-8	xviii

I Kings

2	xviii

Psalms

2:7-12	125
14:1	116
19:7	107
22:25-31	127
24:1	30
25:13	55
32:9	55
32:22	55
82:1-4	125
83	76
110	59
119:13b	16
119:97a	16
119:119b	16
119:99-100	xvi
119:101-106	xvii

Proverbs

6:14	116
12:20	116
14:33	116
17:28	166
26:4	166
26:4-5	165

Ecclesiastes

12:13-14	76

Isaiah

2:2-4	127
9:1-7	97
11:9	127
32:1-9	72
53	101
61:4-6	xiii, 81
64:6	xix, 62
65:17-25	127

Jeremiah

17:9	62, 116

Ezekiel

36:26-27   84, 101

Daniel

2:31-34   97
2:4   87
2:34-35   48

3:1-30   110
3:15   38
44-45   87, 97

Micah
6:6-8   36

Habakkuk

2:4   35

NEW TESTAMENT

Matthew

3:2   96
4:4,   7,   10, 86
4:17, 23   96
5:48   78
6:9-10   51
6:10   97, 98, 102
7:1   27
7:17-19   73
7:20   105
7:21   102
11:2-6   97
12:28   60, 88, 97
15:4   86
18:16   86
19:18-19   86
24:9   38
29:18-20   16, 48, 60, 125, 179

Mark

1:14-15   96

2:27-28   85n
7:9   101

Luke

4:16-30   96
4:21   97
4:43   96
8:1   96
10:9   96
11:20   88, 97

17:21   97
22:42   102

John

4:34   102
6:15   155
14:15   17, 58, 102

14:25-26	60
16:7	61
18:28-40	143
18:36	33, 97

Acts

2:22-36	97
2:32-36	59
7:54-60	7
7:57	91
17:6-7	143
17:16-34	91
17:24-26	xx
28:30	97

Romans

1:18	xx, 116
1:18-25	xix, 118
1:18-32	89, 117
1:26-32	xx
2:14-15	111, 116, 118
2:14-16	117
2:15	xx, 84
2:21-23	148
3:19-20	118
3:21	100
3:21-28	103
3:23	118
4	100
5:20	127
6:14	100, 101
8:22-23	78
11	xi
11:26	136
12:1	28
13	142
13:1-4	44, 150, 151
13:1-7	125
13:8-10	102, 107

13:9	16, 17, 86

I Corinthians

1:2	104
1:13	106
1:17	92
1:18	20, 21
2:14	62
7:2	114
9:9	86
14:14	142
15:23-24	96
15:24-25	97
15:25	127

II Corinthians

5:17	84
5:21	100

Galatians

2:21	103
3:6, 13	100
3:24	102
5:13-14	107
6:2	106

Ephesians

1:20, 22	97
1:20-23	125
2:1	83, 104
2:8	103
2:8-10	35, 100
2:10	104, 105
2:12	56
4:28	82

6:11   143

Colossians

1:13   96, 97

II Thessalonians

2:8   128, 129

I Timothy

1:8   100
3:2   114
4:1   91
4:5   105
5:18   86
6:15   125

II Timothy

3:16   105
3:16-17   85, 126

Titus

2:14   104

Hebrews

8:9-13   84

11:1   175

James

1:25   107
2:10   100, 107
2:17   105

I Peter

2:1-3   104

I John

1:9   102
2:1   101
2:5   58
3:4   101
3:21-24   58
3:24   105
5:3   58

Revelation

19:15   30
22:14   58

SUBJECT INDEX

Abortion, 18, 82, 90, 109, 112
Academic Blackout, xvi
Acquired Immune Deficiency Syndrome (AIDS), xiv
Activism vs. Politics, 35
Adult Gospel, 183-84
Agar, Herbert, 117n
Alexander, J. A., 157
Allen, Ronald B., 107n
Allis, Oswald T., 177
American Civil Liberties Union, 186
American Revolution, 52
American Theological Review, 157
Amillennialism
    Anti-dispensational, 13-14
    Christian Reconstruction, 62-63
    Defeat of Christian Civilization, 72-73
    "Faith in Man," 62-63
    Israel, 137
    Kingdom, 96
    Non-chiliastic, 155
Anderson, J. Kerby, 22
Anglicans, 150
Anti-Biblical Culture, 15-16
Antichrist, 135
Anti-Christian bigotry, 185
Anti-semitism
    Genocide, 6-8
    Prophetic inevitability, 6

Postmillennialism, 132-39, 169-71
Apes, Angels, and Victorians, 167
Aquinas, Thomas, 152
Armageddon, 5
Armageddon Now!, 137
Armenian Christians, 7
Arminianism, xiv, 13, 62-63, 150
Atheist Syndrome, 166n
Augustine, 128, 149, 152

Bahnsen, Greg L.
    By This Standard, 43n
    Chalcedon, xiii
    Common Ground, 91-92
    Debate with H. Wayne House, 177
    General Revelation, 117-18
    Homosexuality: A Biblical View, xiv
    House Divided, 3n, 64n, 87n, 175, 177
    Imminent Return of Christ, 12-13
    Law, 43, 117-18
    Legislating Morality, 117-18
    Postmillennialism, 129
    Theonomy in Christian Ethics, xiii-xiv, 2n, 175
    Westminster Theological Seminary, xiii

Bakker, Jim, 164
Bantam Books, 169
Becon, Thomas, 153
Beisner, Cal, 21
Bestiality, 18
Beza, Theodore, 133, 134
Biblical Law, xiii, xv, 85-87, 151-54, 160
Bibliotheca Sacra, 177n
Billingsley, Lloyd, 7n
Blackstone, William, 114n
Blueprints, xi, 18, 151
Bondage of the Will, 149
Bork, Robert, 113
Brewer, Josiah, 15
Brightman, Thomas, 156
Bringing in the Sheaves, xv, 92
Brown, David, 3n
Bucer, Martin, 133, 153
Bullinger, Heinrich, 153
Bureaucracy, 47, 51
Burke, Edmund, 45
Bush, George, 46-47
By Oath Consigned, xi
By What Standard, xi

Calvin, John, 128, 149, 152, 156
Calvinism, xii, xiv, 148-51, 159
Calvinists, 53, 62, 134, 148-51
Campbell, Roderick, 157
Cartwright, Thomas, 153
Centralized Territorial State, 45
"Certifiable Crazies," 163
Chalcedon Report, xii
Charles II, 69
Chewning, Richard, 17
Chicago Tribune, 184
Chiliasm, 155
Chilton, David
    Covenant, 54
    Days of Vengeance, xvi, 54, 142n, 179n

Great Tribulation, 5n, 67n
Paradise Restored, 6n
Productive Christians in an Age of Guilt-Manipulators, 173
Reformed Theological Seminary, xiv
Christian America, 15
Christian Commonwealth, 112
Christian School, 43
Christian Reconstruction
    "Aberrational," 147-48
    Ascension, 69
    Biblical Blueprint Series, xv
    Biblical Law, 15, 85-87, 151-54
    Biblical Worldview, 20
    Blueprints, xii, 18, 151
    Challenge to Secular Humanism, 21
    Civilization, 15, 30, 154
    Common Ground, xix-xxi
    Comprehensive Evangelism, 34, 77, 83, 155
    Critics, xiii, xvii, 2, 3, 22-23, 160-79
    Decentralized Social and Political Order, 82, 92, 94
    Democracy, 120-22
    Dominion Theology: Blessing or Curse?, 106n
    Dominion by Consent, 93, 122
    Ethics, 143
    Great Commission, 34
    Holy Spirit, 61, 63, 83
    Hunt, Dave, 2
    Indentured Servitude, 10
    Israel, 3-4, 132-39
    Kingdom, 20, 29-31, 96-99, 156
    Law, xviii, 15, 43, 81, 83, 85-87, 99, 100-2, 106-7
    Law of Christ, 106-7
    "Legalism," 20
    Lindsey, Hal, 2

Majority Rule, 122
Minimal State, 92, 126
"Movement," xi, 22, 81
Negative Sanctions, 126
Offense, xviii
Orthodoxy, 147-59, 183
Persecution, 70
Political Action, 125
Politics Fourth, 34, 77, 123-26
Postmillennialism, 82, 87-89, 128-31
Presuppositionalism, 82, 89-92, 148
Progressive Sanctification, 104
Recruiting, xii
Regeneration, 36, 77, 81, 83-84
Revolution, 140-43
"Salvation by Legislation," 124
Sanctification, 103-5
Self-Government, 154
Slavery, 10
Christian Scholarship, 1, 12
Christianity Today, 9, 10, 71n, 89, 175
Chrysostom, John, 155
Church
    Excommunication, 51
    Kingdom, 27-30
Church of the Holy Trinity vs. United States (1892)
Churchill, Winston, 7
Civil Government, 126
Clapp, Rodney, 9, 10, 16
Colson, Charles (Chuck)
    Anti-Christian Bigotry, 186-87
    Biblical Restitution, 10
    Mosaic Law, 17, 83
    Political Illusion, 123
    Prison Reform, 17-18, 82-83
    Reconstructionist, 10, 83
    Schizophrenia, 17, 123
Common Ground, xix-xxi

Common Law (English), 153
Communist Eschatology, 178
Conquest, Robert, 7
Constitution, 10, 113, 120, 123
Cotton, John 120-21, 153, 156
Covenanters, 150
Covenant
    Breaking, xi, xix, 63
    Church, 56
    Civil, 56
    Curses, 57
    Dominion, 56
    Ethics, 50
    Family, 56
    Keeping, xi, 63
    Law, 59
    Lord, 58
    Obedience, 58
    Personal, 56, 77
    Structure, 53
    Suzerain Treaties, 54
    Symbols, 53
    THEOS, 55
Craig, Hays, xi
Craig Press, xi, 178
Cranmer, Thomas, 149
Creation Science, 92
Creeds, 14
Cromwell, 69
Cultural Decline, 46
Cultural Isolation, 29

Dabney, Robert L., 130-31
Darby, J.N., 13
Darwin, Charles, 166
Dallas Theological Seminary, x, 22, 71, 177
Davies, Marvyn, 120n
Davis, John Jefferson, 20-21
Davis vs. Beason (1890), 115
Decentralized Social Order, 92
Declaration of Independence, 120

Debate, 166

Defense of the Faith, x

DeJong, J.A., 122n, 156

DeMar, Gary
  American Vision, xv
  Debate over Christian Reconstruction, 3, 173n
  Democracy, 10
  God and Government, xv, 15n, 93
  Legacy of Hatred Continues, 3, 11, 169-70
  Politics, 93
  Pyramid Society, 94
  Reduction of Christianity, 2n, 36n, 93, 125n, 173n, 175
  Reformed Theological Seminary, xiv
  Ruler of the Nations, 15n, 93

Democracy, 120-22

"Democracy as Heresy," 9

Dennis v. United States, 109n

De Regno Christi, 153

Dispensationalism
  Aberrational, 13, 82, 177
  Activism, 71
  Anti-Reformed Heresy, 13
  Anti-semitism, 138-39
  Armageddon, 5
  Bakker, Jim, 64
  Bureaucracy, 66-69, 71, 73-74
  Cataclysm Theology, 99
  Church Age, 86
  Democracy, 68
  Denial of History, 67
  Escapist Theology, xviii, 15, 70
  Ghetto Theology, 173
  "Great Tribulation," 5, 67
  Hunt, Dave, 15, 66
  Intellectual Error, 5, 177
  Israel, 4-5, 137-39
  Kingdom, 98-99
  Law, 69, 86

Lewis, David Allen, 70

Millennium, 73-74, 86

Novel Millennial View, 14

Pessimism, 67, 72, 88

Political Freedom (morally corrupt), 69

Political Power, 63

Prophetic Inevitability, 6

Rapture, 71

Revived Roman Empire, 88

Revolution, 140

Sensationalism Game, 3-5

Shift, 64

Silence, 64

Social Irresponsibility, 15-16, 89

Swaggart, Jimmy, 64

Theocracy, 68

Dispensationalism in Transition, 177

Dominion
  Biblical Law, 160
  By Consent, 93
  Ethical Service, 141-42
  Inescapable Concept, 57
  Library of Congress, 65n
  Religion, 52

Dominion and Common Grace, 160

Dominion Covenant: Genesis, xv, 56n

Dominion Press, xv

Dominion Theology: Blessing or Curse?, 2, 106n, 177

Downie, Rex, 108n

Eastern Europe, 36

Economics, 50

Edwards, Jonathan, 129-30, 135

Egypt and Bureaucracy, 47

Egypt and Civilization, 47

Eliot, John, 153

English Common Law, 153

Escape Religion, xviii

Eschatology as Test of Orthodoxy, 12-15
Ethics, 50
Evangelicals, 28
Evangelism, 35, 36
Evangelism through Law, 37
Evolution, 89, 128, 166

Federalist Papers, 121
Feinberg, John S., 96
First Amendment, 120
Fools, 165-69
Foundation for Economic Education (FEE), xi
Fowler, Richard A., 85n
Frame, John, 19
Freeman, The, xi
French Revolution, 52
Fundamentalists, 163

Geisler, Norman L.
 Christian Reconstruction, 85n, 92n
 Civil Disobedience, 140
 Civil Government, 87, 108, 110
 Creation Science, 92n
 Dispensationalism, 22, 116
 Schaeffer, Francis A., 140
 Humanism, 90
 Mosaic Legislation, 87
 Natural Law, 17, 22, 108, 110, 116
 Premillennialism, 116, 140
 Religious Obligation, 110
 Ten Commandments, 85n
Geneva Bible, 134
Genocide, 6-8
Gentry, Kenneth L., xiv, 3, 18n, 34n, 175, 179n
Germanic gods, 8

Gerstner, John, 177
Ghetto Mentality, 29
Gillespie, George, 153
God Who is There, xiii
Good Works, 35
Gorky, Maxim, 7
Gouge, William, 156
Government, 44
Grant, George, xv, 52, 92
Green, Ashbel, 153
Green Politics, 46
Greene, Bob, 184
Gross Misrepresentation, 10-12

Hal Lindsey and the Restoration of the Jews, 3n
Hamilton, Bernice, 112n
"Hands Off," 138-39
Harper, F.A., x
Harvard, 15
Harvest House, 2
Hayek, F.A., x
Healer of the Nations, 78n
Heller, Mikhail, 7n
Helms, Jesse, 166
Henry, Carl F.H., 14n
Heresy, 91, 157
Heresy Hunting, 1, 8-9
Hippocratic Oath, 112
Hitler, Adolf 7-8, 121
Hoehner, Harold, 71, 89
Hodge, A.A., 157
Hodge, Charles, 130, 135, 157
Holocaust, 137-39
Home Box Office (HBO), 185
Homosexuality, 18, 90
Homosexuality: A Biblical View, xiv
House Divided, 175, 177
Honest Disagreement, 19
"Honest Reporting as Heresy," 9
Hooper, John, 153
Hoover Institution, ix

House, H. Wayne, 2, 85n, 106, 177
Hulse, Errol, 171
Huguenots, 150
Humanism
  "Cease Fire," 76
  Christianity, 42
  Comprehensive War, 40, 52
  Geisler, Norman L., 90
  God's Law, 77
  Operational Allies, 162
  Politics, 39, 161
  Political Dominion, 40
  Power Religion, 40, 49
  Rejection, xi
  Religion, 38-39, 41
  Sanctions, 52
  Secular Salvation, 41
  State = Church, 40
Hunt, Dave
  Beyond Seduction, 2, 66n, 99n
  Christian Reconstruction, 2, 147, 158, 170, 178
  Confessions of a Heretic, 157
  Dispensationalism, 12, 15
  "Looking for that Blessed Hope," 66n
  New World Millennial Order, 66
  Pentecostalism, 158
  Plymouth Brethren, 157-59
  Rapture, 12, 174
  Schizophrenia, 157-58
  Separation of Church and State, 158-59
  Seduction of Christianity, 2, 174n
  Whatever Happened to Heaven, 2, 12, 173
Huxley, Thomas, 166-67

Ice, Thomas, 2, 106n
Imminent Return, 13

Imprecatory Psalms, 76
Infallibility: An Inescapable Concept, xiv
Institute for Christian Economics (ICE), xiv, xv, 170
Institutes of the Christian Religion, 149
Intercollegiate Society of Individualists, ix
Intercollegiate Studies Institute, ix
Introduction to Christian Economics (1973), xiv
Irenaeus, 152
Irvine, William, 167
Islam, 184
Is Man the Measure?, 90
Israel
  Amillennialism, 137
  Covenantal, 136-37
  Dispensationalism, 137
  North, Gary, 132-33
  Postmillennialism, 132-39
  Representative, 136-37
Is the World Running Down?, 31, 49n

Jackson, Mississippi, xiv
Jerusalem vs. Athens, 90-92
Jesus' New World Order, 48
Jews, 121
John of Antioch, 155
Johnson, Paul, 7n, 8n
Jordan, James B., xiv, 19
Josephus, Flavius, 6n
Journal of Christian Reconstruction, xiv, 154n
Judging, 22-23
Judgment, 27, 76
Judaizers, 100, 101, 103

Kaiser, Walter, 21
Kellogg, S. H., 154
Kelly, Gerard, 114n
Kennedy, D. James, 149
Kenotic Theology, 49
Kevan, Ernest, 107n
Kik, Marcellus, 157
Kingdom
    Already-Not Yet, 96
    Ascension, 61
    Calvin, John, 156
    vs. Church, 27-29
    Civilization, 30, 154, 162
    Coming, 60
    Comprehensive Redemption, 28, 31
    Continuity, 96
    Denying Responsibility, 32
    Earthly, 29
    vs. Ecclesiocracy, 29
    Edwards, Jonathan, 129
    Hodge, Charles, 130
    Holy Spirit, 31, 60-61
    Judicial Redemption, 30
    Judging, 27
    Jurisdiction, 27
    Manifestation on Earth, 27
    Nearness, 96
    vs. "Political Kingdom," 27
    Political Responsibility, 33-37
    Present Status, 97, 129
    Principles, 60
    Reformation, 30-31
    Roman Catholic View, 28-30
    Satan's, 60, 130
    Source, 33
    Transcendent, 33
    Victorious Character, 128-30
    Westminster Larger Catechism, 129
Kline, Meredith G., xi, 54
Knott's Berry Farm, xii
Knott, Walter, xii

Knox, John, 149, 153
Koppel, Ted, 18
Kosster, John P., 166n
Kuhn, Thomas, 41
Kuiper, R. B., 13-14
Kulaks, 7

Last Temptation of Christ, 187
Latimer, Hugh, 153
Law
    Alteration, 43
    Blueprint, 17, 51
    Excommunication, 51
    Holy Spirit, 51
    Jungle, 47
    Legal Schizophrenia, 17
    Natural Law, xi, 17
    Old Testament, 43
    Perpetual Standard, 16
    Prison Solution, 17
    Sanctions, 51
    Social and Political Answers, 43
    Theonomy, 19-20
    Ten Commandments, 18
    Van Til, Cornelius, xi
    Whole Bible, 16
Law of Moses, 151
Law and Society, xv
Lee, Francis Nigel, 178
Leithart, Peter, 3, 11, 93, 169-70, 175
Lewis, David Allen, 70
Liberalism, 127-28
Liberation Theology, 82
Lightner, Robert L., 22
Lindsey, Hal
    "Anti-semitism" Charge, 3, 169
    False Predictions, 6
    Intellectually Corrupt, 169, 178
    Late Great Planet Earth, 6, 88

"Lindsey-Logic," 3-5, 136
Marriages, 170n
Road to Holocaust, 2, 3, 11, 12, 132, 136, 169, 178
Sensationalism, 2, 164
Luhnow, Harold, x
Luther, Martin, 149
Lutheranism, 147

MacDonald, Margaret, 13
Macmillan Magazine, 167
McNeill, John T., 156
Machen, J. Gresham, 100
Madison, James, 121
Madonna, 185
Man, Economy, and State, x
Martyr, Peter, 157
Marx's Religion of Revolution (196-8), xi, 142n
Massachusetts Bay Colony, 152
Masters, Peter, 28, 34, 168
Melanchthon, 149
Millennialism and Social Theory, 171, 176, 179
Miller, William C., x
Minimal State, 92, 126
Mises, Ludwig von, x
Moral Law, 151
Mormonism, 114
Mosaic Law, 20, 22, 151, 153
Moses and Pharaoh, 95n
Moyers, Bill, 123, 162
Murder, 151
Murray, John, xi, xix, 14, 84n, 136, 157
Murray, Iain, 135n
Muslim Nations, 135
Myers, Ellen, 49n
Mysticism, Theology of, 49
Myth of Neutrality, 42, 51-55, 89, 90

National Endowment for the Arts (NEA), 165
Natural Law
Abortion, 109, 112
"Ancient Attitudes," 112
Blackstone, William, 114
Christian Commonwealth, 112
Civil Government, 108
Common Ground, 113-14
Consensus, 110
Constitution, 113
Deism, 116
Ethical Absolutes, 109
Evolution, 115
Geisler, Norman L., 17, 108, 110-11, 116-17
General Revelation, 109, 116-117
Greek Tradition, 110, 113, 115
Murder, 111
Oaths, 113
Polygamy, 109, 114
Pound, Roscoe, 115
Premillennialism, 116
Rape, 111
Reason, 108
Religion, 110
Roe v. Wade, 112
Sanctions, 112
Spanish Thomists, 112
Unbelievers, 111
Unitarianism, xii
Necessity for Systematic Theology, xiv
Negative Sanction, 1
Nekrich, Alexsander, 7n
Neuhaus, Richard John, 1-2, 147-48, 151, 154, 171-72
Neutrality Myth, xii, xiv, 42, 51-57, 148
Newtonian Rationalism, xii
New World Order, 46-50
Ninth Commandment, 164, 169
Nisbet, Robert, 45n, 128

North, Gary
  Bottom-Up vs. Top-Down, 94-95
  Decentralization, 94
  Dominion and Common Grace, 160
  Dominion Covenant: Genesis, xv, 56n
  Healer of the Nations, 78n
  Hyper-dispensationalism, x
  Introduction to Christian Economics (1973), xiv
  Is the World Running Down?, 31, 49n
  Israel, 132-33
  Journal of Christian Reconstruction, xiv, 154n
  Marx's Religion of Revolution (1968), xi, 142n
  Majority Rule, 122
  Millennialism and Social Theory, 171, 176, 179
  Moses and Pharaoh, 95n
  Political Polytheism, 15n, 34, 77n, 114n, 172
  Politics Fourth, 34, 77, 123-26
  Postmillennialism, xi
  Pyramid Society, 94-95
  Religion, 49n, 142n
  Slavery, 10
  Swaggart, Jimmy, 65, 147
  Tools of Dominion, 160n
  Unconditional Surrender, xv, 40n

O'Hair, J.C., x
Oath, 186
One and the Many, x
Origin of Species, 166
Orthodox Presbyterian Church, ix, xiii, 13
"Orthodoxy by Eschatology," 14

Orton, William Aylott, 110n
Oss, Douglas O., 20
Owen, John 134-35, 153, 156

Paganism, 94
Paradigm Shifts, 42
Paraphrase of and Commentary on the New Testament, 156
Parr, Elnathan, 134
"Partnership of Nations," 46
Passantino, Bob and Gretchen, 9, 174
Passport Magazine, 11
Paul, Ron, xiv
Perkins, William, 134, 153, 157
Peters, Ted, 88
Philosophy of the Christian Curriculum, xv
Pietism
  Antinomianism, 173
  Comprehensive Gospel, 35
  Definition, 32
  Dualism, 32
  Evangelism, 35
  Humanism's Ally, 63, 77
  Kingdom of God, 29
  Neutrality, 51
  Sanctions, 51
  Satan's World, 29, 32
  World, 29
Pluralism, 85, 162, 172, 176, 184
Polish Church, 7
Politics
  Activism, 35-36, 161
  Arminianism, 150
  Change, 160
  Fourth, 34, 77, 123-26
  Judgments, 52
  Law, 126
  Messianic, 47, 84, 124
  Ministerial, 44, 52, 124-25
  Religious, 45
  Salvation, 123-26

Political Polytheism, 15n, 34, 77n, 114n, 172
Political Vulnerability, 43
Polygamy, 109
Pope, 135
Postmillennialism
  Augustine, 128
  Calvin, John, 128-29
  Calvinism, 62
  Dabney, Robert L., 130-31
  Definition, 87-89, 154-57
  Edwards, Jonathan, 129-30
  "Faith in Man," 62-65, 72
  Hodge, Charles, 130
  Isaiah's Millennial Vision, 72, 165
  Kingdom, 87-9
  Israel, 132-39
  Lee, Francis Nigel, 178
  "Liberalism," 127-31
  Revolution, 140-43
  Time, 141
Pound, Roscoe, 115
Power Religion, xviii, 40, 49, 52, 71
Poythress, Vern, 19
Premillennialism (covenantal), 14, 65, 87n, 155
Presbyterian Guardian, 14n
Presbyterians, 150
Presuppositionalism, 89-92, 148
Pretribulational Rapture, 13
Princeton, 15
Prison Reform, 17, 82
Progressive Sanctification, 104
Prophecy and the Church, 177
Prophecy 2000, 70
Public Broadcasting System, 162
Public Education, x
Puritans, xii, 53, 150, 152-53

Quantum Physics, xii

Quest for Community, 45

Racism, 166n
Read, Leonard E., xi
Reduction of Christianity, 2, 36n, 93, 125n, 173n, 175
Reformed Distinctives, 20
Reformed Theological Seminary, xiv
Religion and Politics, 37
Religious Conflict, 41
Religious Persecution, 7
Remnant Review, xiv, xv
Republic, 121
Revival, 51
Revolt Against Maturity, xiv
Revolution, 48, 140-43
Reynolds, Barbara, 37
Reynolds vs. United States (1878), 115
Rich Christians in an Age of Hunger, 173
Roberts Rules of Order, xiv
Roepke, Wilhelm, x
Roman Catholic Church, 128-30, 147
Roman Empire, 34
Rosenberg, Alfred, 8
Rothbard, Murray N., x
Rushdoony, Rousas John
  Constitution, 123-24
  Democracy, 124
  Christian Reconstruction, ix-xv, 21, 124
  Fundamentalism, 64
  "Godfather of Christian Reconstruction, 123
  History, 64
  Institutes of Biblical Law, 11, 20, 21, 36, 84n, 175, 178
  Intellectual Schizophrenia, ix
  Law, 11

Messianic Politics, 124
Moyers, Bill, 123
Natural Law, xi
Nature, 116n
One and the Many, x
Orthodox Presbyterian
    Church, ix
Philosophy of the Christian Cur-
    riculum, xv
 Regeneration, 36, 84
 St. Mary's College, ix
 Salvation and Godly Rule, xv
 Social Change, 93
 This Independent Republic, ix
Rutherford, Samuel, 153
Ryrie, Charles C., 88

Sabbath, 85
St. Mary's College, ix
Salvation and Godly Rule, xv
Salvation by Grace, 35
Sanctions, 51-52, 112, 126
Satan's Underground, 2
Schaeffer, Francis, xiii, 12, 121,
    140-41
Schlissel, Steve, 3n
Scofield Bible, 13, 14
Scott, Thomas, 153
Seduction of Christianity, 2
Separation of Church and Society,
    45
Shearer, J. B., 153
Shedd, W.G.T., 157
Shirer, William L., 8
Sibbes, Richard, 134
Sider, Ronald, 173
Shupe, Anson, 172
Sklar, Dusty, 8
Slavery, 10, 109-10, 116
Smorgasbord Ethics, 17
Social Gospel, 82
Social Progress, 160

Social Theory, 17
Socialist-Inspired Millennium, 8
Society and State, 45
Southern Baptist Convention, 19
Southern California Presbytery
    (OPC), xiii
Soviet Union, 7
Sproul, R. C., 13
Spurgeon, Charles Haddon, 148-
    49, 157
Spurgeon's Metropolitan Taber-
    nacle, 28
Stalin, Joseph, 7, 50
Stam, Cornelius, x
Stratford, Lauren, 2
Structure of Scientific Revolutions,
    41
Suffering, 49
Sutton, Ray, xvi, 54, 136-37
Swaggart, Jimmy, 65, 147

Ten Commandments, 18, 85, 151
"Ten Suggestions," 18
Terrorism, 49
Tertullian, 91
That You May Prosper, xvi
Theonomy, 20
Theonomy: A Reformed Critique, 171
Theonomy in Christian Ethics, xiii,
    xiv, 2, 175
This Independent Republic, ix
Thomas Nelson Publishing Com-
    pany, xv
Time, 141-42
Tokes, Laszlo, 37
Tools of Dominion, 160n
Toon, Peter, 133-34
Turkish Massacre, 7

Unconditional Surrender, xv, 40n
Unitarianism, xii, 177

Van Til, Cornelius, x-xiii, 117, 148
Vinson, Fred, M., 109
Virmigli, Peter Martyr, 133
Volker, William, x

Wall Street Journal, 162, 172n
Walvoord, John F., 4n, 98-99, 139n
Warfield, Benjamin, B., 131, 157
Weber, Max, 47
Western Baptist College, 177
Westminster Confession of Faith, 159
Westminster Larger Catechism, 129, 159
Westminster Theological Journal, xi, 20
Westminster Theological Seminary, x, xiii, 13, 14, 19, 136, 170
Wenham, Gordon, 20

Whitby, Daniel, 156, 177
Whitehead, John, 120
Wilberforce, Samuel, 166-67
Willard, Samuel, 153
Wines, E.C., 153
Winthrop, Robert C., 187
William Volker Fund, ix
Williams, Gary R., 22
Wilson, Dwight, 137-39
Wilson, Woodrow, 110
Winthrop, John, 120
Witch Hunt, 8-9, 174
Witherspoon, John, 93
Wolin, Sheldon, 41-42, 45
Wollebius, Johannes, 153
Wormser, Rene A., 116n
Worship, 39

Yale, 15
Young, Curt, 113n

Zwingli, Ulrich, 149, 157